STRANGER IN THE SHOGUN'S CITY

Stranger in the Shogun's City

A Woman's Life in Nineteenth-Century Japan

AMY STANLEY

Chatto & Windus
LONDON

1 3 5 7 9 10 8 6 4 2

Chatto & Windus, an imprint of Vintage,
20 Vauxhall Bridge Road,
London SW1V 2SA

Chatto & Windus is part of the Penguin Random House group of companies
whose addresses can be found at global.penguinrandomhouse.com

Copyright © Amy Stanley 2020

Amy Stanley has asserted her right to be identified as the author of this Work in
accordance with the Copyright, Designs and Patents Act 1988

First published in the United Kingdom by Chatto & Windus in 2020
First published in the United States by Simon & Schuster in 2020

penguin.co.uk/vintage

A CIP catalogue record for this book is available from the British Library

HB ISBN 9781784742300
TPB ISBN 9781784742317

Printed and bound in Great Britain by Clays Ltd, Elcograf S.p.A.

Penguin Random House is committed to a sustainable future
for our business, our readers and our planet. This book is made
from Forest Stewardship Council® certified paper.

For Sam and Henry,
my sweetest and truest loves

CONTENTS

THE PEOPLE OF TSUNENO'S WORLD

TSUNENO'S FAMILY

The reconstruction of Tsuneno's family was among the most difficult tasks of writing this book, since there is no family tree among the Rinsenji records. The relationships here have been reconstituted from birth and death records and mentions in letters (i.e., 'older brother').

Tsuneno's Parents

Emon (1768–1837): Tsuneno's father and head priest at Rinsenji temple
Haruma (d. 1841): Tsuneno's mother

Tsuneno's Siblings

Izawa Kōtoku (dates unknown): Tsuneno's older brother, probably a half brother from a previous marriage of her father's, who was adopted by the Izawa family of physicians in Takada and later became a doctor himself

Giyū (1800–1849): Tsuneno's older brother who inherited his father's position as head priest at Rinsenji temple

Kiyomi (dates unknown): Tsuneno's sister, probably younger, who married a priest in a nearby village

Giryū (1807–1876): Tsuneno's younger brother

Girin (dates unknown): Tsuneno's younger brother who raped Giyū's first wife and was temporarily exiled from the family

Gisen (d. 1848): Tsuneno's youngest brother, who went to study in Edo

Umeka (b. 1815): Tsuneno's younger sister who died in infancy

Toshino (1817–1844): Tsuneno's younger sister

Ino (d. 1840): Tsuneno's younger sister

Giyū's Family

Giyū's first wife: unnamed in the Rinsenji documents, married in 1828 and divorced the following year

Sano (1804–1859): Giyū's second wife and Tsuneno's sister-in-law, mother to Kihaku and four other children

Kihaku (1832–1887): Giyū and Sano's son, who inherited his father's position as head priest

Otake (b. 1840): Giyū and Sano's daughter, whom Tsuneno wanted to adopt

Tsuneno's Husbands

The head priest at Jōganji (m. 1817–1831): Tsuneno's first husband, in Ōishida, Dewa Province

Koide Yasōemon (m. 1833–1837): Tsuneno's second husband, a wealthy peasant in Ōshima Village, Echigo Province

Katō Yūemon (m. 1837–1838): Tsuneno's third husband, a townsman in Takada, Echigo Province

Izawa Hirosuke (later Heizō) (m. 1840–1844, 1846–1853): Tsuneno's fourth husband, in Edo, a native of Kamōda Village in Echigo Province who worked in service to samurai households

OTHER FAMILY MEMBERS, ACQUAINTANCES AND EMPLOYERS

In Echigo

Isogai Denpachi: the Rinsenji temple secretary, also a parishioner
Yamazaki Kyūhachirō: Tsuneno's uncle in Iimuro Village
Chikan: Tsuneno's companion on the road to Edo, a junior Buddhist priest from Jienji temple in Koyasu Village, just outside Takada

In Edo

Sōhachi: a rice store proprietor and Chikan's relative, a native of Echigo

Isogai Yasugorō: Tsuneno's friend from home, a Rinsenji parishioner working winters in the city

Jinsuke: Tsuneno's building superintendent and creditor in Minagawa-chō

Bunshichi and **Mitsu:** Tsuneno's aunt and uncle in Tsukiji

Matsudaira Tomosaburō (c. 1821–1866): Tsuneno's first employer, a bannerman, later known as Matsudaira Nobuyoshi, the Lord of Kameyama Domain

Iwai Hanshirō V (1776–1847): a famous kabuki actor, owner of the rental property in Sumiyoshi-chō where Tsuneno briefly worked in 1840

Izawa Hanzaemon (aka Takeda Yakara and Takeda Gorō): Hirosuke's younger brother, a man of low connections and dubious character

Yado Gisuke: a friend of Tsuneno's, an acupuncturist and native of Dewa Province

Fujiwara Yūzō: an old friend of Hirosuke's, working in service in Hongō

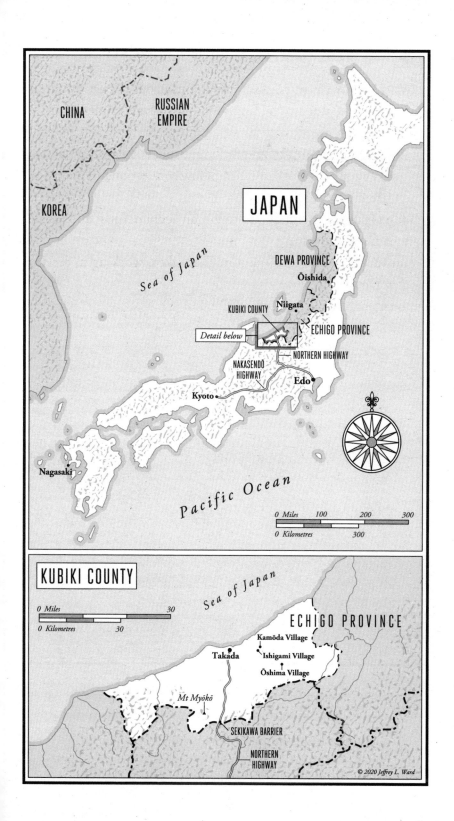

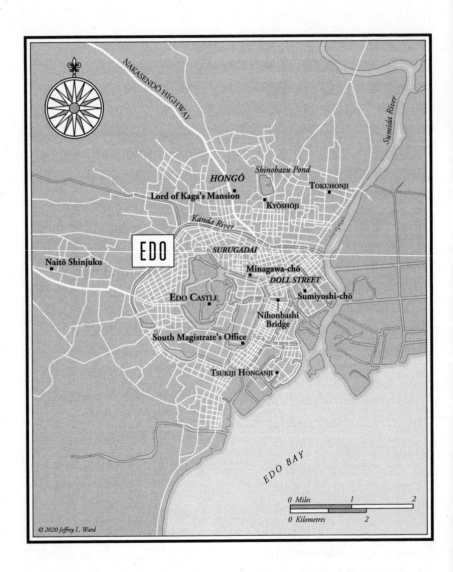

NAKASENDŌ HIGHWAY

Sumida River

EDO

HONGŌ

Shinobazu Pond

Lord of Kaga's Mansion

TOKUHONJI

KYŌSHŌJI

Kanda River

Naitō Shinjuku

SURUGADAI

Minagawa-chō

DOLL STREET

Sumiyoshi-chō

EDO CASTLE

Nihonbashi
Bridge

South Magistrate's Office

Tsukiji Honganji

EDO BAY

0 Miles   1   2

0 Kilometres   2

© 2020 Jeffrey L. Ward

A NOTE ON TRANSLATIONS

Readers in the field of Japanese history will notice that I have translated every Japanese term, even when some of those untranslated terms are commonly used in English-language writing. In the realm of weights, currency and measurements, I have translated *koku* as bales, *ryō* as gold pieces, *bu* as gold coins, *shu* as small gold coins and *mon* as copper coins. I have also converted all traditional Japanese age counts to their Western equivalents. For example, in 1853, when Tsuneno died, she was fifty by the Japanese count, which considered newborns to be one year old, but I have given her age as forty-nine. For ease of reading, I have also converted all Japanese years to their Gregorian calendar equivalents, even though this is not always accurate, because the Japanese and Gregorian years didn't properly align. For example, I render the twelfth month of Tenpō 13 as the twelfth month of 1842, even though it was already 1843 in Europe and the United States. Finally, many of the people I write about changed their names or went by more than one name. For the sake of consistency and readability, I always refer to them by the first version of the name I encountered in the record.

PROLOGUE

On 1 January 1801, the first day of a new century, President John Adams opened the cold, barely finished White House for a public reception. On the other side of the Atlantic, London's church bells rang out to herald the Union of Great Britain and Ireland, and a new flag – the Union Jack – was raised for the first time. Napoléon spent the day plotting future conquests, while Parisians celebrated the traditional New Year in defiance of the French republican calendar, which did not recognise the holiday. The eighteenth century was over, but its waves of revolution were still crashing ashore. Looking ahead, American newspapers made bold predictions, not just for themselves, but for people everywhere. The tide had turned from tyranny to liberty, from superstition to enlightenment, from monarchy to republicanism. In the next hundred years, they agreed, 'a greater change, in the affairs of the world, seems to be promised.'

But across the plains and mountains of their rugged continent, on the other side of a vast and restless ocean, there was no new era to celebrate, no reason to raise toasts or make predictions. On the Japanese archipelago, people followed their own lunar calendar, and only a few even knew the year as 1801. To most, the date was Kansei 12, not a beginning, but a middle. Far away from the Atlantic world's age of revolutions, Japan was coasting through one of the more placid expanses of its Great Peace. It had been nearly two hundred years since anyone in Japan had gone to war. In that time, Europe had convulsed again and again in bloody conflicts over religion, China's Ming Dynasty had collapsed in a continent-shaking cataclysm, kings had been beheaded, new countries had emerged and great maritime empires had risen and fallen. Still, Japan's era of calm persisted. It seemed as though it would stretch forward endlessly into the future.

The day that most of the Western world knew as the first of January 1801 was an ordinary midwinter's day, the seventeenth of the eleventh month of the year. In Japan's cities, elegant women wore layers of padded robes, watchmen scanned the horizon for fire and pedlars sold roasted sweet potatoes on the street. In the countryside, people repaired tools, made ropes, tended their winter crops of greens and radishes, and worried over how to pay their taxes. The harvest season had ended, and all the bills were coming due. In the mountains, peasants piled up timber; along the seashore, they filled barrels of dried seaweed. In farming villages, they assembled bales of rice or soya beans. Sometimes they counted out cash. Every hamlet in each of the sixty-six Japanese provinces owed something: its obligation to the local lord or to the shogun, Tokugawa Ienari, who ruled the realm from his castle in the great metropolis of Edo, a teeming city of 1.2 million.

In the darkest part of winter, as people in the West celebrated, tens of thousands of Japanese tax bills were being written and stamped, copied over in brush and ink, delivered by messengers and passed through the calloused hands of peasants. One of the bills ended up in the possession of a Buddhist priest named Emon. He lived in a village called Ishigami, many days' walk from the great city of Edo's merchant houses and kabuki theatres. His small temple was in Echigo Province, at the foot of steep mountains, in the heart of Japan's snow country. There, among thatched-roofed wooden houses, grassy fields and rice paddies, winter had arrived in full force. Emon's neighbours had already mended their straw boots and snowshoes, reinforced their roof beams, wrapped fragile plants in thick woven mats and hung reed blinds from their windows. By the eleventh month, the snow was several feet deep, and more fell almost every day. When the wind picked up, the snow blew across the fields, piling up in drifts and making it impossible to see the curving pathways and small canals that traversed the village.

Emon's family had lived among the farmers of Ishigami Village for generations. They had been warriors once, samurai. According to their own family history, they had served the great general Takeda Shingen, the Tiger of Kai, famous for his strategic acumen and his distinctive suit of armour, including a helmet crowned with curving golden horns. His armies had fought some of the bloodiest battles of the sixteenth century, during Japan's Warring States Period, when generals rampaged through fields and burned castles, assembling tens and then hundreds of thousands of men as they struggled for control of the archipelago. It was a time when peasants were driven from their villages and armies marched from encampment to encampment; the population was shaken and redistributed across the land. Somehow, when the armies were exhausted and a weary peace set in, Emon's ancestors had ended up in the southern part of Echigo Province.

In the last decades of the sixteenth century, Japan's new military hegemon, the forerunner to the shogun, sorted the population into warriors and civilians. Every head of a samurai household was required to choose his fate. Those who wanted to be warriors had to give up farming and move to barracks in castle towns, where they would stand ready to defend their lords. Those who remained in their villages were ordered to renounce their samurai status and turn in their weapons. Samurai would have the privilege of serving in government and receiving salaries from the shogun or a lord, and peasants would have the assurance that they would never be asked to go to war. Emon's ancestors chose the latter option: they laid down their arms and remained on the land.

Over the years, members of Emon's family farmed and served as village headmen. They mediated disputes, assembled tax payments and communicated with the samurai who administered the area. But one of Emon's forebears chose a different path. He set down his farming manuals, studied Buddhist scriptures and became ordained as a priest in the True Pure Land sect. He gathered parishioners, conducted funeral services, sang hymns and taught the essential tenet of his faith: that anyone who believed in the saving power of Amida Buddha could be reborn in the paradise of the Pure Land, freed from an endless karmic cycle of suffering. He established the little village temple, Rinsenji, where Emon and his family still lived, tending the flock and keeping registers of the living and the dead.

Emon's ancestors' decisions, accumulating over centuries, had consequences that still reached into every corner of his daily life. If his forebears had chosen to be warriors, Emon would have been a samurai, too. He would have worn two swords, a symbol of his warrior status. He would have lived in town, and if he came to the village at all, he would have dressed in formal trousers, his hair gathered into a glossy topknot, every aspect of his appearance announcing his importance. As it was, he wore dull clerical robes and shaved his head. More important, he paid taxes. If Emon had been born a samurai, he would have belonged to the ruling class. He would have issued the tax bills, collected the payments and received a salary for his trouble. He and his male descendants would have been guaranteed an income for as long as their household endured.

Still, even in the middle of winter, as he confronted yet another tax bill, it was difficult for Emon to argue with his ancestors' choices. He was wealthy. He and his wife, Haruma, had already welcomed a baby boy, an heir for the temple, in 1800. With the hope for more children, and the near guarantee of enough money to raise them, Emon's family was flourishing. He gave thanks to the Buddha for his blessings. It had been a difficult year, and most of his parishioners in Ishigami Village were not as lucky as he was. A river upstream had flooded, and the village's ponds and fields had been inundated. The harvest had been terrible, and peasant headmen all across the region had petitioned for relief. Widows and children were starving, they said, and families were fleeing to avoid all the bills they couldn't pay. But Emon faced no such difficulty. For him, a tax bill was not a looming catastrophe; it was just one more document to read and file.

Emon had inherited boxes full of paper, some of it more than a hundred years old, folded accordion-style, stuffed into envelopes and sewn into little books. He had tax bills and receipts going back decades, petitions and notices related to village business, dozens of agreements to pawn land and lend money, accounts of parishioners coming and going, population registers, a record of deaths and posthumous Buddhist names, and even the list of items that the family had purchased for his older sister's wedding. This was not at all unusual. An astonishing number of his countrymen – and -women – were literate. Even in farming villages, as many as one in five men could write, and the number was much higher in most cities. Together, the people of the Japanese archipelago created what was probably the most extensive archive ever of an early modern society: letters drafted by the shogun's women, leaning over lacquer desks in the well-appointed rooms of Edo Castle; proclamations and memoranda from the samurai who promulgated laws and judged criminal cases; planting diaries from the farmers who recorded seeds purchased and fields rotated; ledgers from great merchant houses and tiny local stores; children's lessons scrawled on dull scrap paper; sketches of shrines and harbours and samurai heroes and demons and trees; plans for houses; lists of property values; commentaries on Western 'barbarian' history; lists of the books available in travelling libraries; and poems about nearly everything imaginable.

In the winter of Kansei 12, there was nothing noteworthy in Emon's collection. The contents of his boxes told an orderly and predictable story: the taxes were billed and paid every year, women married in and out, the headship of the Rinsenji temple passed between generations, and the family issued loans and accumulated land. There may have been secrets lurking between the lines of letters, but they were never spelled out. For the most part, the world of the archive didn't encompass much beyond Emon's corner of Echigo Province. In those days, faraway cities were still far away. The shogun in his castle in Edo was an abstraction; his government was a faceless entity that collected revenue. The President of the United States of America, living across the ocean in his new white house, was completely unknown.

But the world was changing slowly, almost imperceptibly, as Emon added to his archive and his family. Soon his collection would contain names and dates he couldn't imagine; it would be the repository of conflicts he couldn't foresee. A few years after the turn of the century, Emon's daughter Tsuneno would be born, and over the next five decades she would cause as much trouble as all of his other nine children combined. Along the way, she would write dozens of letters, all of which her father and brothers kept. She would complain, rejoice, despair, rage and apologise. She would cross out words, correct them and begin again. She would disavow her previous writings and insist that they were never what she meant. She would introduce new return addresses; unknown, eccentric characters; and different vocabulary. She would write until eventually letters to Tsuneno, from Tsuneno and about Tsuneno would dominate the collection. Her rebellion – set down on the page – would inspire more and more writing, in varying voices and formats, as her family struggled to understand, and contain, her messy life. It was as if they believed that a succession of letters and lists might turn her into the sister and daughter they had all expected. Instead, her strong will would reorient the entire archive. Rather than telling the orderly story of a family, it would begin to tell a different story: hers.

If Emon the priest had known what would happen later, the secrets that his collection would accommodate and one day reveal, he might have thought differently about those boxes full of paper. Long after the temple was gone, after the shogun fell and Ishigami Village merged into a neighbouring city, his family's documents would come into the possession of a public archive in the city of Niigata, eighty miles away. The archivists would trace the outline of Tsuneno's story and put one of her letters on a website, and a foreign scholar, sitting alone in her office, would see Tsuneno's words on the screen:

To mother, from Tsuneno (confidential). I'm writing with spring greetings. I went to Kanda Minagawa-chō in Edo – quite unexpectedly – and I ended up in so much trouble!

*

I read Tsuneno's letter over two hundred years after Emon filed his tax bill: a country, an ocean and a world away. I returned to it again and again, in between the classes I taught that winter, reloading the page as the snow blew past my window. When the school year ended, I boarded a flight to Tokyo, the city that used to be Edo. From there, I took a bullet train through Emon's mountains just so I could see Tsuneno's letter in person: the brushstrokes running down the page, the creases still sharp in the paper. I snapped a picture of that letter, and then another, and then dozens more, clutching the table with my free hand, dizzy with jet lag and morning sickness. I was expecting my own child: another firstborn son, another family, another story about to begin.

As I raised my own little boys, I came to know each of Emon's children, starting with Tsuneno, the loudest, the most passionate, the one who seemed to insist on having her story told. The priest left no family tree, so I had to excavate the other names, one by one, out of the tangled masses of hundreds of documents. I met Giyū, Tsuneno's older brother, an uneasy, conflicted patriarch, who kept all the records after Emon retired. I met the youngest brother, Gisen, who composed beautiful, legible letters and called his sister Tsuneno an idiot.

On my computer screen, everyone's scrawled Chinese characters became millions of pixels. I squinted at them, trying to make the squiggles of two-hundred-year-old calligraphy resolve into the more familiar, modern shapes of Japanese words. I spoke and read modern Japanese and I could read nineteenth-century documents in print, but the brushstrokes nearly defeated me. I stared at Tsuneno's letters, in an archaic form of the phonetic alphabet, and spoke them aloud, trying to figure out the breaks between the phrases. I broke the spines of two dictionaries dedicated to the 'destroyed style' of script, leaving crumpled pages behind in a nappy bag, in the kitchen and on the floor of my office. I wrote to Japanese colleagues begging for help; I hired a research assistant for some of the transcriptions. For years, I kept the entire collection of documents catalogued on my phone, just in case I ran into someone who could decipher a difficult passage, maybe at a conference dinner or in the back of a taxi. Eventually, I was able to read most of them myself. Slowly, I pieced together the story: a rebellious woman, a quarrelling family, the last generation of people to know the great city of Edo rather than Tokyo, who would count each of their years according to the old calendar, who would live and die in the shogun's realm.

If Emon had known any of this, he might have questioned his habit of keeping copies and drafts and teaching his son Giyū to do the same. He probably wouldn't have wanted his difficult daughter's story read, much less told. He was not keeping his records for a public archive or a foreign scholar. He would have been amazed, and probably appalled, that a woman, a mother, would fly across the ocean, again and again, leaving her husband and children, just to study his family's correspondence. He would have been astonished that she would be drawn to Tsuneno, of all people, his selfish, aggravating child.

Then again, the family's history had to be remembered somehow, and Emon – like his ancestors and his descendants – lived in a society that compulsively generated and preserved written records. It's hard to say what he would have done differently then, balanced on the edge of what his grandchildren would know as the nineteenth century. At the time, it seemed there was no choice to be made.

Emon filed his tax bill. It was either the last document from an era he didn't know was ending or the first of one he didn't know was beginning. Either way, he was still in the middle of his own story. He was doing the work his ancestors did, paying his taxes and preparing for the future, assembling an archive, still secure in his quiet, snowbound world.

Chapter One

FARAWAY PLACES

Baby gifts arrived at the Rinsenji temple in the spring of 1804, during the early thaw, when the paths through Ishigami Village were choked with mud. The number of presents was limited. This was, after all, the birth of a second child – and a girl. Four-year-old Giyū, his mother's firstborn son, arrived in the dead of winter, and still the temple was swamped with deliveries, package after package of sardines, sake, bolts of cloth, seaweed, dried persimmons and folding paper fans. That was appropriate. This new baby, born on the twelfth day of the third month, received simple, mostly homemade things: sticky rice cakes, sake, a set of baby clothes, dried fish flakes.

She didn't have a name during the first week of her life. It was too soon, when so many infants didn't survive. It would be bad luck, as if the family were trying to hold on to something that wasn't quite theirs. Once the baby lived for seven days, then it would be time to celebrate, to give her a name and welcome her to the community.

When the week of anxious waiting passed, Emon and his family held a small gathering. No records of it survive, but such events were customary, and the temple family fulfilled all the usual social obligations. The guests would have been an assortment of wives and mothers from Ishigami and the neighbouring villages: strong peasants, including the midwives who had attended the birth, and probably a few more refined ladies, Buddhist priests' and village headmen's wives. The baby girl was so new to the world that she didn't yet recognise any of the people who would later become fixtures in her life. She may have slept through the festivities. But considering the personality she grew into later, it also seems likely that she opened her eyes, looked around at the tight circle of women, and wailed.

For a name, the girl's parents had chosen something slightly sophisticated and out of the ordinary: Tsuneno. It was three syllables instead of the more common two, and it took two Chinese characters to write. This child would be the only Tsuneno in her family, most likely the only one in any of the farming villages that surrounded the temple. As long as she kept her name, she would never be confused with anyone else.

In the first months of her life, baby Tsuneno had everything she needed. Her family had old clothes and rags to piece together for nappies, so she could be changed whenever she was wet. She had a mat to sleep on, instead of a dirt floor, and enough firewood and charcoal to keep warm in the long winters. She had a wardrobe: loose cotton robes made up in a tiny size for babies and toddlers. There were lamps and candles to illuminate the shadowy rooms of the temple at night, and on snowy days she could sleep under a puffy patchwork blanket. In the summer, there were mosquito nets over her futon. Her mother could eat enough to produce breast milk – babies typically nursed until around the age of three – and if she couldn't or didn't want to breastfeed, her family could hire a wet nurse. They could also pay a village girl to work as a nursemaid. She could wear Tsuneno on her back and sing her plaintive country songs, and Tsuneno could regard the world from over her shoulder.

There was so much to learn. First, the things that babies need to know: mother's face; father's voice; her older brother's name, Giyū. Next, lessons for toddlers, new vocabulary and rules. The word *shōji* for the paper-covered sliding doors, clattering and delicate, that she shouldn't push her fingers through. *Tatami* for the mats on the floors: they rippled under her bare toes, and she had to remember not to pull at the sweet, grassy straw. *Tansu* was the word for the dresser, which was not safe to climb on, and *hibachi* was for the charcoal brazier that was too hot to touch. *Ohashi* was for chopsticks. There were two words for bowls. *Owan* for the dark, glowing lacquer ones, which were surprisingly light, and *osara* for the smooth porcelain, which could break. It was important to be careful.

Tsuneno also learned social rules, some beyond language, that alerted her to her family's place in their small village. She could get a sense of her status through her neighbours' deferential bows and the quick envious glances of other children. Adults knew the details, and the few who had the time and space to contemplate could perceive the outlines of a longer story. A hundred and fifty years earlier, when Tsuneno's father's ancestors were the Ishigami Village headmen, the main difference between rich and poor peasants had been one of degree: some owned land and others were tenants, but most shared a common occupation, farming, and a similar lifestyle. That had changed by the time Tsuneno's grandfather was born. Prosperous families were finding new places to invest their money and new ways to multiply their fortunes, often at their neighbours' expense. They had opened workshops for the production of Echigo *chijimi* – a kind of fine hemp crepe, bleached on snowfields – or they had become textile dealers, middlemen between producers and merchants. They bought local rice and brewed sake or bought eggs and sold them to city people. Or, like Tsuneno's family, they invested in religious education, established temples, performed funeral services and collected offerings. When they made money from these endeavours, they opened pawnshops, lent money and, most important, invested in land. Already in Tsuneno's great-grandfather's generation, half the land in Ishigami Village was held by people in other places. By the time she was a child, one family – the Yamadas of Hyakukenmachi, an easy walk downriver – had holdings in nearly thirty villages.

Tsuneno's parents and grandparents were investors and planners. They had to be, since even substantial fortunes could be lost quickly through bad harvests and mismanagement. But families like theirs also spent money freely on the small things of everyday life. They bought sets of bowls and plates for a few hundred coppers each. They bought books, too, to be read and lent to the neighbours, and low desks for writing. They spent heavy, ridged gold coins on futons, thick blankets and finely woven mosquito nets, and they also purchased silk kimonos and obis for special occasions and heavy coats for the winter. With the small change left over, they bought snowshoes and wooden clogs for the children. When the tea had been drunk, the bowls had broken, the coats had worn out and the mosquito nets had torn, they bought more. Consumption had become an endless occupation, and their houses filled with more and more things for their children to name and count.

In Tsuneno's house, which was attached to the temple, some of those everyday things were funded by donations from parishioners, who gave cash, rice and vegetables in gratitude for the Buddha's compassion. Snow country people were known for their piety, not only because their lives were so difficult but also because the revered founder of the True Pure Land sect, Shinran, had lived there for a time in the early thirteenth century. He had been exiled from the capital for his heretical teaching that salvation depended on faith alone: anyone who called on Amida Buddha could be reborn in the paradise of the Pure Land. Even worse (at least from the standpoint of the clerical establishment), Shinran rejected priestly celibacy. Instead, he had married an Echigo woman, Eshinni, who established the role of the priest's wife as a religious leader.

Some adherents of other Buddhist sects – such as Zen, Nichiren and Shingon – still looked down on True Pure Land believers. Those who belonged to austere monastic traditions, in which clerics refrained from eating meat and remained celibate, often thought True Pure Land priests like Tsuneno's father were too invested in worldly success, too covetous of riches and too indulgent in earthly pleasures. True Pure Land priests had wives and children, and they enjoyed a lifestyle much like that of prosperous laypeople, all funded by gifts from parishioners. ('This is truly a sect that treats the people with extreme greed,' a critic wrote.) But even those who condescended to True Pure Land believers could recognise the strength of their devotion. They tended to raise large families, believing that infanticide – fairly common among other peasants – was a sin. In some circles, this was regarded as an admirable commitment to principle. In others, it was a sign of irrational zealotry or even barbarism: raising large broods of children as if they were dogs or cats.

In the end, Tsuneno's parents had eight children who survived infancy. Childbearing was part of Tsuneno's mother's vocation, as central to her faith as singing hymns and saying prayers. The True Pure Land sect's scholars taught that raising a child to become a priest or priest's wife was a gift to the Buddha equal to 'all the treasures that fill three thousand worlds'. So Haruma tended to her babies, and then her growing children, while she fulfilled the other duties of a village priest's wife. Every day, she placed offerings of food and flowers on the altar before an image of Amida Buddha. She kept house, entertained parishioners with tea, and ministered to the women of the village. As the 'guardian of the temple,' Haruma taught her sons and daughters that devotion could be embodied, that consistency and discipline were testaments of faith.

Tsuneno and her siblings learned about religious implements the way that peasant children learned about threshers and fishing nets. Their days were perfumed by the smouldering incense on the altar and punctuated by the deep, hollow sound of the bell calling people to the main hall for worship. Tsuneno learned to roll the cool beads of a rosary between her palms as she prayed. She memorised the first, most important prayer, Namu Amida Butsu (Hail Amida Buddha), something even a toddler could say.

Outside the temple, Tsuneno learned things that all Echigo children knew. She grew up speaking the local accent, switching around her *i*'s and her *e*'s just like everyone around her. In winter, she learned to 'paddle' through powdery snow in straw snowshoes and to clear a path by 'digging' rather than 'shoveling.' In spring, when the snow froze hard, she learned how to walk on ice without slipping and how to laugh at her little brothers and sisters when they fell. She probably knew how to win a snowball contest, how to design a snow castle, and how to build a little cooking fire by scooping out a hollow in the snow and spreading rice bran under the kindling. If she didn't, her brothers certainly did.

One of Tsuneno's older brothers, Kōtoku, had been adopted by a doctor's family living in the nearby town Takada, where a local lord had his castle. Most of the town's twenty thousand residents lived in dark, narrow town houses tucked behind unbroken rows of eaves. In winter, they climbed to their rooftops to clear the snow, then dumped it out into the middle of the road. Kōtoku could have taught Tsuneno how to scramble up to the top of the snow heap. By midwinter, it was so high that they could look down at the rooftops and out towards the mountains.

There was a measuring pole ten feet high set out in front of Takada Castle, and in the worst winters snow buried it completely. Echigo's children learned to speak of blizzards and frozen horses as if such things were ordinary. They were not impressed with giant icicles, even when they grew inside their houses, extending from the rafters nearly to the floor. They were accustomed to spending days in the dark because all the doors and windows were snowed over and couldn't be cleared. Little girls filled the dull stretches of time with singing and clapping games or with stories: *Once upon a time, a fisherman named Urashima Tarō rescued a turtle. A woodcutter and his wife found a tiny baby inside a hollow bamboo stalk. A weaver girl fell in love with a cowherd.* An outsider might have thought the winters were quaint, even cosy, and children may not have minded. But for their parents, there was nothing romantic, or even pleasant, about the winter. It was a test of endurance. The region's most famous author, Suzuki Bokushi, wrote: 'What enjoyment is there of snow for us in Echigo, where foot after foot falls year after year? We exhaust ourselves and our purses, undergo a thousand pains and discomforts, all because of the snow.'

But at least everyone knew what to expect. It would be 'freezing from equinox to equinox,' as the older people said, and sometimes farmers would need to shovel out the fields so that they could plant their rice seedlings. But eventually the rivers would thaw, the ice would retreat from the valleys, and in the fourth or fifth month all the flowers would bloom at once.

In the short summers, when the snow had cleared, Tsuneno learned the contours of her village. Ishigami extended to the shore-lines of Big Pond and Little Pond, the reservoirs used to flood the rice fields in the spring. Like all children, she first measured distance in time and footsteps – she could walk all around Big Pond within the space of a morning – while the adults around her rendered the same distances in numbers and noted the figures for their records. To Tsuneno, Big Pond was just a vast glittering lake, but to men like her father, the details were important: the height of the embankments, the surface area of the water, the level of rainfall, and the date on the calendar when the floodgates would be open and the muddy fields would fill with water.

As the men in Ishigami made measurements and drew brightly coloured maps of local rice paddies and pathways, all of the Japanese islands were being charted and measured more precisely. Just before Tsuneno was born, the cartographer Inō Tadataka had surveyed her part of Echigo, equipped with a compass, a sextant and his knowledge of the stars. He had followed the Sea of Japan coastline from the northern tip of the main island of Honshu down to the port of Naoetsu and turned inland towards Takada. From there, he set out for the mountains, naming the villages he passed and noting the number of buildings in each. Later, he turned his surveyor's diary into a map of southern Echigo, which he presented to the shogun. He rendered all the turns and inlets of the Sea of Japan coast, the town of Takada, all the little villages along the Northern Highway, and the distinctive peak of Mt Myōkō, a familiar sight on the horizon whenever the clouds cleared. But Ishigami Village was still too small and remote to have a place on his map – even Big Pond and Little Pond were blank space. They would have to wait a few decades to appear on a comprehensive map of the province, and by then Echigo would be called Niigata Prefecture.

Meanwhile, a child could make her own map of the woods and fields around Big Pond, noting the cicadas seething in the grass and the clicking black dragonflies tracing circles over the water. Stands of cedar trees bracketed the shore; water chestnuts and lotuses floated on the water's surface. There were also other, mysterious things. They lurked in dark forests and in the depths of the ponds. Tsuneno couldn't see and touch them, but she knew they were there. All the children did – it was common knowledge. Water sprites splashed in Big Pond, and goblins with long red noses darted among the trees. Even ordinary animals had hidden lives. Badgers were tricksters, and foxes could turn into beautiful women. An industrious rabbit lived in the full moon and spent every night pounding sticky rice cakes.

In books, the forests were no longer enchanted. Precise illustrations of all the plants and animals appeared in thick, dense volumes, which were available for purchase from travelling booksellers. Like cartographers, Japanese natural scientists were charting the world of Tsuneno's childhood, making detailed observations and measurements. They classified what they found as medicinal herbs, 'products', or natural objects, inspired by the categories named in Chinese texts. But that would soon change. Far away in Bizen Province, a boy a little older than Tsuneno was studying 'Western learning' and puzzling out the foreign sounds and letters of Dutch books. In time, he would write a *Sutra of Botany*, arguing that the Japanese should adopt the classification system devised by the Swedish botanist Linnaeus. For the first time in Japan, the cedars in the forest and the lotuses on Little Pond would be called plants.

For Tsuneno, there were no 'plants', but there were other kinds of knowledge waiting between the pages of books. When she could be trusted to sit still and not spill her ink, probably around the age of seven or eight, she began her formal education. This was not taken for granted in rural Echigo. Only a few years before Tsuneno was born, a woman from a nearby village was forced to apologise to her in-laws for wasting time learning to read and write. But Tsuneno was not an ordinary peasant. A sophisticated girl, and a desirable bride for a priest or village headman, would have to be able to write graceful letters, read poetry and, in some cases, even keep family accounts. What if Tsuneno's mother-in-law kept a housekeeping diary and expected her to follow written instructions? Or what if Tsuneno didn't know how to arrange plates on a tray properly and wanted to look up the answer in a manual? There were expectations for womanly competence, and Tsuneno had to keep up. Parents all around were purchasing copybooks and hiring tutors, and their daughters were practising literacy: drafting simple letters to their friends, entering numbers in ledgers and keeping short diaries.

By the time Tsuneno first knelt at a desk to dip her brush in ink, her brother Giyū, who was about four years older, had already begun lessons. He and Tsuneno might have attended the same village school, since teachers in some places taught boys and girls together, or one or both of them might have studied with a tutor at home. But even if they sat side by side, they followed different curricula. Both siblings started with the forty-eight letters of the Japanese phonetic alphabet, which were much more difficult to master than they seemed because each of them could be written in a number of forms. From there, Giyū might have continued with the *Primer on Names* so that, in the future, he could correctly address the ordinary Kōheis, Denpachis and Jinbeis who populated the countryside. Then he learned how to write the names of the provinces, as well as the counties of Echigo and the neighbouring villages. He already knew these places as collections of trees, fields and houses – they were home – but now he would learn how officials saw and classified them. Eventually, the shapes of the characters would become as familiar as the mountains on the horizon, and he would barely have to think about how to move the brush when he identified himself in an official document: Giyū of the Rinsenji temple, Ishigami Village, Kubiki County, Echigo Province.

In order to understand his place in the world, Giyū also had to learn about the political structure of the realm. He came to know, vaguely, that he lived in the land of the gods, the ancient deities whose ranks included everyone from the Sun Goddess, mythical progenitor of Japan's emperor, to the local guardians of ponds and mountains. Although Giyū was a Buddhist, the profusion of other gods would not have bothered him. Most ordinary people thought of 'the gods and the buddhas' in the same category, and the veneration of Japanese deities didn't interfere with their devotion to the Buddha.

The gods' territory was indistinct. Giyū might have guessed that their realm roughly corresponded to the dominion of the emperor, whose family had ruled Japan for over a thousand years. The emperor appeared in history books and literature, but in Giyū's time he was not a politically important figure. He lived cloistered in his palace in the city of Kyoto, composing poetry and conducting esoteric rituals. The real power in the realm was the shogun, the military leader who ruled from Edo Castle. He directly administered about a third of the land in Japan, including Giyū's own village: the taxes that Giyū's father paid went to the shogun's coffers in Edo. The remainder of Japan was carved into domains administered by powerful lords. They collected their own taxes, and some of them were more amenable to the shogun's authority than others, though they all performed their obedience by spending one year out of every two in attendance on the shogun in Edo. In all, there were nearly three hundred domain lords, far too many for Giyū to remember. And since most domains didn't have contiguous boundaries, he couldn't study their shapes on a map. But he had to know the important domains in Echigo Province, especially Takada, since it was the closest.

Giyū studied some basic Buddhist doctrine, since he was destined to be a priest. Later, he would go to a main temple to be ordained. For now, still at home, he puzzled over the language of official correspondence, an awkward classical Chinese-Japanese hybrid style that no one ever spoke, a vestige of the time when classical Chinese was the sole language of government. Japanese and Chinese shared a set of complicated characters, but they were completely different languages with different grammars. Giyū sometimes had to rearrange the order of the characters when he read the hybrid style out loud. 'With fear and trembling we humbly present the following request,' he read, half-backward, learning the correct way to open a petition to the authorities. He would use the same hybrid style, with fewer obsequious flourishes, for the certificates and contracts that sealed everyday agreements among commoners: 'An Agreement to Send a Person into Service', 'An Agreement to Borrow Money' and 'An Agreement to Sell Land'. There were correct forms for all of these documents, but luckily they could be looked up in a convenient manual.

Giyū also studied straight classical Chinese, because it was still the language of ancient history and philosophy. He could write poetry in the Chinese style, an accomplishment that made him proud. He bound his compositions in a book and wrote his name with bold characters on the cover. Judging from some of the references he made in later letters, he was interested in Confucian treatises, which distilled the wisdom of the ancient Chinese philosopher who taught about the cultivation of the self, the virtues of good rulers and the correct conduct of relationships. Parents were to be obeyed and venerated, and, conveniently for Giyū, who eventually had eight younger siblings, older brothers were to be respected.

Tsuneno and her younger sister Kiyomi, who was close to her in age, learned some of what Giyū and their other brothers did. They studied basic Chinese characters – they, too, could write 'Ishigami Village' and 'Rinsenji' – but they never had to study the convoluted language of bureaucratic memoranda or copy out petitions for tax relief. They probably didn't study much classical Chinese, either, although Tsuneno must have acquired at least a passing familiarity with *The Classic of Filial Piety*, an ancient Chinese text that purported to represent a conversation between Confucius and one of his disciples on the importance of revering one's mother and father. Years later, Giyū quoted the famous first passage to her in an angry letter, confident that she would understand the reference.

But Tsuneno and Kiyomi also learned many things their brothers did not. They must have encountered primers for girls, which were so popular that the most famous were reissued and reprinted hundreds of times. The main text in each book was always dull and didactic. 'The only qualities that befit a woman,' *The Greater Learning for Women* said, in gracefully rendered, meticulously glossed Chinese characters, 'are gentle obedience, chastity, mercy and quietness.' Luckily, there were always appendices with more interesting content. *The Treasure Chest of the Greater Learning for Women* had illustrated versions of the most famous chapters of the eleventh-century classic *The Tale of Genji*. *The Women's Amazing Library* had an entire section about removing stains: for lacquer, use miso soup; for tooth-blackening powder, warm vinegar.

There were also pages and pages of pictures. Some depicted

contemporary women from all kinds of backgrounds – aristocrats, samurai, and commoners – looking stunningly beautiful as they worked at traditional women's occupations. Among them were tidy mothers teaching children to write their first letters; vain young women examining themselves in mirrors; industrious peasants spinning cotton or scrubbing laundry in great bamboo tubs; waiflike girls raking salt from the seashore; tough city women hanging noodles, dyeing paper and stringing rosaries; and naked abalone divers plunging into the waves, their hair streaming behind them. Occasionally, there was a sullen little girl moping while her mother worked. There were also historical figures and characters from fiction: delicate, round-faced ladies wearing heavy, twelve-layered robes, the heroines of *The Tale of Genji*. There were even, on occasion, foreigners: paragons of feminine virtue from ancient China, who wore strange gold ornaments and appeared near craggy mountains, often accompanied by elderly, neatly bearded men.

Each page was another lesson in the brilliant variety of women's experiences, a glimpse into a life in another place, and occasionally another time, among a different kind of people. The ordinary shops and windy salt fields, the well-appointed rooms looking out into gardens, the city courtyards where women were hanging noodles to dry, even the fishing boats – they were like nothing a sheltered girl from inland Echigo had ever seen. Tsuneno knew she had as much chance of encountering these things as she did of travelling to ancient China and speaking to the sages: she was expected to grow up and marry into a family much like her own. The very first line of *The Greater Learning for Women* instructed the reader not to hope for anything else. 'To be a woman is to grow up and leave for another household,' that is, to marry. It admitted no other possibility. So while her brothers studied the practical administration of the shogun's realm and the divine mysteries of the Pure Land, Tsuneno also divided her imagination between two opposed spheres: the confines of the marital household, a world of thrift and dull obedience, and the expansive universe of female beauty, furnished with gold, exotic prints and brocade, and available – at least in theory – to every little girl.

To make her way in either world, Tsuneno would need to be able to sew. Fortunately, making up an unlined kimono was not particularly difficult. Most of the seams were straight, there was only one standard size for the fabric, and the piecing was simple: squares, right triangles and rectangles. But there was always a right way and a wrong way to sew, just like there was a right way and a wrong way to sleep, walk and open a door. Girls should sleep with their arms and legs pulled in close to their bodies, walk so that their footsteps could barely be heard, and open doors so that they made as little noise as possible. Sewing was one more form of discipline and self-cultivation, which could chafe at a little girl who would rather look at the pictures in books or play in the snow. But as the venerable *Greater Learning for Women* said, and most of the other books repeated in some form or other, 'Of the many skills necessary to become a woman, needlework is the most important.' Many years later, a woman who recalled her childhood in the countryside would say, 'I was bad at sewing and calligraphy, and was scolded at home, told "you're not a girl."'

The right way to sew was with loose stitches for kimonos, so that they could be taken apart easily to be washed, and with tiny invisible stitches for handkerchiefs. For tricky silk crepe, which could stretch out of shape when seamed, the correct approach was to stitch a perfectly straight row along the edge of the fabric to guide the hand. For crinkly silk, it was to wipe away wrinkles with a dampened handkerchief before beginning. For thick fabrics, it was to use hempen thread rather than silk. The right way to sew was quietly, with perfect attention to the task at hand, so that seams could be matched up neatly. To avoid tangling the thread into knots that couldn't be undone. To measure carefully so that fabric wasn't cut in the wrong place, so that mother didn't have to smooth out the scraps and recycle them in a patchwork coat or as nappies for the new baby.

Tsuneno and Kiyomi had three little brothers, so they had to be careful with their tools and not leave them lying around for the toddlers to find. Needles were sharp, and they were also expensive, because they had to be forged and tempered by skilled artisans. When a needle broke it had to be disposed of carefully, or even donated to the Buddha, which would make an appropriate end to its service. There were less exalted tools, too: flat wooden rulers, knives to cut through fabric, puffy pincushions, and sharp little hooks to pull out stitches. When they weren't needed, they were kept in lacquered boxes or sewing chests with tiny drawers. But they came out nearly every day, because there was always sewing to be done. In varying stages of difficulty, it was enough to keep a little girl busy: the manufacture of children's clothes and little bags and wallets aprons for the servant girls, and quilted winter coats and blankets; the laundry sewing, when kimonos were taken apart to be washed and then pieced back together; the cycles of mending: letting the fabric out of seams, replacing cuffs and hems and linings, and patching tears and holes.

Most of this was daily upkeep, the ordinary tasks of running a large household in a place where most clothes were not purchased ready-made. But there was also an element of planning for the future. Whatever the three sisters made for themselves would one day be added to their trousseaus. At their weddings, the coats and robes and socks and handkerchiefs would be displayed at their in-laws' houses for all the neighbours to see. There would also be shoes and furniture, futons, boxes of tooth-blackening powder, fresh ink and paper for writing, and possibly a box of gilded clamshells whose insides were painted with lines from famous poems. They were meant to be used for a matching game, in which the first and last lines of the poem were paired, just as the bride and groom would be on their wedding night. The trousseaus would also contain a sewing box for each sister, so that they could start their own households and make new lives elsewhere, without their parents and brothers and without one another.

Yet sewing lessons suggested other possible futures for little girls who were attuned to them. Needlework was a skill that could be turned in a few different directions – seamstresses worked in the employ of many wealthy households, and poor women in cities supported themselves through piecework. Women who learned to weave or spin could migrate to towns like Kiryū in Kōzuke Province, which was home to great silk-weaving workshops. But even for a girl who never planned to work for wages herself (and Tsuneno had no reason to believe she would ever have to), sewing created new possibilities, if only in the imagination. It was tedious to piece together yet another old robe after it was taken apart to be washed, but it was always possible to daydream about making similar stitches in lavender silk, with a pattern of delicate white cherry blossoms, and pairing it with a red lining with a geometric pattern, and maybe a light pink underrobe. Or a plaid seafoam green, with a purple polka-dotted hem, paired with a dull brown obi.

The illustrations in the primers for girls weren't in colour, but the elegant women reading by the gardens must have been wearing something like that, or even something better, which no one in Ishigami Village could possibly imagine. What were those women reading? What did they talk about? Where would they go next?

What kind of life could Tsuneno have if she could dress like that?

*

As Tsuneno practised her stitches, she was also piecing together the remnants of Japan's cosmopolitan past. By the time she left her childhood behind, she had dozens of pieces of clothing packed away in a standing dresser and overflowing into other chests and baskets. She had a lined robe in wisteria-coloured silk crepe, printed with a fine pattern, and another in black, in a different fine pattern. She had one in stripes with a Chichibu silk lining and another in a coarse silk weave. She had over a dozen cotton-padded robes for winter, in reddish 'hawk' brown, in the duller shade of 'tea', in white-figured satin, and in all kinds of stripes. For layering, she had over-robes in light pink damask and deep black satin, and for summer, unlined robes in striped and patterned pongee and cotton. Every single piece was of domestic manufacture, but they all owed their existence to an era of global trade that had long passed by the time she learned to sew.

The cotton that formed the majority of Tsuneno's wardrobe was not native to the Japanese islands. Instead, it had been introduced from South Asia by way of China and Korea sometime in the fifteenth century, and it was cultivated widely by the sixteenth century, though not in quantities sufficient to meet the demand for clothing. Silk had been produced in Japan since ancient times, but in the case of this textile, too, demand for finished cloth outstripped the supply. As a result, Japan started to import vast quantities of Chinese silk. In those days, during the tumultuous Warring States Period, the Japanese were notorious pirates and ambitious traders. Setting sail from Japan's Inland Sea, they had raided the Chinese coastline and ranged as far as Southeast Asia, where they traded camphor, rice and silver in exchange for guns, deerskins, gunpowder, textiles and sugar. The precious metals that fed this trade were hauled out of newly opened Japanese mines at a staggering rate. Violent boom-towns sprouted up across the archipelago, populated with greedy prospectors, bandits and overwhelmed administrators. What began as regional commerce in the South China Sea – Chinese silk in exchange for Japanese silver – became a global trade in the early seventeenth century. The newly formed Dutch East India Company, which established trading posts throughout the Indian Ocean and Southeast Asia, began to send ships loaded with silk thread and Indian cotton textiles to Japanese ports.

But in the middle of the seventeenth century, after the Tokugawa family of shoguns was securely ensconced in Edo, Japan retreated from the tumultuous arena of global politics and military conflict. By the 1630s, the shogunate had become increasingly concerned about the influence of Christianity, which it viewed as an evil foreign religion, after a group of rebels that included a number of prominent Christian converts launched a massive uprising on the southern island of Kyushu. The shogun issued edicts barring Western traders and diplomats from Japanese soil, with the exception of the Protestant Dutch, who were permitted to come to port at the southern city of Nagasaki. They had earned this exemption by convincing the Japanese that they, unlike their Catholic competitors, had little interest in proselytising. Around the same time, the shogun forbade his subjects to travel beyond the Ryūkyū Islands in the south and Korea in the west. This meant that Japanese who remained abroad at the time of the edict were effectively exiled.

At the same time that the shogunate limited foreign travel, it tried to maintain, and even expand, foreign trade. But Japan's mines were failing, and within decades the shogun's men began to worry about the quantity of precious metal leaving the archipelago. In 1668 the shogunate halted the export of silver entirely, and restrictions on the export of copper followed in 1685. Meanwhile, new edicts curtailed silk imports from China. Within decades, Japan produced enough silk, and then cotton, to satisfy its own market. Dutch and Chinese ships still arrived at Nagasaki bearing luxury textiles, but much of the trade shifted to ginseng and sugar, medicines and foreign books, all things that Japan could not generate itself.

Yet more than a century later, memories of an earlier era of global trade in textiles still surfaced unexpectedly in Tsuneno's wardrobe. She had a robe in Nankin stripes, which referred to the Chinese city of Nanjing a major silk-producing area. She also had a few sets of Santome stripes, which were named after the seventeenth-century Portuguese colony of São Tomé, near Madras. Before the Dutch East India Company trade, Japanese had not been accustomed to wearing stripes at all; even the word 'stripes', *shima*, came from the word for 'island', signifying that the textile design had come from abroad.

The reminders of seventeenth-century trade were elsewhere in Tsuneno's world, too. The tobacco grown in villages near Ishigami, which filled the long pipes of sophisticated women, originally came from the New World. So did the sweet potatoes grown on sunny hillsides, which supplemented the diets of poor peasants and were sold on city streets. The clocks that some wealthy families had in their homes were domestically manufactured adaptations of European models. There was also a range of products, most very expensive, that came in through more recent trade. These included the swatches of calico that fashionable women wore sewn into fantastic patchwork robes; the eyeglasses sold in city stores and, occasionally, by pedlars travelling the countryside; the magnifying glasses that appraisers could use to examine the scratches on swords; the telescopes that allowed aspiring astronomers to study the heavens; and the Dutch books that had taught the cartographer Inō Tadataka about surveying and would one day inspire a young scholar to write a *Sutra of Botany*.

Due to the influence of an earlier era of global connection and the continuing presence of a few important trade goods, everyday life in Japan was still connected to the material culture of the rest of the world. Japan, like Europe or North America, was a place where young women wore cheap cotton prints to work, prosperous men carried watches, and people consumed sugar with tea. But in Japan, women wore their cotton prints as kimonos with wide silk sashes, the watches counted uneven hours named for the animals of the Chinese zodiac (the Hour of the Dog, the Hour of the Horse), and the sugar came in brightly coloured rice flour dumplings served alongside unsweetened green tea. The German doctor Engelbert Kaempfer, who had resided at the Nagasaki trading settlement for two years in the late seventeenth century, was not exactly correct when he described Japan as a 'closed empire'. But it was a sheltered place, inaccessible to most foreigners and at a remove from global markets. Its cultural practices reflected the distance.

Yet during the years of Tsuneno's childhood, the world was coming closer all the time. The only boats on Big Pond were little skiffs belonging to local fishermen, but on the surrounding seas the water was crowded with more and different kinds of ships. Fortified hulks carried opium from Calcutta to the southern coast of China, where they anchored in coves and awaited the rowing boats that would smuggle their black, sticky cargo ashore. Canoes travelled along coastlines from the Arctic to Alta California loaded down with sea otter skins, which were traded to merchants on American ships with tall wooden masts and complicated rigging. They brought the otter furs to Hawai'i and Canton, shipped North American ginseng to China, delivered Fijian dried sea slugs to Manila, and brought Kaluan wood to Honolulu. Whalers, outfitted with harpoons and giant cauldrons, chased their prey all over the northern Pacific, while seal hunters drifted into inlets, scooped up the animals from rocks, and clubbed them to death. Meanwhile, boats of almost every description carried people from one end of the ocean to the other, sometimes against their will. Merchant vessels kept Indian prisoners among the cargo and delivered them to a penal colony in Penang, and massive British ships used the technology of the Atlantic Ocean's slave trade – shackles, iron collars, and chains – to transport London's convicts to Australia's Botany Bay.

As this traffic circled closer to the Japanese archipelago, children along the coasts that Inō Tadataka had so carefully surveyed began to encounter new, bigger boats with triangular canvas sails and strange flags. In 1807, people in Hitachi Province, bordering the Pacific, sighted a foreign ship along their coastline for the first time since 1611. Over the next forty years, they would see more than a hundred. Most of those who made their way into Japanese waters were whalers working the 'Japan Grounds' in the northern Pacific. Herman Melville, who was fascinated with Japan, wrote about the ships and their crews in *Moby-Dick*: 'If that double-bolted land, Japan, is ever to become hospitable, it is to the whale-ship alone to whom the credit will be due.' But there were also adventurers and surveyors, including a group of Russians circumnavigating the world, fortified with wild garlic and salted reindeer from Kamchatka, eager to name Japanese capes and mountains after Russian military heroes.

Most of these ships didn't land. The few whalers who tried to come ashore wanted provisions, particularly fruits and vegetables to ward off scurvy. The ordinary Japanese who encountered them learned that they liked sour plums, hated fried tofu and smelled terrible. The Russians, less desperate and better supplied, wanted to establish diplomatic relations and trade, and the officials who encountered them learned that they were imperious, demanding and hostile to questioning. Both groups of interlopers were given basic provisions, but they were all sent away and asked not to return.

Meanwhile, Japanese sailors, setting to sea in increasingly large, sturdy and well-supplied boats, found themselves meeting with foreign ships or drifting to faraway shores. During severe storms, Japanese crews would cut down their masts to avoid capsizing, which left them at the mercy of the currents. Some sailors drifted for months, surviving on fresh fish, seabirds and whatever they had in their stores, and landed in the Philippines, the Aleutian Islands or the Olympic Peninsula. Others were rescued by passing vessels and suddenly found themselves among crews of strange men speaking English, Russian or Spanish. A few Japanese castaways managed to be repatriated, occasionally by foreign captains who had ulterior motives, such as opening trade relations. The returnees were subjected to prolonged interrogation by samurai officials, who gathered their intelligence on foreign lands and then often forbade them to speak to others about what they had seen and heard.

Japanese officials' anxiety about the outside world mounted around the turn of the nineteenth century, fuelled by encroaching ships and new knowledge. The samurai Honda Toshiaki, who was, like Tsuneno, a native of Echigo Province, wrote startling tracts urging Japan to begin an aggressive programme of exploration, expansion and foreign trade. He proposed to establish commercial relations with Russia and send Japanese trading ships across the oceans. He wanted to colonise the far northern island of Karafuto (now Sakhalin), following the example of England, 'a nation about the same size as Japan' that had built a maritime empire. But he was an iconoclast who did not resemble any of the people Tsuneno knew. He thought that priests chanting in Sanskrit sounded 'like croaking frogs' and complained that Buddhism caused people to 'waste their time in total ignorance'. He also insisted that Chinese characters were overly complex and made people inclined to dilettantism; he suggested that all Japanese should be written in a phonetic alphabet. Shogunal officials did read his work, but they thought he was eccentric, and they did not heed his advice.

When the Napoleonic Wars finally reached Japan, in the form of a British warship, the shogun's men were not prepared. The ship sailed directly into Nagasaki Harbour, flying a Dutch flag, in early autumn of 1808. The samurai assigned to naval defence stood down, thinking it was a Dutch East India Company vessel. They were shocked when the sailors disembarked and took Dutch hostages – part of the hostilities in Europe – but they had no choice but to offer provisions in order to secure the safe return of the Dutchmen. The ship was so well armed and fortified that it looked to them like a floating castle. In the end, the harbour magistrate committed suicide to atone for the gravity of his error. Meanwhile, Russians, spurned in their efforts to open trade, conducted a series of raids in the far north, burning villages and disrupting fisheries. At one point, they planned to kidnap all the Japanese occupants of Karafuto and send them to Alaska to establish a colony there. This never came to pass, but the shogun's men were alarmed and determined not to be caught off guard again. When the Russian naval ship *Diana* landed on an island off the coast of northern Hokkaido in 1811, the Japanese took the crew hostage and kept them prisoner for three years, asking again and again about Russian intentions in the north.

Finally, in 1825, the shogunate issued the Edict to Repel Foreign Vessels, which instructed Japanese to fire on all Western ships attempting to cast anchor in any port other than Nagasaki. Any vessel that landed was to be burned, and the crew was to be executed.

*

While little girls in places outside of Japan learned to fear cast-iron cannons, 'disease boats' bearing mysterious illnesses, and the 'white men with horrible looks' who might haul them into ships and carry them away, Tsuneno could not have spent much time wondering about red-whiskered foreigners. They had no place in Ishigami Village, and they did not appear in any of the stories she was told. The goblins in the woods and the water sprites in Big Pond must have seemed more real. In any case, there were other things to fear, like hungry bears in summer, and sudden avalanches that buried entire villages in the winter, and epidemic diseases, like measles and smallpox, that ravaged families. At Rinsenji, Tsuneno's three-week-old baby sister, Umeka, died in the early spring of 1815, when Tsuneno was eleven. Her father, Emon, had been away for the baby's birth and never met her; her brother Giyū, only fifteen years old, was left in charge. It was the first time he had to shoulder the responsibilities that would be his when he succeeded his father as head of the household. He arranged for another temple to conduct the funeral services, accepted the candles, vegetables and coins that his neighbours sent as consolation gifts, and kept track of how much he had spent on rice and tofu to feed the mourners.

As her family prayed for Umeka's rebirth in the Pure Land, Tsuneno could turn her thoughts to an equally alluring and faraway place: the shogun's capital of Edo, the greatest city in the realm. Edo was where most of the books in her father's collection were published, where villagers migrated to work as servants and labourers in the winters, and where the Echigo crepe sellers went to meet wholesalers. A single city block there could contain more people than lived in all of Ishigami and the two neighbouring villages combined.

Tsuneno's corner of Echigo Province seemed remote, but it was only about two weeks' walk over the mountains to the capital, and news always came back, not only in books, prints and maps but also with migrants who walked the highways home in the spring, carrying the latest gossip along with small fistfuls of gold coins. They told their neighbours' wives and children of the strange customs in a place where it almost never snowed, where black demons walked the streets on New Year's Eve, plain for everyone to see, and an exorcist might snatch one up and throw it into the sea. They related the amazement they felt when they saw the riverbanks explode with bright white plum blossoms and green willows in the early spring, or when they ventured outside on winter nights to find naked young carpenters running through the streets, chanting the prayer to Amida Buddha and stopping intermittently to douse themselves with water, offering their momentary suffering as a testament to their faith. No one in Echigo would have done that, no matter how pious they were – they would have frozen to death.

Above all, those who returned from the city told stories about Edo's prosperity: its rows of stores extending for miles in every direction; its hordes of vendors, bearing things they'd never seen and didn't know they wanted; its cavernous merchant houses; and its multitude of hairdressers, street cleaners, night soil collectors and laundresses, who seemed to be everywhere, offering services and demanding tips. In Edo, there was an unimaginable number of things to buy, but there were even more ways to make money, and sometimes it was hard to distinguish between labour, entertainment and extortion.

Edo was familiar to the men in Tsuneno's family, who could speak with authority about friends and temples and city neighbourhoods. They had connections in Kyoto, the emperor's city, as well: the head temple of their sect was there, and they had made the necessary pilgrimages several times. Emon had been there when he was a young man, and Tsuneno's brother Giyū went as soon as he was ordained, in 1821. But the family had more associations in Edo, which was closer, and which loomed larger in the minds of most Echigo people. Tsuneno's uncle, the black sheep of her father's generation, had been adopted into a temple family in the downtown neighbourhood of Asakusa years before she was born, and the family kept up correspondence with a few Edo temples. Tsuneno's little brother Gisen would be sent there to study one day. He wouldn't inherit the temple – he had too many older brothers – but he could be very well educated, and it would also be useful for the family if he made the circuit of True Pure Land religious institutions and kept up with the latest news.

None of the women in Tsuneno's family went to Edo, or if they did, their trips never made any impression in the temple's archive. But the capital meant something to them, too. For women who had spent their lives in provincial villages, 'Edo' was an invocation of a different kind of life. It was shorthand for fashion and sophistication among country girls who did their hair in the 'Edo style', even though it had little resemblance to how city women wore theirs. It was an entertaining story for mothers and daughters who sat by the hearth on winter nights interrogating well-travelled guests about how city people celebrated the New Year. It was both an opportunity and an impossible standard for young women whose Edo-raised teachers told them that they wore their obis too low, spoke too roughly, greeted guests inappropriately, and didn't even understand how to walk down the street. Most of all, it was a dream of escape for the rebellious, discontented and desperate women who felt they had nothing left to lose.

Miyo, a village girl in Echigo, hated the fiancée her older brother had chosen. She begged to be sent into service in a distant province, perhaps envisioning a future in Edo, where many of her neighbours had gone to work. Riyo, an unhappy wife in Sagami Province, abandoned her husband and took off for the city with her two-year-old. She found a job as a wet nurse for a samurai family and started over. Taki, a pawnbroker's daughter in Musashi Province, ran away with her husband, who didn't get along with her parents, and the pair settled in a rented back-street tenement. Sumi, a peasant girl from Hitachi Province, absconded with a man who promised to take her to Edo. When her older brother came to look for her, she told him that she didn't care what kind of work she had to do or even if she died – she would never leave the city. Michi, a peasant daughter sent to serve a high-ranking lord, flatly refused to return to the countryside. She said there was nothing for her to do back home, so she married an Edo samurai and stayed.

There were others, too, women in unimaginably faraway places who flipped through pictures, listened to stories, envied their brothers and plotted their escape. By the early nineteenth century, this was a long and broad tradition, running from the rural women who streamed into Venice in the wake of the late-seventeenth-century plague epidemic, through the English dairymaids who left the countryside for London in the seventeenth century, to the country girls who crowded into Paris during the Age of Enlightenment. In 1616, an English maidservant testified that she had 'come from her father against his mind to dwell in London.' In 1644, a Finnish girl ran away from a detested husband and entered service in Stockholm; when her husband came to look for her, she fled the city with her new master. Marie-Anne Lafarge left her village for Aix in the 1780s because she believed that her parents favoured her brothers and sisters. Annushka, a contemporary of Tsuneno's, abandoned a faithless lover in the Russian countryside and went into service for a Frenchwoman in St Petersburg.

For young girls who hated village boys; daughters whose fathers beat them; bored women who couldn't face another day staring at barley fields, cows or rice paddies; dreamy teenagers who wanted the dresses they'd seen in pictures; wives whose husbands were boring, abusive or just too old; and brides who were disappointed on their wedding night, the city was a beacon. It was a possibility. It was a story they told themselves about what might happen in a crowded, anonymous place where not everyone was a peasant, where no one knew their families, where they might disappear and reemerge as entirely different people. Wherever the rise of the market economy had expanded the territory rural women could traverse in their own imaginations, they left. They believed that something different – something better – was waiting.

Tsuneno couldn't imagine any of these women, though they certainly lived in the same world as she did. They, too, had learned to sew with silk and cotton thread (though probably not many had learned to read). They, too, wore printed stripes, drank tea and ate sugar when they could afford it. They were following similar pathways through different landscapes, moving through places Tsuneno would never visit, speaking languages she would never hear. She was preoccupied with familiar things: the brothers she loved and resented, the snow that fell year after year, the dragonflies on Big Pond, the books in her father's library, the needles in her mother's sewing box, the silk robes packed away in her chest. The incense on the altar. The village that was yet to appear on a map of the province. The cedar trees that were waiting to be 'plants'.

Yet somehow, amid all of this, in a place that was being categorised and mapped, in a country where the outlines of the natural world were being retraced and the stakes of a new age of empire were just becoming clear, she, too, looked up and imagined a different kind of life. Was it the pictures in her books? The habit of envisioning the Pure Land, which inspired her to imagine other distant realms and better possibilities? Or was it some overheard conversation about the city, possibly concerning the plans for her little brother Gisen's future? Maybe it was just a vague sense that a life like her mother's would never be enough.

Or maybe it was years later, when all her conventional plans for her life had collapsed, when she was staring down a future that suddenly seemed unbearable, that the idea took shape in her mind. Whatever the reason, at some point Tsuneno came to understand the problem that would define the rest of her life, and to perceive it as something that had been true for a long time. It was one of the first things she ever wrote in a letter, something she had already told her family many times before she finally put it in writing: 'I wanted to go to Edo, but you wouldn't let me go.'

Chapter Two

HALF A LIFETIME IN THE COUNTRYSIDE

I n 1816, Tsuneno left Rinsenji for the first time. She wasn't going to Edo or anywhere else nearly as exciting. She was headed to an inland river town called Ōishida in Dewa Province, in the north. It wasn't exactly the opposite direction from the city, but it might as well have been. No one in Echigo read about Ōishida. No one dreamed of going to Dewa, unless they were cartographers or adventurers, the kind of people who might be interested in rugged mountains, wild forests and bears. Dewa was even colder than Echigo. In the winter, the fir trees, encased in heavy snow, would look like grimacing monsters frozen to the hillsides.

It was a difficult journey from Ishigami Village to Ōishida, over 180 miles. Tsuneno could get there by boat, sailing up the Sea of Japan coastline and then upriver. Or she could go on foot, along the coastal road and through the mountains, following in the footsteps of the haiku poet Matsuo Bashō, who had famously made the same journey in 1689. Bashō had travelled with a single companion, also a poet, seeking a kind of rootlessness that was akin to enlightenment. 'The months and days are the travellers of eternity,' Bashō wrote. 'The years that come and go are also voyagers.' He wanted to be unencumbered, so he brought very little: an old hat and a raincoat, brushes and ink to write. Tsuneno's trip was different. She travelled with attendants and luggage, weighed down by expectations. She was on her way to fulfil a promise. She was going to be married. She was twelve years old.

Tsuneno had always known that she would be married someday. Every girl did. She also knew that she had little choice in the matter: girls of her status did not select their own husbands. Instead, their parents made plans for the future. While Tsuneno was occupied with her sewing and her books, her parents, Emon and Haruma, searched for an appropriate groom. They sent letters back and forth, employed intermediaries, negotiated payments and exchanged gifts; bought mirrors and cosmetics, clothing and furniture. They had to pack carefully, because they were sending Tsuneno to a distant province. It was too far for her to come home for the customary one-month return, when a bride travelled to her parents' house for her first visit as a married woman. Once she was gone, she could send letters, but she would be alone with a new family in a strange place.

Tsuneno's parents weren't thoughtless or unkind. At twelve, Tsuneno was young to be married, but her aunt Chisato had been a thirteen-year-old bride. Girls who married that early might struggle more than older girls did with homesickness, but they would usually be granted a grace period to adjust to their new households' – and their new husbands' – demands. At twelve, most girls weren't even menstruating yet, and there was a general understanding that a girl under the age of fourteen or so could be too young for sex. In this regard, Emon and Haruma could be reassured that they had arranged the best match they could, and they could trust Tsuneno's new in-laws. The groom was a True Pure Land priest like Emon, and the two temple families had been friends and correspondents for generations. Tsuneno's new home, Jōganji, was a prominent temple, and the town of Ōishida was busy and prosperous, home to about a thousand people. In some ways, it was a step up from Rinsenji and Ishigami Village, even if it was farther from the realm's great cities.

Ōishida was famous for safflowers, which blanketed the valleys to the south in fields of vivid gold. When Bashō visited in the seventeenth century, he described how the town's poets tended their old-fashioned verses as if they were flowers from half-forgotten seeds. In reality, the work of cultivation was left to peasants in outlying villages, who went out to harvest on misty mornings in early summer, when the plants' spiky leaves were coated in dew. They plucked the blossoms, processed them into compact yellow-orange discs, then sold them to middlemen who loaded them onto packhorses bound for Ōishida's warehouses. In town, another set of labourers bundled the packages onto boats, which followed the course of the Mogami River towards the Sea of Japan. Eventually, the safflowers would be off-loaded in the emperor's capital, Kyoto, where they would be used to make cosmetics and textile dyes. Peasants labouring in the fields around Ōishida sang: 'I too want to go to the capital, on a black horse, with the safflowers.'

Tsuneno was born and raised in the rice fields of Ishigami, but she came of age amid the tiled warehouses and white sails of Ōishida. She arrived at her husband's temple as a girl, young even by the standards of her time, and was transformed into a full-fledged adult. Marriage did that for women, though it wasn't the same for men. If boys were peasants, the border between their childhood and adulthood was marked by a coming-of-age ceremony, when their hair would be cut short and they would change their clothes and assume new names. From then on, they could carry portable shrines through the village during festivals and even, sometimes, officiate at weddings. For Tsuneno's brothers, who were priests, the transformation point was different: it came when they were ordained. But for women – all women, peasants or samurai, priests' or merchants' daughters – the wedding ceremony was a universal divide. Whoever you were, and wherever you came from, marriage made you a woman. You would emerge with blackened teeth, painted carefully with metallic-tasting powder, to mark your new status. You would probably wear shorter sleeves and a rounder hairstyle. Even if the marriage failed, you would never be the same.

There were other, equally profound changes below the surface. At first, Tsuneno must have been fascinated with the stranger who had suddenly become her husband. As she moved through the familiar cycles of bells and prayers and offerings – the rhythms of her childhood, transposed to a new setting – she must have studied how he moved and ate and snored. She must have scanned his face and listened for his silences, considering all his preferences and habits, comparing him to her father and grandfather and older brothers. She had to try to accommodate his demands, even if they seemed strange and uncomfortable. That was what young brides were supposed to do, what all the books for girls told them to do, and even the most stubborn twelve-year-old would have found it difficult to disobey. She must have learned and changed in her pursuit of something ordinary: a slightly grander version of her mother's life.

But Tsuneno, who would later write so vividly about her struggles, never addressed those first years as a bride in a strange country town, far from her family. By the time she put brush to paper, her early marriage was so distant, or so thoroughly buried, that it never surfaced.

*

While Tsuneno was away in Ōishida, her brothers and sisters struggled with their own marriages. Kiyomi, the sister closest to her in age, had also married into a True Pure Land temple, but her new village was only a short walk away. It was close enough that she could borrow a miso bucket from her mother; her husband and her brother Giyū corresponded about how much they paid labourers to shovel snow. It was a familiar kind of life: the village temple, the same web of friends and neighbours. But it still wasn't easy.

Kiyomi had a sharp tongue, and her husband complained that she took offence at the slightest criticism. She didn't tend the altar to his satisfaction, and she wasn't welcoming to the parishioners. It was becoming difficult for him to fulfil his responsibilities as priest, because running a village temple was a job for two people. In truth, the situation was making him question his own judgment. He wrote to Giyū, explaining that he was reaching the end of his patience. Could Giyū talk some sense into his sister? But either Giyū declined or, more likely, his intervention was ineffective.

Eventually, Kiyomi's retired father-in-law took matters into his own hands. 'Kiyomi is acting like a criminal,' he wrote, 'and I won't stand for it. I'm preparing a cage for her. I've already started construction.' It wasn't the most unthinkable punishment for a wayward wife – even a difficult lord might find himself locked inside a wooden cage, with gourmet meals and murmured apologies passed through the bars. But it was humiliating – a forceful, public assertion of the family's power over the individual. Cages were in courtyards or in front rooms, where people from the community could see that the punishment was underway. In fact, that was part of the point, to save the family's reputation by displaying its resolve.

Over the years, Kiyomi learned her place. She stayed with her husband and had at least two children. Their arrival was celebrated with gifts and announcements, and she remained the mistress of the temple. But for the rest of her life, she might have shuddered whenever carpenters came to her house, thinking about her father-in-law, seeing the bars of a cage.

Giyū's transition to married life was equally difficult and humiliating. Just after he first married, in 1828, his father, Emon, went on a long pilgrimage, leaving Giyū in charge of Rinsenji. Giyū was only twenty-eight, but he had been the head of the household and the head priest for five years. It was long enough to learn the role: he knew where he was supposed to sit, what he was supposed to say, and who was supposed to listen to him. But he hadn't quite grown into his authority, and he still had trouble asserting himself, especially when his father was away and he was left alone to manage the five younger siblings who were still at home. The minute they sensed weakness, they were relentless. His brothers tried to sit in his place and ignored him when he told them to go buy firewood. His little sister Ino, still just a child, mocked him in front of the parishioners. Meanwhile, he was supposed to teach his bride, Rinsenji's new mistress, the ways of the household. It was a heavy responsibility, and he felt it keenly.

The first month of his marriage went as well as he could expect. At least, there was nothing out of the ordinary, nothing he would need to write down. That changed, suddenly, after his wife went on the customary first visit back to her parents' home. When she returned, it was as if an entirely different person had appeared in her place. She refused to obey any of Giyū's instructions and pointedly ignored his lectures about Buddhist and Confucian morality. She neglected basic household tasks and alienated his youngest sisters, Toshino and Ino, who complained about her to his mother. When he confronted his bride, she answered sullenly: 'I'll do as I like. And you do as you like, too. Get a prostitute or a concubine – I don't care.'

Giyū was shocked. This was not the way women talked. It was certainly not the way a young bride was supposed to speak to her husband. He might have been alluding to sex when he discussed her neglect of household duties. Certainly, a wife was expected to accommodate her husband's demands in that realm. Her blunt refusal, in such crude, explicit terms, was astonishing.

Giyū decided he had to divorce her, even though he was reluctant on several counts: his father was still away, an early divorce was embarrassing, the family had just spent a fortune on the wedding, and, perhaps most important, it seemed as if his wife might be pregnant. But what could he do? He couldn't be expected to put up with a rebellious, unpleasant wife. Finally, he summoned all his courage and confronted her. He was planning to call for the go-betweens in the morning so that they could inform her parents: the marriage was over.

Giyū might have expected resigned silence, sullen acquiescence, or maybe even an insincere promise to try harder. He wasn't prepared for what actually happened. His wife, who had spent months in open rebellion, began to cry so hard she could barely speak. When she finally recovered her composure, she told him something so terrible that he could barely comprehend it. In the fifth month, she said, just before she had left for her parents' house, she had been sick and lying in her room when a man broke in and raped her.

With that startling confession, Giyū's wife's fury seemed to dissolve into despair. For the next two days, she refused to eat; instead, she sobbed and begged for forgiveness. Giyū was shaken. Rather than calling in the go-betweens and preparing a notice of divorce, he waited. It turned out that she really was pregnant, and he couldn't know if the child was his, since there was no exact method of dating conception. As far as Giyū was concerned, it might not have mattered. According to his own account, he had been planning to write out a notice of divorce even when he had every reason to believe she was carrying his child. For him, his wife's conduct was the most important factor: he had the temple to think of, after all. Like his sister Kiyomi's husband, he would find it difficult to go on as head priest with a wife who wouldn't cooperate.

For Giyū's wife, that autumn and winter must have been agony. As the puddles in the courtyard clouded over with ice, she wrapped her obi a little higher towards her ribs every day, feeling her centre of gravity shift. Maybe she regretted her impulsive confession and wished that she had been able to swallow her rage. Or maybe she went on, dull and hostile, trying to force Giyū to send her away, so that she could leave and start over. But maybe she and her husband maintained a brittle peace, having reached some agreement that he never wrote down. She might have known her days at Rinsenji were numbered. She might have been biding her time.

In early spring, roughly nine months after she was raped, Giyū's wife went home to her own parents' house to give birth. At first, no one needed to know that anything was wrong. New mothers often spent those anxious days in the care of their own parents. But the days stretched into weeks, and Giyū never sent for her. He never even inquired about the baby. That was when her parents knew that something terrible had happened. They sent inquiries, engaged go-betweens and offered apologies (for what, exactly, they may not have known). But Giyū wouldn't tell them anything. Was he trying to spare their daughter? Trying to protect his own reputation? He would only say, in the vaguest possible terms, that the marriage had failed. Eventually, he sent a notice of divorce.

Giyū never searched for his wife's rapist, because he already knew who it was. It was his younger brother Girin. But Giyū couldn't quite bring himself to write it down. Instead, in a long memo for his own records, he juxtaposed an account of his wife's assault and his brother's punishment, leaving a blank space where the link between them should have been. 'Girin's misconduct in the fifth month of last year does not need to be related here,' he wrote. After a long discussion of his problems controlling his brothers, he concluded, conveniently, that the conflict with Girin 'was all my wife's evil doing'. By then she was long gone, and she and her child would never be mentioned in the Rinsenji records again.

Giyū remarried the following year. His second wife, Sano, survived her first year of marriage, took on the role of 'guardian of the temple', and lived a quiet, blameless life. She never caused the kind of trouble that would create a written record, and while she must have been able to write, nothing in her hand survived. When she died in 1859, she was given the second character of Giyū's name to take with her into the afterlife. She was, apparently, a perfect match.

But who could say what made a lasting marriage? Sano may have been wary, scarred by her own unwritten history. Or she may have sensed a silence where there should have been a story, hidden somewhere in the strange pauses and averted glances when her brother-in-law Girin's name was mentioned. Or maybe she did hear the story about her predecessor, as well as others. Women at Rinsenji talked. By the time she was married, Sano was already twenty-five. She had lived long enough to know about men, their loyalties, and what they might do to protect themselves. She was old enough to understand the risks of speaking too directly.

Sano kept quiet and stayed busy. Between 1832 and 1842, she had five babies. She could count on the help of servants, Tsuneno's little sisters and her still vigorous mother-in-law, but her days were occupied with infants and laundry, fevers and tantrums, broken dishes and runny noses. There were rooms to be swept and servants to be supervised, a husband to tend to, village women to visit, and always more offerings to be laid on the altar. During those years, she was the vital centre of the household and everyone depended on her efforts. She must have known she was fortunate. Her marriage endured, and all of her children survived. Her household was secure, she didn't have to work in the fields, and she never had to worry about how to afford miso, sake or lamp oil. If it wasn't enough, if sometimes, during her prayers to Amida Buddha, different, harsher words echoed in her head, she didn't let on.

Sano was bound by duty and routine, by the presence of children who needed her, by a workable, durable marriage, and maybe also by love. There were tense silences at Rinsenji, but there were also expressions of affection, usually among siblings and between parents and children. Tsuneno wrote warm letters to her mother and often asked after Sano. She sent them gifts and was concerned when they were ill. Giyū loved his brothers, or at least he insisted that he *should* love them and they should love him back. Tsuneno, writing much later, agreed. No matter how much she argued with Giyū, he was still her older brother.

But if Sano and Giyū loved each other, those bonds were forged outside the space of documents, somewhere in the temple's enduring silence.

*

In the fall of 1829, when Tsuneno had been married for thirteen years, her younger brother Girin arrived in Ōishida unexpectedly. She might have suspected something was wrong. He was old enough to be married and start his own life, but instead he was spending the days studying with her husband and helping with services at Jōganji, and he seemed to have no immediate plans.

Then again, Tsuneno was preoccupied with her own affairs. She had just returned from a long trip to Kyoto with both her mother-in-law and her own mother. It was a journey of nearly five hundred miles, and they had stopped at Ishigami Village on the way. Finally, she saw a city – the well-dressed crowds on Sanjō Bridge and the splendour of Higashi Honganji, the head temple of her branch of the True Pure Land sect. Overcome with the excitement of her first big trip, she may not have noticed that Girin was miserable, consumed with self-loathing. But he couldn't forget. When he wrote home to Rinsenji, he said that when he thought about his life – the terrible things he had done, his regrets, and the lies he had told – his hair stood on end. He didn't mention his brother's first wife, but he didn't have to. Giyū knew what he meant.

The year after Girin arrived in Ōishida, a fire ripped through Jōganji and burned it to the ground. If people knew where the fire started or had suspicions, they didn't create and preserve a record. Whatever blame and recrimination followed the blaze, it was either ephemeral or carefully hidden. Only accounts of the damage endured: the temple next door to Jōganji lost its main hall, the family residence, the belfry, the storehouses, the walkways through the garden, and even the outhouses. Thankfully, the gold images of the Buddha on the altar, the temple death register and an assortment of paper documents were spared. But Jōganji lost its entire collection of sutras, sacred Buddhist texts that Tsuneno's in-laws had been collecting for generations. It was a perfect lesson in the ephemerality of earthly things, but it was heartbreaking.

Over the following years, the temple was rebuilt, the blackened gravestones were tended, and the Jōganji archive of sutras was partially, and painstakingly, reassembled. But the family couldn't be salvaged. In the autumn of 1831, as Tsuneno's husband tried to reconstruct his ancestors' home, she travelled back to Echigo. An official notice of divorce followed.

By then, Tsuneno had lived in Ōishida for over half her life. She had attended fifteen years of festivals and memorials and readings from the sutras. She had learned her parishioners' names, greeted their children and offered condolences at their funerals. Hundreds of people had been her husband's responsibility, and hers. She had mastered the routines of the household, changing with the seasons. She had rushed around before the New Year, with frozen breath and aching hands in the early mornings; she had listened to the rain on spring nights when the Mogami River ran so quickly that they could hear it from the temple. She had accepted gifts of summer vegetables on days when tall birds stood still in the fields and cicadas cried in the trees. She had greeted unexpected visitors, left on trips, and managed all kinds of domestic catastrophes. But now those were memories – she would never go back.

Tsuneno's family might have tried harder to save the marriage if her husband hadn't lived so far away. As it was, there was little they could do. Giyū replied to the notice of divorce with a graceful letter of acknowledgement. 'My parents are devastated,' he wrote, 'but they accept that it's fate and there is nothing to be done. They are grateful to you for taking her in while she was still very young and caring for her for the last fifteen years.' As far as the family's records were concerned, that was the end of the story.

Maybe Tsuneno loved her husband and wrote home to her mother marvelling at her good luck. Maybe she had miscarriage after miscarriage and watched him slowly lose interest and his ultimate rejection broke her heart. Or perhaps it was the opposite: she dreaded every night and put him off with a thousand excuses. She could have found a lover – a young priest or a servant girl – and got caught up in a passionate, doomed affair. Or she might have endured fifteen years of shouted insults, fists and bruises, and spent part of every day staring blankly, planning her escape. She might have set the fire: a moment alone in a room, the lantern carelessly, casually overturned, a silent retreat.

More likely, the truth was mundane: her mother-in-law urged her to be patient, but she never could hold her tongue; the pickles she made were always too salty or not salty enough, she alienated the servants and was unkind to the neighbours, and her husband finally tired of arguing with her. Whatever happened, there is no record. It's possible that even Tsuneno didn't think any of it was worth remembering.

*

A divorce wasn't necessarily a catastrophe. Although every girl could expect to marry, everyone also knew that marriages didn't necessarily last. By some counts, nearly half of women ended up divorced from their first husbands. Divorce was a practical solution, a safety valve for a family system where so much depended on the compatibility of young couples. Newly married people usually lived with their in-laws, and the success of the household relied on the labour and goodwill of the new wife (or, sometimes, husband) who had joined the family. If the bride or groom was found lacking in some fundamental way, then it was best to call off the marriage and try again, cycling through partners until the best match was found. This rule applied for both men and women. People might wonder why Tsuneno had been sent home, whether there might be some essential problem with her character. They might also wonder why she had never had children, which, for some families, would be an equally important question. But a divorce wouldn't necessarily make her unmarriageable.

In some ways, the problem for Tsuneno was that her first marriage had lasted as long as it did. If she'd divorced quickly and returned home at the age of fifteen, or even twenty, then her prospects would have been much better. Women who divorced in their twenties almost always remarried, but those who were older struggled. Tsuneno was twenty-eight and right on the edge. Her father worried that she might be too old to make another good match.

It took over a year to arrange another marriage, but finally a prominent local family made a proposal. They were farmers, not priests, and their village, Ōshima, was up in the mountains. But they were wealthy and socially appropriate. It was a relief. Tsuneno was lucky.

In the first days of the chilly summer of 1833, as anxious peasants hoped for a break in the clouds, Giyū threw himself into the process of planning parties and drawing up shopping lists for his sister's wedding. Tsuneno's trousseau required special attention, in part because its contents would be displayed at her in-laws' house. Giyū was always concerned for propriety, and he knew his family needed to make a good showing. Of course, since he was a man, and a priest, he couldn't know exactly how a married woman should be outfitted. He usually wore dull clerical robes, and the vagaries of style were beyond him. Luckily, there were women around – including Tsuneno, Sano and his mother – who could weigh in on the details. 'Should this unlined kimono be striped silk crepe or should it have a fine pattern?' someone jotted down in the margins of a shopping list. 'The fine pattern is better,' came the decisive answer.

In the end, the bill for new clothing totalled more than twelve gold pieces, which Giyū paid out in instalments over two weeks.

Tsuneno's much younger sister Toshino was also getting married that summer, and outfitting two brides at the same time was a strain. Giyū gratefully accepted a gift of fifteen gold pieces from Tsuneno's future in-laws, with the understanding that it would be used for her trousseau.

It was an auspicious start, even if the weather was gloomy. As peasants waded out into the rice fields, still wearing their padded coats, Giyū hosted a party. He distributed sake and snacks to thirteen parishioners, tipped the cook one gold coin, and gave two hundred coppers to the local beggars, who expected alms on the occasion of a wedding and could cause disruptions if they weren't paid. The usual people were in attendance – the immediate family, of course; Tsuneno's brother Kōtoku's wife, who showed up with a new baby and a nursemaid; Kiyomi's beleaguered husband (the incident with the cage behind him, hopefully); and the go-betweens who had arranged the marriage. They were outnumbered by the servants – well over a dozen, including six strong men just to carry Tsuneno's furniture from one house to the other.

The walk to the groom's house in Ōshima took most of a day. It was all uphill, on muddy, slippery paths, past terraced rice fields, where seedlings were planted two or three deep in rows that marched into the mountains. The fields were dark and murky, and the tips of the plants barely poked through the water. They were growing too slowly – anyone could see that. It wouldn't be a good harvest. Still, weddings were good luck, and people lined the road to see the bridal party pass, shouting at them, every so often, to stop and sing songs of celebration.

Ōshima Village was remote but not isolated. It hosted a market three times a month, and it was a stop on a minor highway leading through the mountains. In summer, when Tsuneno arrived, travellers and packhorses were still coming through, bringing news with them. It would be much quieter in winter, because the road would be impassable. The province's major artery, the Northern Highway, would also be snowed in, but it had the advantage of being strategically important. If an official message was on the way from Edo to the Sea of Japan coast, peasant labourers in flat, weighted shoes would be sent to stomp on the snowdrifts so that messengers could fly through. But there would be no need to send anything important through Ōshima's hilly little highway, so no one would clear it. The village would wait, quietly, for the spring.

Every fall, before the snow blocked their way, many of Ōshima's young people followed the road down out of the mountains and southeast to Edo. The area had little to offer them besides tedious work in the fields, and they could earn higher wages as servants and labourers in the city. Some went for years without contacting their relatives because they were illiterate and couldn't send letters. On at least one occasion, the villagers pooled their money to send a man to check on the migrants. Most were still where they said they would be, but some had thoroughly disappeared and were never heard from again. Those who returned encountered the reflexive suspicion of mountain people. Two years after Tsuneno arrived in Ōshima, a group of seven men who had come home after spending the winter in the city were accused of bringing back a strange disease and spreading it among their neighbours. The village headman made them agree to pay the medical expenses of everyone affected.

In Ōshima, Tsuneno belonged to a farming family for the first time. Everyone in her household engaged, to some extent, in the muddy, tedious labour of making things grow. The project consumed their minds even as it strained their muscles. There was something new to think about every day. If peasants just planted last year's seeds in the soil, pulled weeds, and hoped for a harvest, they risked catastrophic failure. And those who failed had no security. Eventually, they wouldn't be able to pay their taxes, their households would fracture, they would have to indenture their children to brothels or dance troupes, and they would be left to wander the roads as beggars.

The first decision in a farmer's year was which strain to plant, and there were many choices: catalogues offered seed varieties with enticing names like White Beard and Princess Crane. It was best to vary the proportions, taking into account the previous year's yield, always balancing risk. For the same reason, it was advisable to intersperse rice with other crops: wheat for 'good' fields, soya beans for mediocre ones, millet where nothing else would grow, and buckwheat at high elevations. Once planning was over, success or failure was a matter of timing. Farmers needed to know how long to soak the seeds, when to begin ploughing, when to transplant the seedlings and when to flood the paddies. They could consult almanacs and manuals, or they could watch the clouds and feel the soil. Fortunate, literate families could look back through their own diaries. Successful farmers left little to chance.

But in 1833, the year Tsuneno arrived in Ōshima, even the best planning couldn't compensate for the weather. The rainy season had arrived on schedule, with its light mists and heavy downpours, and the fields were flooded in the usual way. But the fog never lifted. Peasants waited in vain for the hot, sunny weather that would encourage green shoots to emerge from the muddy water. Instead, it rained so hard that fragile young plants were submerged for days at a time. Late summer brought a freak snowstorm and an unprecedented early frost. When it was time to harvest, farmers were only able to salvage a third of the rice crop. Tsuneno's hungry neighbours, mountain dwellers who rarely saw the ocean, travelled to the seashore, waded into the surf and tried to gather seaweed.

One bad harvest could be endured: samurai officials granted petitions for tax relief, domain lords forbade their subjects to brew sake or send grain out of their territories, towns and villages opened their rice stores, and wealthy merchants donated money and food to their neighbours. Tsuneno's new family had money and influence; they probably gave alms to beggars and helped to draft the relief petitions. Then they awaited the next planting season, a little anxious because poor peasants had spent their money on food and had little left for seed rice and fertiliser. Luckily, the weather in 1834 was warm and dry. But starving farmers had eaten some of their seedlings, and even before the autumn came it looked like there might be a famine. Villages to the east of Ōshima pooled their money and rushed to buy relief rice. They were prescient. The harvest was only 60 percent of what it should have been.

During Tsuneno's second winter in Ōshima, she watched her neighbours struggle. But everyone thought the crisis would be over after one more good year. Peasants scanned the sky, counted the days, and waited. And waited. The spring of 1835 was freezing and the snow was late to melt. Farmers brought in less than half the usual rice crop, and the soya bean harvest was so bad that no one could make miso. Tsuneno and her family could still eat, but cooking was tricky. Every measure of rice and every cup of soy sauce was precious. In the autumn, when a large, wealthy peasant family might pickle nearly a thousand radishes to get through the winter, the stakes were already high. The mistakes that might ordinarily be tolerated of a new bride working in an unfamiliar kitchen could be fatal in a year when rice bran was expensive and miso was impossible to get.

After the gloomy New Year of 1836, when only the very luckiest families could eat the traditional sticky rice cakes and drink sake, it snowed heavily. Two miles from Ōshima, the headman in Mine Village panicked. More than half the families in his village had run out of food. They could try to forage mountain vegetables, kudzu, reeds and water oats, but in early spring there were still nearly ten feet of snow on the ground, and the late thaw would make it impossible to gather new leaves in time to stave off starvation. Meanwhile, the families who could still eat had nothing to give them. At planting time, peasants wouldn't have the money to redeem all the farming tools they had pawned. Even if they didn't eat their seed rice, they wouldn't be able to plant. It seemed as though half the village would starve to death.

By late spring, hungry farmers were so weak that even those who had seed rice and tools couldn't work. The fields stood empty, infested with bugs. By the end of the year, Murono, another village near Ōshima, would mourn eighty deaths. The number was staggering, disorientating, a catastrophe in a place where farming communities typically contained only a few hundred people each. The fatalities weren't spread evenly among villages – some were larger and better prepared, others poorer and more vulnerable – but in the area as a whole, the annual death rate nearly tripled. The headman in Murono wrote that the harvest in 1836 was 'the worst of all time.'

Tsuneno was in no danger of starving, but she wasn't entirely sheltered. Her husband, Yasōemon, had spent all four years of their marriage waiting in vain for something to change, for the weather to clear, for the rice plants to grow. The failure was utterly beyond his control. There were opportunities in famine years – if he still had cash on hand, he could buy fields and woodlands cheaply. Still, he was a farmer, and Tsuneno was now a farmer's wife. Ultimately, they had to make the land yield something. It was little consolation that others were suffering more: entire families of poor peasants had deserted their fields to stumble down Ōshima's main road, and harrowing stories drifted back from villages even deeper in the mountains.

Back at Rinsenji, Tsuneno's family was forced to economise. Giyū sold off a stand of woods that included over three hundred trees, then wrote to a correspondent to whom he owed money and apologised that he couldn't pay his debts. He also exchanged letters with Tsuneno's former husband in Ōishida, who reported that the formerly prosperous town was devastated. The Mogami River had flooded, taking seventeen houses with it, and the years of bad harvests had left over twenty of his parishioners' families with nothing. People were so desperate that they had cut down two-thirds of the cedar trees near town, either to use as fuel or to sell to anyone who had money left to buy timber. Witnessing the suffering of ordinary people, he pondered the impermanence of the world, a fundamental Buddhist teaching, and dedicated himself to his prayers. He found some hope in his faith. In the next life, at least, all believers would be reborn in the Pure Land.

As winter turned to spring, everyone prayed, for the living and – increasingly – the dead. Across Japan, at the height of what would later be known as the Tenpō famine, fatalities measured in the hundreds of thousands. It was hard to say how many died of hunger and how many died of the epidemic diseases – typhus and dysentery – that ravaged the weakened population. The mountainous region between Echigo and Kyoto lost over 10 percent of its people. There were wild reports out of the northeast: half the peasants in one domain had died and some of the survivors had resorted to cannibalism. Even reliable accounts described people reduced to eating grass and straw sandals, roadways strewn with emaciated corpses, and gravediggers too weak and exhausted to continue their work.

In the summer of 1837, even with the hope of a good harvest on the horizon, Ōshima was still suffering. It was a year of broken families, and not only because so many had starved, fallen sick, and died. Poor families were sending away daughters-in-law to eliminate extra mouths to feed, and vulnerable people were disappearing. Tsuneno's marital family was not poor or marginal, and her husband, Yasōemon, wasn't desperate enough to send back a wife of four years because he couldn't afford food. But he also wasn't willing to struggle through a difficult marriage. He and Tsuneno had no children. Her sister Toshino, who was only eighteen, had given birth to a healthy girl in the freezing summer of 1835. But Tsuneno, thirty-three years old, was already middle-aged, at least by village standards. There might have been some expectation that she could have a baby early in the marriage, but it was extremely unlikely that she could give birth to a first child so late. Month after month, as Yasōemon toiled uselessly in the rainy, chilly fields, they lost hope. In better times or with a more compatible wife, Yasōemon and his parents might have decided to adopt an heir. People did it all the time. But in the eerily quiet summer of 1837, Yasōemon decided to cut his losses.

Giyū heard about the divorce from his uncle, who had received the information from the go-between in Tsuneno's marriage. Yasōemon was in the middle of rice planting, but he said that he would return all of Tsuneno's things later. The following day, he sent his own letter. 'Nothing especially bad has happened,' he explained, 'but household affairs are not proceeding smoothly.'

Giyū had heard those words before. It was almost the exact same language he had used when he divorced his traumatised pregnant wife, nearly a decade earlier. Maybe Tsuneno's fertility was the issue, but Yasōemon had tactfully failed to mention it. He even agreed that Giyū could keep the fifteen gold pieces that his family had contributed to pay for Tsuneno's trousseau. It wasn't poverty that had compelled him to cut ties with Tsuneno; it was something else, something he wasn't saying. If he wanted to know, Giyū would have to hear the story directly from his sister. But he knew from his own experience that sometimes it was better not to ask.

Tsuneno left Ōshima and descended the foothills through the haunted, broken countryside. In the middle of the devastation, Rinsenji was more or less as she had left it. Her little sister Toshino was married and gone, of course, and her sister-in-law Sano was chasing around yet another toddler. But the temple's death register recorded more names than usual that year: ten, as opposed to four or five. And there were other signs of strain in the family. Two of Tsuneno's younger brothers were also divorced, including Girin, who had somehow found his way home from Ōishida and back into his family's good graces. And her father was declining. He died in early autumn, a few months after she returned to Rinsenji. The family mourned, and Giyū worried. Now he really was the head of household, in fact as well as name, and he was alone with his responsibilities. As he often did, he turned to writing, ending an account of his father's death with a list of his troubles: 'This year Tsuneno, Girin, and Gisen all divorced. The temple is struggling, and we will have to help our poor tenants make it through the winter.'

It wasn't clear how much of the family's troubles could be blamed on the famine. Emon was already old and weak, and the three divorces in one year might have had more to do with the idiosyncrasies of the family than the devastation that had claimed so many of their neighbours. The more important question, now, was how to go on.

*

Tsuneno's third new beginning came earlier than anyone might have imagined. Only months after she returned home, Giyū entertained offers from four potential husbands. The prospect of an alliance with a prominent temple family must have been attractive, and the open question of Tsuneno's fertility must not have bothered them. Tsuneno's mother conferred with Giyū and they chose another peasant, this time from a village on the broad plain near the castle town of Takada. The area as a whole was more prosperous than the mountains, with general stores that sold sake, tobacco, dried squid and sandals. Some houses had waterwheels; in good times, they rented them out to townspeople who wanted to polish their rice.

Initially, Tsuneno agreed to the match. But by now she was thirty-four. She wasn't the twelve-year-old who had travelled the long road to Ōishida, unsure of what to expect. Twice now, following her family's plans had ended the same way: with a notice of divorce and another round of wedding planning. This time, Tsuneno would make the choice. About a week after the engagement was decided, her uncle came by the temple when Giyū and her mother were both out for the day and Tsuneno seized the opportunity to change her fate. She told him that she didn't want to marry the peasant. She much preferred another candidate, a priest.

If Tsuneno's aim was to get out of her engagement, she succeeded. But for some reason, she didn't end up marrying the priest she claimed to prefer. Within two months, Giyū found a fifth candidate, a man in Takada, and negotiated an entirely new match. Tsuneno agreed. At that point, she probably had little choice.

Giyū planned the wedding, again. This time, twenty-three hungry peasants descended on the temple and drank two and a half gallons of sake. They also devoured two pounds of whale and eight large blocks of tofu, along with pickled and boiled radishes. Rinsenji was ready for the crowd. Sano set out soup bowls for ordinary sake and rice bowls for cloudy, unrefined sake. She was an accomplished hostess; it was part of her job as the head priest's wife. But the main wedding party, a few days later, was quite small, comprising only Tsuneno, Giyū, the go-betweens, and a few servants. The group walked the short distance to Takada, stopping a few times to distribute sake to people along the street and once so that the women in the group could rearrange their hair. By the time they arrived to deliver Tsuneno, they were well coiffed and probably slightly drunk. The servants, who received gold coins for their trouble, were always happy to celebrate another wedding, but Giyū hoped it was the last one.

Tsuneno's third husband's house was in Inada-machi, a peripheral neighbourhood across a narrow river from the rest of Takada. Still, it was by far the most sophisticated place Tsuneno had ever lived. The castle town featured bathhouses, hairdressers and even theatres. In midwinter, while the villages were sleepy, waiting for the thaw, Takada felt alive. Businesses remained open, and people scurried from place to place through a maze of snow tunnels. They couldn't see the mountains or the stars. The spring would be blinding, a sudden flood of sunshine after months of dim, filtered light. In the meantime, they wrapped themselves in padded cotton and ventured out, trying not to mind the cold.

But Tsuneno was stuck inside. Barely six weeks after the wedding, she contracted an eye disease that left her incapacitated. Her family sent a gift: a box of miso, a few pickles and rice crackers. The messenger returned to Rinsenji with adzuki beans and the distressing news that Tsuneno was too sick to know what she was sending. A few weeks later, the go-between in the wedding expressed concern over Tsuneno's health when Giyū visited to pay him for his services. Giyū was so worried that he rushed to Takada, carrying a small gift of sake for Tsuneno's husband, and ended up spending the night. Days later, Tsuneno recovered enough to visit home, but the family continued to worry, and they sent her blankets and money.

In the end, Tsuneno's third marriage lasted four blurry, claustrophobic months. She was divorced before the last of the snow melted. For the second time in a year, a group of men from the village carried her furniture home.

*

All through the rest of 1838 and into 1839, Tsuneno was desperate. She had never recovered from the illness she suffered in Takada, and her ailments seemed psychological as well as physical. She wrote later that she had intended to die. Giyū attributed her suffering to her personal failings: 'She was married, but the marriage failed due to her selfishness, and soon after she was divorced her health deteriorated.' He had little patience for his sister's weakness. His wife, Sano, was expecting another baby at the end of the summer, and the house was full. He started making plans to send Tsuneno away. Perhaps there was a widower somewhere who needed help with housework and wouldn't mind an older bride with an unfortunate history.

'If I stayed at home,' Tsuneno wrote later, 'they were talking about sending me to another terrible place to marry a widower. I was terrified to disobey, but I didn't want to marry a widower. I was being forced into something that I just refused to do.' She didn't want to cause trouble, and she knew her mother and her brother thought her behaviour was intolerable. 'I understood that my own unacceptable conduct had tried my family's patience,' she wrote.

She had already failed at marriage three times, and this instance of disobedience would only confirm her brother's low opinion of her. But she knew she couldn't marry again. She had to summon her courage. 'When I wasn't brave,' she reflected later, 'I got caught up in unpleasantness no matter what I did.'

She refused every proposal. Later, she described her resistance as a wooden door reinforced with metal. It was one of the only times she used a metaphor; she usually confined herself to literal descriptions. But the image of the door must have appealed to her. It was a plain, ordinary thing, but it was far stronger than it looked. It wouldn't break, no matter how many times it was hit. It would stand for years, ugly and battered. But eventually, it would warp so badly that it could never be opened.

There had to be something else: a proposal she could make herself. Another option, so she wouldn't have to spend the rest of her life saying no.

She could go to Edo.

For years, Tsuneno had told her parents that she wanted to go to the city, but they wouldn't hear of it. She also told her uncle and her favourite brother, Kōtoku, who was a doctor in Takada, but they wouldn't listen. She told friends and near strangers, until it seemed like everyone in the county knew, but she couldn't find a way to get there. Women didn't travel to Edo by themselves. She thought she might be able to hire an escort from a messenger service, but for that she would need money and an opportunity to escape.

In the late autumn of 1839, Tsuneno told Giyū and her mother that she wanted to visit Kōtoku and then go from there to a hot spring in Kōzuke Province, which was, conveniently, in the direction of Edo. It would be good for her eyes, she said. She packed carefully, choosing mostly new clothes that would be suitable to wear on a late-autumn trip. She sold many of the items from her trousseau to a man in Iimuro Village, just next to Ishigami, and left three gold pieces with her uncle who lived there. She trusted him. Then she wrapped herself in a long black coat and set off on foot for Takada.

She never arrived at Kōtoku's house. Instead, she stopped on Shimogomachi Bridge, which spanned a little stream in the heart of Takada's commercial district. There she had planned to meet a young man named Chikan who was a junior priest at a village temple nearby. She already knew him – her family had friends and acquaintances at temples all over the county, and he had visited Rinsenji a few days earlier. At the time, she had told him that she wanted to go to Edo. He replied that he had relatives in the city, including his uncle's two brothers. They would welcome her there. Maybe he and Tsuneno could go together.

When Tsuneno met Chikan on the bridge, he said that he was about to leave for the city with his aunt. Tsuneno was also planning to leave, but not quite so soon. She had wanted to hire an escort from a messenger service, she said. He dismissed the idea. It wasn't necessary. He'd be her escort; it would be no trouble. She'd need money for the trip, of course, but she could pawn the clothes she was carrying, and that would probably be enough.

Tsuneno considered her options. She had no reason not to trust Chikan. After all, he wasn't a strange person from another province and he came from a temple family, just like her. He spoke to her kindly, as if she were a younger sister. He was travelling with his aunt, and he said he had relatives in Edo. She would have company, people who knew the road, and a place to stay when she reached the city.

It was the first day of the tenth month of the year, and already the wind had picked up behind the mountains. The first snow would come soon, and then another grey winter. In a few weeks, the roads would be buried. If she left, it would be difficult for anyone to come after her. On the other hand, it would be impossible to get home.

A few blocks to the south, her brother Kōtoku was waiting with his wife and family, expecting her any minute. To the west was Rinsenji, her mother, her sister-in-law Sano and her children, the endless conversations about marriage, an existence that had become intolerable. Surrounding her were the inns and shops of Takada. Packhorses and travellers crossed the bridge, everyone with somewhere to go. And beyond them was the northeastern countryside, the fields and mountains where she had spent half a lifetime. Thirty-five years of tar-black nights, blinding sunshine on snow, and thick icicles like giant white radishes hanging to dry. How many more years did she have left?

To the southwest was Edo, and in front of her was a man waiting for an answer. Would she go, now, and leave everything? She looked at him, standing on the bridge.

The door swung open.

She said yes.

Chapter Three

TO EDO

At first, the process of planning to leave appeared to be ordinary, a series of mundane activities. From the outside, they looked like the kind of errands any woman might pursue on any typical day. But Tsuneno knew that each was a little betrayal. They added up to a decision that could never be undone.

First, she made a quick inventory of everything she had carried to Takada: padded robes in striped silk crepe and cotton, lined underrobes in scarlet crepe and brown patchwork, a patchwork undergarment, a long winter coat, an unlined robe in glossy silk, a mirror, a box of hairpins and a set of patterned handkerchiefs. She was wearing an unlined robe and a black coat. Those she would keep; they would have to be warm enough for the journey. The rest could go. She made a bundle and handed it over to Chikan, who had found an intermediary who would take them to a pawnshop and exchange them for cash.

Tsuneno hated parting with her clothes. It was not only because they made her who she was – the priest's daughter in warm padded robes and tidy, pinned hair. They were also her creation, the product of years of patient labour and good judgement. Giyū had always thought her attachment to her things was unreasonable.

They had once argued bitterly over a robe she had made for her first husband. Giyū had tried to buy it – he gave her husband money for it – and he was incredulous when Tsuneno demanded that he send it back. 'It was my work and skill,' she'd insisted. 'She's ridiculous,' he'd scribbled to himself, finding a familiar outlet for his frustration in writing.

Now, ten years and three divorces later, Tsuneno handed over her clothes, mirror and hairpins to be exchanged between strangers. She wouldn't watch as the pawnbroker assessed them, and he wouldn't care who had stitched and unstitched her robes, where she had worn them last, or how they had ended up in his possession. He wouldn't ask who needed the money and for what purpose. Pawnbrokers rarely asked; they just accepted clothes and handed over coins and receipts.

Tsuneno knew a little about pawnshops, because her brothers had a habit of pawning things for spending money. One of her younger brothers had once got into serious trouble for pawning Giyū's silver pipe, along with a little bag that Tsuneno had sent from Ōishida, and several dozen books from the library, including, ironically, the five Confucian classics.

Village women used pawnshops, too, but they had to be especially careful not to be cheated. Back in Ōshima Village, a well-known story about a girl named Towa illustrated the point. Her father had been the wealthiest man in the village next door, and he had leveraged all his connections to marry her off to a prominent merchant's son in Takada. It was a brilliant match, and Towa was sent off in the very best style a peasant could manage. But she soon found that the silk and cotton robes in her trousseau, which had so impressed people in the village, were considered dowdy and outdated in Takada. At the age of thirteen, newly married and far from home, she desperately needed to fit in. So she sold several items to a used-clothing dealer, hoping to use the proceeds to buy better things. The dealer and his mother took the measure of this scared, awkward girl and decided she was an easy mark. They never gave Towa all the money she was promised, and she ended up in debt to the store where she went to purchase new clothes. When her husband and in-laws found out, they sent her right back to her village with a notice of divorce. Who could trust a bride who was devious enough to secretly sell things and stupid enough to be cheated? Eventually, Towa's father had to go all the way to Edo to bring the clothing dealer to justice. Her family was humiliated, and she had no prospect of making such a good marriage again.

Tsuneno should have known as well as anyone how easy it was to be cheated, how a woman could be ruined by a single bad choice. She certainly knew how clothing could make a person, and she should have realised how its loss could multiply, too quickly, until it consumed a marriage, an identity, a life. But she had already made her decision to leave, and pawning her clothes was the cost.

The intermediary came back from the pawnbroker with a ticket and three gold pieces. Chikan took the cash – for the journey, he said – and the intermediary kept the ticket. Tsuneno was left empty-handed, with just the list she had memorised: the brown patchwork, the scarlet crepe, the hairpins. It was the beginning of an equation that she would continually rebalance, day after day, as autumn turned to winter. These were the things she had lost. This was how much they were worth. This was the price she had paid.

Before she left Takada, Tsuneno wrote a letter to her uncle. He was holding three gold pieces for her – the proceeds of her earlier sale – and if he went straight to the pawnshop, he could redeem her things before the interest started accruing. She related a version of her story, a first draft that she would revise later, changing the details as she wrote to different people. She hadn't been feeling well, she wrote, so she was going to visit hot springs along with a group of five men and eight women she'd met in Takada. Her old friend Chikan was among them, and when he said he didn't have travel money she'd pawned her clothes, hairpins and mirror to help. After explaining the mechanics of the transaction, she added, almost as an afterthought: 'By the way, as I've been telling everyone over and over again, I really want to go to Edo if I get a chance. So if I end up going there, I'll write to you right away. There's a group heading to Edo, and they're all very good people, so you don't have to worry about me.'

She wrote confidently, in complicated Chinese characters, as if she expected to be forgiven for the decision to pawn everything and leave with a strange man. It was as if she believed that her uncle would find her money, go directly to the pawnshop and redeem everything. As if everyone were kind, all her calculations were accurate and every loss could be recouped. Tsuneno might have suspected that her accounting was still in process and that, in the end, the equation wouldn't balance. But for the time being, she didn't let on. There would be time for more letters later.

*

Tsuneno and Chikan left Takada on a familiar road, the same one they would have taken if they were walking back towards the countryside. At first, it still might have been an ordinary day. The path, wide and marked with stone lanterns, led into the mountains south of Takada and climbed towards Mt Myōkō, the farthest, highest peak on the horizon of Tsuneno's childhood. There was a small hot spring town at the base of the mountain, Akakura, where Tsuneno and Chikan stayed for a few nights and prepared for the rest of their journey. There Tsuneno wrote another letter to her uncle, again in perfectly formed characters. Later, she would claim that Chikan was looking over her shoulder and telling her what to write. The letter was another version of the same story, with one change. Now, she wrote, she was definitely going to Edo, where she would be staying with one of Chikan's relatives. She posted the letter, addressed from 'Tsuneno in Akakura', and continued on her way.

Akakura was a short walk from Sekikawa Barrier, one of the many checkpoints along the roads where samurai guards in the employ of the domain lords or the shogunate checked travel passes. This was part of the security apparatus that the Tokugawa shogunate had established in the seventeenth century, intended to monitor the movements of people who might present a threat to the still fragile Great Peace. Sekikawa was one of the realm's most important guard posts, because it was just beyond the point where the Northern Highway turned towards Edo. Any lord on the Sea of Japan coast who was planning rebellion would lead his troops through Sekikawa, and his women, who lived as hostages in Edo, would pass through in the opposite direction to flee to safety in their home provinces. As a result, the Sekikawa guards refused to admit women who didn't have passes, and those who did have the necessary documents were carefully scrutinised.

Tsuneno had a good excuse to pass through – her cover story was that she was going to a hot spring to recuperate from an illness, and that would have been enough to procure a pass from the magistrates in Takada. But the barrier was always a problem. Even with a pass, Tsuneno could still be detained or required to produce a bribe. And how was she supposed to explain Chikan? It was easier to bypass the armed guards and the barrier post and follow the unmarked paths laid down by thousands of women who had made the same choice, knowing that they were unlikely to be apprehended. There was a way through the barrier, if she was willing to crawl through a dog door. She could go at night and hope the guards looked the other way. Otherwise, she could leave the shogun's highway and walk along a path that passed the base of the mountain, then wound through rice fields and forests, across grassy plains, and through villages of resentful, suspicious peasants. In either case, she needed to hire a guide, and it would cost a few dozen copper coins, at least. It was another risk, another price to be paid and added to the account.

Back on the highway, Tsuneno and Chikan joined other men and women travelling in the same direction, over the mountains and towards the capital. Some were destined for Zenkōji, a spectacular temple that attracted thousands of pilgrims. Others were the last, desperate refugees from the famine. Still more were regular travellers and seasonal migrants, Echigo peasants who left in the autumn and would return in the spring. The people in Edo called them grey starlings, because they were drab, noisy and hungry, and they flocked to the city every winter. Many would find work as servants. They would rely on their masters for a few months' room and board, and they would come home clutching gold coins. Others, rough, burly men, would find work in the city's bathhouses, where they would carry water and stoke fires. Or they would polish rice, crushing unhulled grains in huge mortars. It was heavy, exhausting labour. City people joked that new arrivals from Echigo were so tough, and so naïve, that they lugged their own stone mortars down the highways to Edo.

Tsuneno and Chikan followed the road from station to station. There were places where inns lined up in a pleasant row, lights glowing from the paper-covered windows; places that looked rough and half-deserted; places where gaudily dressed women lined up in the streets and pulled at men's sleeves; places where the horizon was clear and they could look back towards Echigo. It wasn't too cold yet, but the nights were long. Chikan paid for rooms and bought food, rented cooking utensils and bedding. As the Northern Highway turned into the Nakasendō Highway leading to Edo, their supply of coins steadily decreased.

Somewhere along the way, after the rest of the travelling party had departed, on a rented futon or a dingy tatami mat or the cold ground, under a shared blanket or a canopy of branches, in the still quiet of the early morning or amid the drunken music of a late-night party, Tsuneno suffered a loss that she couldn't measure in coins. It was hard to put a name to, and there was no need to commit the details to memory; she couldn't append them casually to the end of a letter, and anyway, they wouldn't have been easy to forget. Later, when she described the incident, she was vague, using the vocabulary of marriage, which she already knew well. She told her uncle, 'On the way, Chikan started saying, "You know, I have relatives in Edo and they would never turn you away – why don't you marry me?" And I tried to refuse, but we were on the road. And he talked about all the things that might happen to a woman alone; but it wasn't a real warning, he was making fun of me. The others who had been travelling with us had left by that point, so I had no other choice: I did what he wanted.' In writing, she was even more circumspect. She alluded to Chikan's 'impure intentions' and lamented her own misguided faith in him. 'After all,' she wrote, 'he wasn't a strange person from another province.' But in the end, 'though it was never my idea to do anything so terrible, Chikan was scheming to make me his wife.'

Tsuneno circled around a pain she couldn't name precisely. She didn't have the words to describe sex with a man she would not have chosen, under circumstances she couldn't control. It might not have been rape according to the legal definition: the shogun's laws equated rape with physical force, and Chikan's weapons were words. His was a familiar, acceptable kind of violence, the same kind of presumption and entitlement that lay at the heart of every arranged marriage. It was exactly what Tsuneno had left Echigo to avoid. She had insisted over and over again that she would rather die than remarry. Yet given the choice between sex with Chikan and the uncertainty of being alone on the road, she had decided to keep moving forward.

It was hard to reconcile the swings in her behaviour – her rebelliousness and then her acquiescence – but in the end, it was all part of the same calculation. There were some risks that were acceptable and others that were not, and the only goal was to move towards a life that held some hope of change, where she wouldn't be buried alive under a dying old man, in a lonely little village.

Yet even if Tsuneno survived the moment, there would always be long-term costs to what Chikan had done. She had run away with a strange man, but her brothers still might have forgiven her if she insisted that she saw him as a relative, perhaps an older brother. And if Chikan had behaved accordingly, her brothers might even have recognised him as a fellow cleric, the closest person she could find to an appropriate escort. But running away with a lover was a different kind of rebellion, one that she couldn't explain as easily. Although Chikan's behaviour wouldn't necessarily be recognised as rape, her involvement with him definitely qualified as illicit sex, which the shogunate defined as sex that was unsanctioned by a woman's head of household. Technically, this was a crime and the shogunate could order Tsuneno punished with exile. That was unlikely, since no one would report it. The more likely consequence was that Giyū would be enraged. He would see her behaviour as a blow to the household's reputation, another black mark for a family that had seen its share of scandals.

For Tsuneno, Chikan's behaviour would be a lasting reminder of her own bad judgement. She had put her trust in someone who was unworthy of it. Maybe that proved that Giyū was right: she couldn't be left to her own devices. She had to be married, safely in someone else's custody, tucked away in some corner of Echigo, if only to keep her from hurting herself and her family. In general, women were weak, and even those who weren't particularly stupid knew nothing about the world. Their little plans and calculations were nothing when set against the chaos of the road and the sharp minds of men. How could a sheltered priest's daughter possibly navigate a city like Edo, especially if she was so naïve that she trusted someone just because he had a familiar accent? What had she been thinking? The question would haunt her for years; she would always be trying to find an answer, an excuse, a story.

One of the last sights along the Nakasendō Highway on the way to Edo was a tall Chinese hackberry tree. Its leaves were turning yellow at the edges. A sign announced that it was a 'tie-cutting tree', and the shrine beside it was piled high with small offerings and paper petitions. According to lore, a person who wanted to be released from a relationship could peel off a piece of the tree's bark, steep it in hot water and serve the brew to his or her unsuspecting partner. And then, as if by magic, their karmic tie would be loosened and a tightly knit fate would unravel. The path forward would smooth itself out like untangled silk thread, straight and uncomplicated.

Tsuneno might have stopped at the tree and tucked a piece of the bark in her sleeve. She might have left a few coins. Or maybe she gave the shrine a backward glance as she remembered the ties she had already cut, the three husbands she had left behind and family she might never see again. It's possible that her bitterness

towards Chikan only developed later, when she had seen through
to the end of their story.

Tsuneno herself could never decide on one version of her past.
She had reasons to dissemble, and her memory was an unreliable
guide. Part of her path was unknowable. There were too many
options – detours and reversals. She travelled the Nakasendō or
turned down an entirely different, unmarked route. She passed
by the tree or stopped to make an offering. She looked down at
the road or back towards the northern horizon. She thought of
the city in her future or the home she'd left behind.

The important thing – the crucial and irrevocable part of the
story – was that she was moving forward. Her momentum carried
her. Edo was just ahead.

*

After nearly two weeks on the road, on the sixth day of the tenth
month of 1839, Tsuneno and Chikan finally reached Edo. This
might have been a dramatic moment, but it wasn't clear where
the countryside ended and the city began. Edo had no wall surrounding it. There was no gate to pass through and no guard to
bribe or petition for entry. Rather than relying on a perimeter of
stones and plaster, the shogun who planned Edo had chosen to
fortify his headquarters from the inside, using a system of moats
and mazelike, gated streets to block the approach to his castle.
He had made the plan of the city its armour.

Without city walls, Edo was free to expand. Over the centuries,
it had radiated outwards in a spiral pattern, gradually swallowing
up outlying fields and villages and turning them into hundreds and
hundreds of city blocks. As a result, by the early nineteenth century
even the shogun's men could not discern the city's boundaries. In

1818, an official put the question to his superiors: 'The shogunal inspectors do not have any documentation to answer the question of where the capital begins and ends. When we tried to investigate, we found that understandings varied, and it was impossible to get a definitive answer to the question.' All of Edo belonged to the shogun, but he had little interest in the details of city government, and no one else had jurisdiction over Edo in its entirety. The City Magistrates governed the commoners' districts, the Temple and Shrine Magistrates took charge of religious institutions and their lands, and the shogunate's Grand Inspectors watched over the domain lords' compounds and samurai barracks. But once the question of the entire city's boundaries had been asked, it had to be answered, so one of the shogun's elders commissioned a map. It showed Edo Castle in the centre, as always. It was the heart of the city and, as far as the shogun's men were concerned, the reason for its existence. A black line around the castle circumscribed the territory of the City Magistrates. A red line traced a larger circle, and the key to the map declared that the territory within that boundary was Edo.

If Tsuneno and Chikan followed the path of the Nakasendō Highway, they passed over that red line when they entered Itabashi Station. In some ways, it must have seemed exactly like the other post stations they had seen on the way from Takada: a series of inns, a weary procession of travellers, the smell of dung from the packhorses, a rush of messengers running through with packages, and one of the shogun's wooden signposts listing a series of prohibitions. But in the afternoon or evening, the difference was clear. Travellers could hear it in the music that floated down from the teahouses along the Shakujii River, where the banquet rooms were stacked three storeys high. Inside, groups of men were shouting and laughing, teasing the waitresses who came and went through sliding doors delivering tray after tray of sake. Some of them were the scared young girls familiar from other stations, overwhelmed by their bright robes and heavy makeup. But others were elegant geisha. Up close they might have seemed a little old, a little tired, maybe a little let down by careers that hadn't gone as they'd hoped. But many were veterans of Edo establishments, still in command of their art and their audience. When they played the latest songs, accompanying themselves on the shamisen, travellers felt like they'd arrived at last.

There were also darker, subtler signs that Tsuneno and Chikan had reached the edge of the capital. During the famine, emaciated and dead-eyed people from the northeast had stumbled towards Edo, assuming, correctly, that the shogun's city would be well provisioned. The shogunate, concerned for security and its own reputation for benevolence, had operated a relief kitchen in Itabashi to cater to them. But hundreds had already died in the mountains surrounding the station, and desperate, exhausted migrants still collapsed on the streets. The head priest at Itabashi's largest True Pure Land temple had gone out in person to gather the dead. He assigned Buddhist names to anonymous strangers, conducted memorial services for them, and buried them in the temple precincts. Their gravestones remained, and later there was a memorial to both the priest and the people he had buried. It was a sign of the kindness that desperate migrants might encounter, but also a warning of the end they might meet.

After Itabashi Station, Edo looked like the countryside again. There were fields on either side of the road, now dry and golden after the harvest, and stands of decorative trees. Every so often, there would be a gate to a shrine or a new-looking storehouse belonging to some lord or other. Some of these places were actually blocks under the jurisdiction of the City Magistrates, but some of them weren't even marked on the maps of Edo. In person, they looked like villages, and their residents were mostly farmers.

Gradually, the landscape changed. Trees and shrubs and fields gave way to the blank faces of warrior barracks. These long, low-slung buildings seemed identical and, at first glance, anonymous, but the names of the samurai who owned them were noted on maps of Edo, and each household's crest was imprinted on a front-facing tile at the peak of its roof. A few of these buildings were auxiliary residences and villas for great lords, but most of the plots were small, and they didn't belong to famous men. Only minor retainers of the shogunate had their main residences here, so far from the city centre, a stone's throw from rice fields and orchards. Tsuneno knew two boys from home, the Izawa brothers, who had gone to Edo to find employment in samurai households. Maybe she thought of them as she passed, wondering whether they might be living behind similar walls and fences, or hoping they had managed to land positions somewhere more exciting.

Then, to the left, just as it was starting to seem like this monotonous streetscape was all there was to see in Edo, there was a jarring interruption: the brilliant red gates to the Lord of Kaga's mansion. Solid and massive, set against a background of drab grey stones, white walls and dirt, they seemed to vibrate with colour. In Edo, a city where every architectural feature had a corresponding law or regulation, red gates were permitted to domain lords who ruled entire provinces and those who had married the shogun's daughters. The Lord of Kaga, Maeda Nariyasu, was both. His province, a beautiful stretch of land along the Sea of Japan coast, produced over a million bales of rice every year. He had commissioned the mansion's most striking gate in anticipation of his marriage to the shogun's daughter, and it was reserved especially for her.

What would Tsuneno see if she passed through that gate? A lord's compound wasn't a place that ordinary people could enter without permission, though some had tried and succeeded. One was a thief called the Mouse, whose exploits had captivated the city fifteen years before Tsuneno arrived, back when the red gates were still under construction. The Mouse would break into mansions by scaling the walls or squeezing through gaps in the fences. Sometimes he made off with as many as a hundred heavy gold pieces at a time. At one point the authorities apprehended him, had him tattooed and exiled him from the city. But even that didn't stop him. When all the compounds on Lords' Row near Edo Castle were hit, one after another, everyone knew that the Mouse had returned. Finally, in 1832, he was caught in the act. This time, there wasn't a second chance. The City Magistrate passed judgement: the Mouse was to be led through the city and executed. People who were lucky enough to catch sight of him on the way to his death, when he was escorted through the city by dozens of men brandishing lances and pikes, still talked about it. They said he was ordinary looking, just a little small, which explained how he had crawled through the gaps in so many fences.

If Tsuneno gazed up at the heavy roof of the Lord of Kaga's gates, it would have been difficult to imagine even peeking into the compound, much less scaling the walls. The fences, barred windows, and solid stone foundations looked impregnable, and they were meant to: they advertised the lord's duty to defend the realm. Just beyond the walls, the rooms on the perimeter of the compound belonged to rank-and-file samurai in Maeda's service. They had just arrived from their home domain, along with dozens of horses and countless boxes of luggage and weapons, and they would be with their lord in Edo until he was allowed to take his leave in the summer of the following year. Their job was just to be there, looking official if necessary, augmenting the lord's prestige. They occupied themselves drinking, composing poetry, sleeping late, playing card games and cooking sad little meals with rationed rice, pickles and sardines.

The centre of the compound was a mystery, even to the lord's men, who were never allowed inside. But spaces like these were easy for Tsuneno to imagine, because girls grew up reading about them and seeing them in illustrated books. She could picture long hallways of gleaming wood and wide rooms covered in fresh matting, lacquered trays and porcelain cups, a haze of drifting incense. The sliding doors wouldn't clatter when they were opened. There would be hushed, elegant conversations: discussions of novels, gossip about handsome actors and long descriptions of plays that no one had ever seen. Very high-ranking ladies would not go out to the theatre with ordinary people. Instead, they would spend entire days comparing hairpins, making balls out of string, or arranging little dolls in front of miniature go boards and thimble-sized teacups. They would play games and pluck instruments and obsessively plan their rare outings to temples. And they would be impeccably dressed. They ordered everything from Edo's finest clothiers: imported velvet sashes and entire kimonos done up in calico, and padded silk nightclothes adorned with hand-painted flowers and embroidered dragons. Even Tsuneno, who had an impressive wardrobe by rural Echigo standards, couldn't possibly imagine how much it all cost.

Just past the Lord of Kaga's red gates, the numbered blocks of Hongō counted down from six to one as the Nakasendō Highway, now just a city street, made its way south. Here the walls and fences of the samurai quarters gave way to a different kind of urban landscape, oriented towards the street instead of turning away from it, and the clean lines of the warrior districts were replaced by a jumble of rooftops and entryways jutting into the roads. Each of the blocks was a social and administrative unit with its own regulations and employees. Its membership was drawn from the families who owned the buildings on either side of the street. Groups of blocks were assigned to commoner ward headmen, who then reported to the samurai in the City Magistrates' offices. Unlike the invisible boundaries between the city and the countryside, the borders between the blocks were marked on the landscape in the form of wooden gates. They were closed at night, part of the security apparatus that made the external fortification of the city unnecessary. In the morning they were thrown open so that the lifeblood of the city – its commerce – could flow unimpeded.

For Tsuneno and for the other travellers on the road, the six blocks of Hongō merged into one thoroughfare – from the miso wholesalers in Hongō six, setting out their barrels filled with deep maple reds and pale wheat golds; through the well-known pharmacist in Hongō five, who specialised in remedies for children; to the landmark store Kaneyasu in Hongō three, which had sold tooth-polishing powder for generations. The store's advertising strategy was famous: employees stood in the road screaming at the top of their lungs, extolling the many virtues of 'milky fragrant powder'. People used to say Kaneyasu marked the border between Edo and the countryside – 'until you get to Kaneyasu, Hongō isn't Edo' – but that was before the city expanded so drastically, back when there was no map or red line and Edoites had to rely on a colloquial understanding of the city's boundaries.

The crowds grew thicker as Hongō turned into Yushima, a patchwork of warrior residences, shops, and temple and shrine lands. There were samurai on errands, stiff shouldered in their starched overskirts, their long and short swords hanging from their sides. Attendants kept pace behind them. People just in from the countryside lugged boxes on their shoulders and pulled wagons. There were working animals, too: horses and massive black oxen fitted with wheeled carts. The flow of traffic carried them all southward – towards the Kanda River and the great shrine Kanda Myōjin.

If Tsuneno passed the shrine, she would have recognised it as a landmark. Kanda Myōjin was noted in all the guides to Edo's famous places, and its soaring evergreens featured in prints of the most scenic spots in the city. It held its festival, Kanda Matsuri, every two years in the middle of the ninth month, and the last one had been just weeks before Tsuneno arrived. Commoners from the surrounding districts had flooded the streets with drums and banners, wearing straw hats crowned with red flowers, waving fans and playing flutes, celebrating the founding of the shogunate, the gods of the shrine, and their own survival. Each block had its own float, and some were more than three storeys tall – silk-robed ancient courtiers loomed over the rooftops, along with a cockerel, a long-tailed phoenix, demons, a gnarled blue octopus, masses of enormous flowers and a rising sun wreathed in brilliant rays. If Tsuneno could make it through two years in the capital, she would be there to see the procession and Kanda Matsuri would be her festival, too.

From the shrine, the Nakasendō sloped towards the banks of the Kanda River. Edoites called the road along the Yushima side of the river Dumpling Hill, another warning: if a traveller slipped off the road and tumbled down the muddy embankment, she would end up looking like a round, roasted dumpling. But the day Tsuneno arrived was bright and dry, and there was no danger of falling. If she looked down, she could see clear to the riverbanks below the road, where small boats unloaded their cargo to oxcart drivers who delivered to lords' mansions, warehouses and stores that were inaccessible by the inland waterways. The drivers were rough men, often migrants like those who had come along the roads with Tsuneno. They piled into the back rooms of the oxcart masters' houses, and whenever there was business they were dispatched and paid a daily rate. Tsuneno would have considered the oxcart men beneath her notice, and other Edoites barely acknowledged them. They were outsiders: not renters or landlords, not apprentices, not even tenement people. But they were everywhere, carrying palanquins in the streets, fighting fires, pulling handcarts and raising scaffolding. Theirs was the common fate of the migrant: to make the city work without ever quite belonging.

Across Shōhei Bridge, the Nakasendō delivered travellers onto a raised bank planted with willow trees. This scenic promenade continued all down the Kanda River, and though it was hard to tell during the day, it was notorious as a night haunt of streetwalkers. Past the willow trees was a small wooden gate, and then a vast plaza called Yatsukōji. A firemen's guardhouse stood in the corner, where a low-ranking official of the shogunate waited among long hooks and ladders, ready to take reports of fires. Another official was posted in the Yatsukōji fire tower, a famous sight of Edo, which rose several storeys over the tiled rooftops. If the guard posted there saw a fire, he would bang a great drum or ring a bell, picking up the pace as the flames drew nearer.

Everyone in Edo, even newcomers, knew how often and how catastrophically the city burned. They'd heard of the sparks that escaped from charcoal braziers and caught the wind; they'd been warned of carelessly tended lanterns that tipped over and incinerated rooms. They knew stories about arsonists: a spiteful servant who wrapped smouldering cinders in an old cloth and stashed the bundle under his master's staircase; a desperate girl who set her parents' house on fire so she could escape and meet her lover;

an enterprising man, hoping for a job, who burned a store so he could get credit for fighting the flames. They had learned to be watchful in the cold, dry months of winter, when fires traced erratic paths, burning through the wooden frames of homes and stores, racing across bamboo fences and scaffolds, jumping plaster walls, consuming everything in their wake. And they had learned to recognise the aftermath: dead bodies and smouldering debris, stacks of furniture that people had salvaged and piled high in the middle of the street, and piles of timber where houses had been pulled down to create firebreaks.

The year before Tsuneno arrived, part of Edo Castle had burned, then a large swathe of the downtown district of Kanda was incinerated. A few weeks later ten blocks of the commoner neighbourhood of Kōjimachi were reduced to ashes, and in late winter a fire in a samurai's residence tore through hundreds of commoners' houses and destroyed one of the City Magistrates' offices. The year so far had been quiet, but the tenth month was only the start of the season. The Yatsukōji fire tower was a reminder of the danger, a kind of a warning in itself, even on a clear, quiet day when the drums and bells were silent.

Across the dusty plaza, the road into the heart of the city skirted the northern fringe of Kanda Market, where stores offered an astounding array of fruits and vegetables, as well as eggs and seaweed. To Tsuneno, who had survived the Tenpō famine in the mountains of Echigo, the market's abundance would have seemed like a miracle. Merchants were setting out persimmons from Nagano and tangerines from Wakayama; they had expensive matsutake mushrooms and winter greens laid out in baskets. And due to the unseasonably warm weather, prices were the lowest they had been in years. But Kanda was a wholesale market, so Tsuneno couldn't stop there and buy a single persimmon or winter squash.

The people of Edo bought their produce from neighbourhood stores and, on occasion, directly from peasants who came into the city and set up makeshift stands.

In fact, though its displays were impressive, Kanda Market was struggling. It had maintained its place in the city for over a hundred years, but Edo's economy was changing, fast. There was no way for Tsuneno to see it from the outside, certainly not on that first brilliant day in early winter, when the places she'd seen on the map suddenly exploded into noise and colour. Everything in the city was new to her, and long-term trends were imperceptible. But the Kanda vendors knew a change was coming. They could hear it in tense meetings of the wholesalers' union, where they discussed how to compete with upstart suppliers who didn't follow their rules or carry their tax burdens. Experienced travellers knew it, too. They could catch glimpses of a looming crisis on the roads, where more people were coming into the city than leaving. And residents of back-street tenements could feel it, even if they couldn't explain it. There was a tension that hadn't broken, still building, day by day.

In Edo Castle, the shogun's high-ranking officials understood the problem. Edo had survived the famine through the desperate efforts of the City Magistrates. They had estimated that fully half of the commoner population – nearly three hundred thousand – required emergency relief. Now prices seemed to have stabilised, but hungry newcomers were still coming in. What would happen in another bad year?

To Edo's traditional elites – the samurai in the castle, the commoner ward headmen and the wholesalers at Kanda Market – the city was familiar. Clattering oxcarts and looming fire towers held no surprises; they didn't need to be warned about the bad ends people could come to in a large, anonymous place. But they perceived other threats. To them, danger had a form, a shape. It looked exactly like Tsuneno: an exhausted stranger in an old robe, sharp-eyed and hungry, looking around the city like it was everywhere she'd always wanted to be. The warning was as plain as her Echigo accent, as clear and insistent as a fire bell, heralding a crisis in the making, coming nearer all the time.

*

Tsuneno's immediate destination lay in the western reaches of Inner Kanda, in a crowded, nondescript neighbourhood that backed up against the moat of Edo Castle. At midday, some of the stores were open to traffic, welcoming visitors in to see the displays of sweets or tools; others were shut tight or half-closed, discouraging curiosity. In early evening, the entrances would be flanked by tall lanterns, each resting in its own pool of light.

Shopkeepers and their employees occupied the buildings fronting the street. Some of them had lived on the block for generations, but nearly all of them were renters. The people who owned the buildings and the land lived in other neighbourhoods, even other cities. In some parts of Edo, massive firms owned flagship stores surrounded by affiliated buildings and property that sprawled across several blocks. But Inner Kanda was not that kind of place. An 1843 ranking of nearly two hundred of Edo's richest commoners included only one man from the neighbourhood: a high-end clothier named Sanmojiya Ichibei. His neighbours were undistinguished shopkeepers who sold sweets, tea, medicine, tooth-blackening brushes and small metal goods.

Chikan's relatives lived in the second block of Minagawa-chō, a dead end that backed up against the estate of a doctor whose family had served the shogun for centuries. The block's few resident landlords were people like him: skilled commoners who had been granted property, stipends and nominal samurai status in return for their service. Among them were artisans specialising in gold leaf and lacquerware, some of whom maintained workshops just across the moat on the grounds of Edo Castle. That was the only remotely interesting thing about Minagawa-chō, which was so obscure that most people had never heard of it. Even people who had been there sometimes confused it with its better-known neighbour, Mikawa-chō.

Chikan and Tsuneno were looking for a rice shop called Daikokuya. Its proprietor, Sōhachi, was somehow related to Chikan. He had done fairly well for himself, at least by the standards of an Echigo migrant. Many of the men who started as rice polishers dreamed of opening a store like his. They could start out with just a mortar and pestle, then save up to rent a storefront. If the store was a success, it would be cluttered with dishes, barrels, scoops and straw-wrapped bushels and it would be noisy with the clattering and pounding of rice-polishing machines.

At first, the master of the store would have to learn how to operate the polishing machine himself. It was hard work, but easier than a mortar and pestle. The assembly looked a little like a wooden giraffe, with a long, straight neck swinging into the air and a hard head crashing to the floor over and over again. That was the pestle. The mortar was a heavy bowl set into the floor. The worker ran the machine by mounting it and pressing hard on a pedal, looking a bit as if he were riding the giraffe. It was sweaty, undignified labour, so eventually – the master hoped – someone else would do it, maybe a young man dispatched from an employment agency. Then the easier, happier work would fall to the proprietor and his wife, who would rinse the rice in wide baskets and funnel the grains into little wooden boxes. If the proprietor was a sociable type, he could make the evening rounds of the back alleys, selling a scoop of rice at a time, hearing all the gossip.

During the famine years, rice sellers like Sōhachi came under pressure. Their little stores were located at the exact point of tension between the large rice wholesalers, who wanted to charge market prices, and the people of the city, who feared they would starve. Whenever rice became too expensive, proprietors of the neighbourhood stores worried about riots. During the severe Tenmei famine in the 1780s, prices spiked to the point that a good day's work for a pedlar or pieceworker would barely buy four servings of rice, with nothing left over for rent, fuel or other food. In the summer of 1787, for days on end, rioters targeted the city's rice wholesalers, retailers, sake brewers and anyone else they blamed for shortages and high prices. They smashed mortars, tore furniture apart, trampled clothing in the mud and threw kitchen utensils into the sewers. They tossed bushels of rice into the street and split them open. Their carelessness was a point in itself: they were protesting hoarding, but they weren't stealing. The grains went skittering uselessly across the alleys, and still the cooking pots in the tenements stayed empty. In the end, after days of chaos, several hundred stores were smashed. Most were wholesalers and sake brewers, but several dozen were retail rice shops.

The unrest in 1787, known as the Tenmei Riots, made the shogun's officials realise that they had lost their grip on their own city. This was no ordinary peasant uprising: for the first time in well over a century, they encountered a genuine popular threat to their rule. Two years later, in Paris, a group of market women enraged over the price of bread stormed the Hôtel de Ville, forcing it to open its stores, and then continued to Versailles, where they and thousands of their fellow protesters forced the king to return to the capital. This uprising, only a few months after the fall of the Bastille, was part of the massive wave of urban unrest that helped bring down the Old Regime in France. Although this turn of events in Europe was impossible to foresee in Edo, the shogun's men were not alone in apprehending the revolutionary potential of angry urban rioters. After the city was pacified, the shogunal elders launched a series of new administrative measures known as the Kansei Reforms, including the provision of a city savings association. The reforms, introduced between 1787 and 1793, were intended to ensure that the city 'at the knees of the shogun' would never face a similar crisis again.

The Tenpō famine in the 1830s severely tested this strategy. As rice prices rose, wealthy commoners in Edo braced for riots. They put off construction projects, in part because they didn't want labourers to assemble near their stores. When tenants stopped paying rent, threatening signs appeared on gates and walls, and rumours of violence spread through the back alleys. The great merchant houses were forced to open their storehouses and distribute rice and cash. Meanwhile, the shogun's men worked feverishly to keep the city calm. They established soup kitchens and distributed rice rations to hundreds of thousands of people. Officials also tried to keep rice affordable for those who still had cash. When prices spiked, they mandated lower retail prices and broke the stranglehold of Edo's established rice wholesalers. For three years, between 1836 and 1839, anyone could bring rice into the city and sell it. Still, stores like Sōhachi's had trouble finding suppliers, and the shogunate found it necessary to lend them emergency provisions, warning that unrest would ensue if they closed.

Thanks to the combined efforts of the shogunate and the major merchant houses, the expected riots never materialised. Prices returned to their pre-famine lows, and by the time Tsuneno arrived at Sōhachi's store in 1839, a good day's work for a pedlar could buy over twenty servings of rice. It appeared that the worst was over, but the people of the city were still wary. That autumn, during the season for moon viewing, they joked, 'Even when we're looking at the moon, we're talking about prices on the rice market.'

Even if Sōhachi had been inclined to be hospitable, it wasn't a good time for a person in his business to host unannounced guests, especially people from the country with no employment prospects and no plans to leave. He was furious at the imposition and made it clear that Tsuneno and Chikan couldn't stay at his store. He said he would send Tsuneno out to work as a maidservant if she couldn't find somewhere else to go. From his perspective, it might have been an offer, but from hers, it was a threat.

Chikan had promised Tsuneno that his family would welcome her. He'd told her that it was 'no trouble' if she came along with him to the city. He said that his relatives would never leave her homeless. But those guarantees, like so many other things he'd said, turned out to be lies.

*

That night, the sixth of the tenth month of 1839, Tsuneno might have wished to reverse the course of her story, to go back to Takada and choose another companion, another day, and another opportunity to make her escape. For a moment, she might have wanted to go all the way back to Rinsenji, to make different decisions, to stay home or to get married. But there was no going back, and Edo didn't stop for anyone.

At Itabashi Station, prostitutes painted over their bruises and stabbed pins through their stiff, lacquered hair. If they were lucky, they might be able to sneak something to eat before they were called out to parties. If they were really lucky, their guests would get so drunk they'd pass out. The music floated towards the river as always, the same sad songs that the geisha had played yesterday and would play again tomorrow. Rowdy guests clapped and stomped and hooted – drinking games. The girls laughed, as expected, and their giggles echoed all up and down the main street of the station.

It was quiet in the Lord of Kaga's residence. The labourers tasked with sweeping leaves out of the garden returned to their crowded common rooms, and others left to stand guard for the night. Ladies-in-waiting helped the lord's wife, the shogun's daughter, change into her padded silk nightclothes. Maids rearranged the furniture, set out futons and filled water jugs, and kitchen servants made sure the fires were out. In a few hours, they'd have to light them all over again.

The men in the barracks retired to their rooms, where they worried over their account books or flipped through the latest version of the Edo warrior register so that they could orient themselves in a sea of unfamiliar faces. Others wrote long letters home. They inquired after their wives and children. They complained that Edo was dirty. The pickles weren't like the ones they were used to, and all the persimmons seemed small and bruised. And why was it that that the 'Edo hairstyles' people wore in Kanazawa were nothing like the hairstyles that people actually wore in Edo? They wrote about some of the outings they'd planned for the next few weeks: a visit to the used-clothing stores in Hikage-chō to look for new hats. Maybe a trip to see Mt Atago, where you could look over the whole city and see if it really was as flat as everyone said.

At Kanda Myōjin, the priests and their servants were still recovering after the commotion of the festival. From the quiet grounds of the shrine they could see all the way to Shōhei Bridge. There, on the embankment, streetwalkers waited under the willows. Some were thin and sickly, and some were wrinkled and pockmarked.

But with their thick coats of makeup, it was hard to tell, even under the light of a nearly full moon.

In Yatsukōji, the guard on fire watch climbed to the top of his tower and settled in for a long night. It was clear and the beginning of fire season: a time to be vigilant. A few blocks away, merchants responsible for bringing grapes to Kanda Market waited for the next shipment. In some years the grapes spoiled in transit, and then they couldn't be presented to the shogun. Sometimes the highway was better, and sometimes the sea route. They wouldn't know until the cargo arrived.

Elsewhere in the neighbourhood of Kanda, shopkeepers sat up thinking about profits and losses, while their servants bedded down in back rooms and tenements. Parents tried to get their babies to sleep. The ward headman, a famous writer named Saitō Yukinari, scribbled a brief entry in his diary. A geisha had sent him a gift of persimmons and grapes, perfectly seasonal. Otherwise, there was little to report. Stray dogs howled, nighttime vendors packed up their stands, and the block's watchmen closed their wooden gates.

Somewhere in the second block of Minagawa-chō, Tsuneno spent her first night in the city. People all over Edo were remarking on the warm start to the winter, but Tsuneno had no nightclothes and no futon. She had no extra clothes. She had no money. She had no friends and no prospects. Chikan was a useless liar, and Sōhachi was threatening to send her to work as a maid. Nothing about her first day had gone as planned. Back in Echigo, her family would be receiving her letters from the road any day now. They'd realise she had run away, and her brothers would be furious. Her mother would be heartbroken. They might never write back. She'd thought her situation there was unbearable, but what had she traded it for? 'I struggled so much . . . ,' she wrote later. 'I don't even have the words to describe it.'

Chapter Four

A VIEW FROM A
TENEMENT

With no money and no immediate prospect of a job, Tsuneno could not do much in her first days in Edo. It was hard enough just to get her bearings. From the main streets of Inner Kanda, the order of the city was comprehensible. It looked more or less like it did on printed maps: a series of blocks divided from one another by gates and fencing. But the back alleys were different, dark and unpredictable, as if the passages between the stores' facades led to an entirely different world.

Tsuneno walked down pathways so narrow that the eaves of facing buildings nearly touched. Two adults could pass each other, but if one of them happened to be a pedlar with baskets slung over his shoulders, then the other would have to step aside. Below her feet, uneven flagstones were set into packed dirt. Along the row houses, sliding door followed sliding door. On the walls and gates, there was a confusing proliferation of signs. A notice for an employment office. A flyer for a play. A reminder to be careful with fire. An advertisement for a patent medicine that was good for haemorrhoids. None of them looked official, and they obviously weren't permanent. Some were worn away and half torn down.

It was clear that there was no plan at work. None of the paths seemed to go very far before they stopped and veered off at right angles. Then there would be a new series of doors and a new series of bewildering signs. Or, suddenly, a tall storehouse belonging to someone on the main street.

Sometimes the wells and outhouses were set out haphazardly in the middle of the pathways, but sometimes they occupied their own little clearing alongside an overflowing rubbish bin. These were the only places where it was possible to look up and see more than a sliver of sky. But it was better to keep looking down. There were plants, baskets, toddlers and dogs underfoot, and the ground was wet where people had been doing their laundry.

It seemed that no one made any distinction between indoor and outdoor space. Tools, noises and smells spilled out onto the pathways, and people conducted their personal business in plain sight. They went to and from the bathhouses nearly naked. And since some of the outhouses had only half doors, men urinated while talking to their neighbours. In the middle of the chaos, it was obvious that Tsuneno was in Edo – where else would be this crowded and loud? – but it was hard to tell exactly where she was or how to get out.

Was this what Tsuneno had come all the way from Echigo to see? Chikan didn't care. He was almost out of money (at least, that was his story), and this was the only part of the city he could afford. When Sōhachi failed to welcome him, he had arranged to rent an alley tenement room. It was an easy transaction, even on short notice and without much cash. In order to rent a room any-where within an Edo city block, Chikan needed a guarantor to sign a document attesting to his status and promising that he wouldn't do anything illegal. The landlord would be called to account if his renters got in trouble with the City Magistrates' offices, and he didn't want to assume that risk alone. In theory, Chikan's guarantor should have been one of his relatives or someone else who had a close relationship with his family. But like so many things in Edo, it didn't actually work that way. There were just too many newcomers. By the time Chikan and Tsuneno arrived in the city, a class of professional guarantors brokered deals to rent out rooms. They signed the same documents over and over again, stamping their seals to boilerplate language about security and responsibility. They charged fees, but they didn't ask many questions. They were confident that they would be able to find their clients if they got in trouble or skipped out on the rent. As a rule, guarantors knew the city well and had some rough connections.

When his documents were all in order, Chikan made a deal with a man named Jinsuke. He was the tenement superintendent and, in the absence of the landlord, the boss of their little fraction of an alley. The block was divided into deep, narrow lots. Each contained about three buildings that faced the street. These were large shops and residences, and if the landlord lived on-site he and his family would occupy one of them. Behind these grander homes, long row houses containing one or two dozen tenement rooms were set perpendicular to the main street, stretching back towards the ends of the lots. Since most landlords didn't live on the block or they were large businesses and not individuals, they hired superintendents to take care of dealings with the city administration, along with rent collection and all the other tedious problems that came with having tenants. The superintendents' compensation came in the form of housing, so they typically lived in the back alleys, too. Sometimes they were like community leaders, even surrogate parents. Some even covered for renters when their payments were late. But Jinsuke was not that type of person, and Tsuneno disliked him intensely.

The room itself was a 'three-mat', only six feet wide and nine feet long. A very tall man could have grazed both walls with his fingertips, and two adults could barely set out their futons side by side. Even the next size up – a four-and-a-half-mat room – was unbearably cramped for more than one person. A few decades before Tsuneno arrived in the city, the writer Shikitei Sanba joked: 'They say that someone who lives in a four-and-a-half-tatami room is like an inchworm: all bunched up now so they can stretch out later.' This implied a kind of ambition on the part of Edo's tenement dwellers, who could endure discomfort in the hope of upward mobility. In Tsuneno's case, the three-mat room was the opposite: the end point of a precipitous downward slide. It was the smallest, and probably the filthiest, place she had ever lived.

From the packed-dirt entryway, which was just about big enough to hold two pairs of sandals, there was a step up into the main room. Inside, there was enough space to set one tatami mat lengthwise, and then beyond it two more stretching side by side towards the back wall. Otherwise the room was bare; tenements didn't typically come furnished. And there was no room for furniture, anyway. If Tsuneno had extra clothes, which she didn't, she would have to hang them on the walls or stack them in baskets. If she had a futon, which she didn't, she would have to roll it up and shove it in the corner. During the day, this one room would need to be the living and eating space. And it wasn't pleasant. The only light came from a window facing into the alley. Since most tenement houses consisted of two rows of units facing opposite directions, both the side and back walls were shared. The sun would have to be at exactly the right angle for light to fall through the slatted window. The back of the room was permanently sunk in shadow.

Beside the room's entrance, on the same level, there was a tiny, wooden-floored space for holding water buckets. Next to it was the place for cooking, too small to be called a proper kitchen. It would fit a miniature charcoal brazier and maybe a box of rice. There wasn't room to cook more than a pot of rice at a time, so everything else would have to be prepared well in advance or bought ready-made from pedlars. And the brazier would need accessories: after the charcoals inside were lit, Tsuneno would have to use a pipe to blow on them to get them to ignite. All those things – the brazier, the pot, the pipe, the charcoal and the boxes and buckets – would have to be purchased. There were shelves on the wall next to the door, which would be useful if she ever had dishes, trays and chopsticks. They couldn't be set on the floor: in a three-mat, there was barely enough room for one person to crouch next to the brazier.

Much later, Tsuneno would become accustomed to life in Edo's back alleys. She would get to know her neighbours and learn how to ignore the loud arguments that echoed through the walls. She would figure out how to stand in line at a well, how to share a toilet with dozens of strangers, and how to buy charcoal by the scoop. She would even come to prefer her life in the city to the more comfortable existence in Echigo. But during her first weeks in Minagawa-chō, she could barely describe her situation except to say how awful it was.

Tsuneno was probably worse off than most of her neighbours, men and women who belonged to the more stable part of Edo's lower class. A few worked as servants who didn't live in, and others were palanquin bearers who propped their palanquins outside their doors when they weren't working. More were pedlars. They departed every morning, far more cheerfully on sunny days than on rainy ones. For hours they made their rounds, selling things like candles, sweets or hot peppers. Other alley dwellers used their tiny rooms for commerce. Sellers of used dishes set them out by the door, teachers had pupils come in and set up their own desks, and employment agents entertained walk-in clients. But most of the tenement people were small-scale artisans. It was amazing how many different types of things they could fabricate in their back-alley rooms. People were dyeing and stencilling cloth and carving woodblocks for printing; they were making wooden tools and eyeglasses; they were weaving tatami mats and smoothing boards and assembling musical instruments. They did all of this in full view of the alley, with their sliding doors thrown open to catch the light.

These busy people kept tabs on their neighbours. They gathered around the well, at the bathhouse and at the barber. They even chatted across the alleys while they were working. Men flung boasts and insults back and forth in narrow spaces, put-upon grandmothers criticised their daughters-in-law, and pompous old men bored everyone with peevish complaints. There was always something to say. There were people who liked to borrow things and wouldn't return them; whiny, sticky-handed children who wiped their noses on adults' kimono sleeves; no-good men who spent all their families' money at brothels; lazy women who made their husbands fetch water from the well; and haughty girls who criticised their mothers' clothes. No one was immune to criticism or exempt from speculation. Buyō Inshi, an Edo samurai, claimed that back-alley women couldn't wait until their menfolk left for the day so that they could 'get together with the other wives in the neighbourhood or on the same row to talk about how useless their husbands are.'

In Minagawa-chō, people probably had something to say about Tsuneno and Chikan's relationship. But it wouldn't have been a major scandal, and it certainly wouldn't have provoked any special concern from the commoner headman, who was in charge of keeping track of the population and communicating with samurai in the City Magistrates' offices. Until it was time to compile the population register every year, it wasn't always clear who was living with whom and why. It was also hard to distinguish permanent residents from people who were just crashing or passing through. Most Kanda tenement rooms contained three to five people: couples, families and a smattering of single bachelors, widows or widowers. Sometimes three generations would live under the same roof, or an unmarried aunt or uncle would be attached to a family with young children. But there were also more unorthodox configurations. It wasn't unusual to find an adult brother and sister living together, hosting a dependent who wasn't related to them at all. In this context, it wasn't strange that Tsuneno and Chikan weren't married. No one had a marriage certificate anyway, so Tsuneno could claim whatever she wanted.

The stranger thing about Tsuneno and Chikan was that they had no work: no occupation, nothing to sell and no idea what they were doing. During her first days in Minagawa-chō, Tsuneno's eyes were still bothering her, and it was probably enough for her to figure out how the alleys intersected, to find the wells and latrines, and to learn the faces of the familiar people on the block. There was the superintendent, Jinsuke, of course, and Chikan's relative, the rice store proprietor Sōhachi. Then there was the gate guard, who received his salary from the block. He was the closest thing the neighbourhood had to a public face. He had purchased his first name, along with his post, from an association that controlled guard positions, which were valuable because they came with access to an income and a living space. Then he installed himself and his family in a hut just to the side of the block's main gate. From there, he could watch everyone coming in and out. That was his official job, along with breaking up fights, finding things that people had lost, and generally maintaining order. But the salary wasn't great, so men like him usually established side businesses selling things, which they lined up on the little window that looked out towards the gate. They offered the exact kinds of items you might suddenly need, break or run out of on short notice: straw sandals, brooms, tissues, candles, roof tiles (used for grilling fish, not repairing the roof) and braziers. In the early winter, when Tsuneno arrived, they also sold grilled potatoes.

Amid the chaos of the alley, Tsuneno occupied herself writing letters home. On the tenth day of the tenth month, two days after she moved in, she composed several at once. One was a short note to her brother Kōtoku, informing him of her new address. It was accompanied by another, longer letter. The address was accurate, but the letter wasn't. She complained that she was freezing, which was probably true, and that she was still wearing only one unlined robe, which probably wasn't true (later, she wrote that she had a coat, a much more likely story for someone who had come through the mountains in late autumn). But the exaggeration underscored her main point: Kōtoku needed to send her clothes, immediately, before the snow fell in the mountains and ruined the roads. She knew exactly when the express services would leave Takada for Edo: the official express, used for domain business, departed on the first, the eleventh and the twenty-first. Obviously it was too late for the eleventh, she wrote, but Kōtoku should try to make the twenty-first. 'It's snowy there,' she wrote, 'so please send my things as quickly as you possibly can, and hurry while the roads are still good. It gets colder here every day, and I have nothing to wear.'

Next, Tsuneno composed a chilly and precise letter to Giyū. It issued specific instructions for how he should redeem the clothes she'd pawned on her way to Edo: 'As for the money . . . I left some cash with Uncle Kyūhachirō. It won't be enough, so please sell my chest and my wardrobe.' These were the two most expensive things purchased for Tsuneno's trousseau, but it would be impossible to send them to Edo. They were so heavy that it had taken a group of men to move them home when she divorced for the second time. Asking Giyū to sell them was a clear message that she never intended to live in his house again. She went on to request the futon and quilt she'd left in her bamboo chest, as well as a cotton-padded robe, which she'd left hanging. There were two aprons, mirrors, a pillow and shoulder padding in her long chest. Giyū should send those, too. As for the rest of her things, he should take good care of them for her, and she would send word when she needed them. He should also send the address of the family's acquaintances in Edo. At the end of her letter, she added a postscript: 'At some point, I want to go into service for a great lord and learn the manners and customs of the upper class. When that happens, I will need to have my bamboo chest and all my things sent here.'

Behind the bravado, Tsuneno's situation was deteriorating. On the fourteenth or fifteenth day of the month, about a week after he arranged to rent the room, Chikan left. He said he was going to Shimotsuke Province, to the north of the city. Maybe he was angry with his relative Sōhachi for being unwelcoming. Maybe he was disappointed that Tsuneno was less compliant in Edo than she had been on the road. Maybe he was always planning to deliver Tsuneno to the city and abandon her. Or maybe he really did have some mysterious, pressing business in Shimotsuke, a strange place where Tsuneno had never been. Before he left, he gave her one gold coin. It was all that was left of the clothes she had pawned in Takada and all that was left of him. Tsuneno never saw him again.

She might have cried, or laughed, or yelled so loud that her neighbours shouted back. Or she might have been quiet, relieved to be rid of him. She never wrote about what happened. But it didn't really matter what she did – she had a problem. The coin Chikan had left her was a lot of money for the average Edo tenement dweller. It would take a pedlar at least three good days to make that much. It could buy enough food for a few weeks, if she was careful. But it wasn't nearly enough to set up house. It wouldn't even pay for one good unlined robe. And she desperately needed her clothes. Without them – without her money, without her family, without the one person in Minagawa-chō who knew where she came from – how would she know what to do next?

During those weeks in the tenement, Tsuneno was anonymous for the first time in her life. She looked around at the women her age and saw no one she recognised. Back in Echigo, an arch of an eyebrow or the curve of a hairline was all she needed to place a girl precisely within a family, in a constellation of villages and relatives, in a galaxy of people who had known one another's names for generations. The people she encountered were her grandfather's cousins' neighbours, her sister's in-laws, or her husbands' families. They were her childhood friends, girls who knew which pickles were her mother's speciality, who might have recognised one of her lined robes if she left it behind at someone's house. They might have been able to distinguish her brothers by their voices and known which one was her favourite. Some of the older women could probably state with authority that she was prettier, or uglier, than her grandmother had been when she was young.

But here, in Minagawa-chō, Tsuneno's name meant nothing. Her accent only placed her somewhere in Echigo, the snowy province where the bathhouse attendants came from and the hired hands disappeared to every summer. She probably didn't look like a peasant who'd spent a lifetime hunched over in a rice field, but no one could have known from looking at her that she was the daughter of a priest or that she had dozens of silk robes packed in a chest hundreds of miles away. And what did it matter? There were other girls with country accents, from Echigo or closer by – Kōzuke, Shimotsuke, Musashi – who had never worn silk. Most of them couldn't even write a letter. But they had clean, padded cotton with fine, bright stripes. Their immaculate collars and carefully placed hairpins vouched for them, saying they belonged in Edo, even if their names were made up and their only relatives were languishing in dismal villages or crowded into tenements. And at least they had somewhere to go every day.

Tsuneno had none of that. But she did have other advantages. She had been raised the daughter of a True Pure Land priest, and in her experience a temple in her sect would not turn away a priest's daughter. No matter how small Rinsenji was, or how far away, someone would know the temple's name. And no matter how she looked, she knew how to comport herself – she had once been the mistress of an important temple, even if it was in a little river town in Dewa Province. So Tsuneno left Minagawa-chō in the middle of the tenth month and headed south, towards the largest True Pure Land temple complex in Edo, Tsukiji Honganji.

*

The main road from Minagawa-chō to Tsukiji led back through Kanda Market, over Imagawa Bridge, and on towards Nihonbashi. This was the commercial heart of the city, a place that made the western districts of Inner Kanda look almost as sleepy as Takada. Great merchant houses lined the streets. The biggest was Mitsui Echigoya, which even people from small villages like Ishigami knew. By Tsuneno's time, the Mitsui conglomerate had several holdings and subsidiary businesses: it lent money and owned real estate,

including many of the tenements in Inner Kanda, and it took care
of money orders for the shogunate. But the flagship was still a retail
store, a landmark with tiled roofs, crisp blue banners, and armies
of tidy uniformed apprentices running in and out with packages.

Echigoya sold kimonos and obis in all the latest styles and
fabrics: silk, hemp, cotton and even imported calico and velvet.
The store had allowed same-day cash purchases well before its
competitors, which sold on credit and settled at the end of the
season. This practice allowed Echigoya to sell at lower prices and
to cater to people without established accounts and reputations,
the perfect strategy for the expanding, anonymous city. Over a
hundred years later, it was still a business that relied on the quick
thrill of impulse shopping. The main floor was always stocked with
new things, and it was wide open to the street, welcoming pass-
ersby, trying to tempt them into spur-of-the-moment purchases.

Inside the store, dozens of clerks took orders and settled
accounts, clicking the abacus and making out receipts as they
went. Their names were brushed onto oversized banners hanging
from the rafters, which made it easier for shoppers to find their
favourite salesmen and their assistants. But despite their prominent place in one of the city's most famous institutions, the clerks'
situation was more precarious than it looked. The Edo branch of
Echigoya employed hundreds of them, and most had been hired
as children. For years, they worked as all-purpose errand boys and
assistants, until at last, at their coming-of-age, a bare majority
became full-fledged clerks. From there, they climbed an arduous
path towards promotion. Very few would ever reach the highest
positions, which would provide them with a salary adequate to
support a family. In the meantime, middle-ranking clerks lived in
quarters provided by the company, taking pride in their impressive
wardrobes, saving their wages for outings at lower-end brothels.

Beyond Mitsui Echigoya's blue banners, there was a different type of commerce, less organised and hierarchical, conducted in copper coins rather than gold pieces. Pedlars crowded the street, bent double under bundles of kindling or dragging long poles of green bamboo across the ground. Some were swarthy men in from the countryside balancing baskets of greens or flat bamboo trays with large silver fish. Others were selling blank white lanterns in a variety of shapes and sizes. Smart young men sat beside them, ready with brushes and ink to write names on the lantern faces. Surprisingly attractive women gathered small crowds around them as they danced and sang – it turned out that they were selling hard candies. They competed for attention with the dapper young men who walked monkeys on leashes. Exhausted old ladies passed carrying heavy loads of charcoal on their backs, their faces black with soot. Old men tottered by, wheeling noisy carts piled high with bird and insect cages. Women in head scarves stood still beside displays of potted plants and flowers. Occasionally, there was a lumbering figure who looked like a sumo wrestler from a distance. Sometimes he would turn out to be an ordinary-sized pedlar wearing dozens of straw baskets, sieves and whisks. Other times he was actually a sumo wrestler.

Did Tsuneno want eggs? There would be a man somewhere with dozens laid out on a mat. Sugar candies? She could look for the stand with an umbrella shielding them from the winter sun. Did she break a sandal? She could buy a new one from the old man at the guard station. Need a cup of water? A pet goldfish? A new set of brushes? She could wait a few minutes and someone would come by. In the meantime, would she give alms to a child on pilgrimage? Did she have spare copper coins for a beggar? Did she want to hear a song played by a blind musician? If not, did she have any old clothes she wanted to sell? Did she have any unwanted paper? She could give it to the men with the strange haircuts, members of one of the local outcast groups. They sold scrap to the used-paper dealers, who would recycle it and sell it back to her as tissues.

Everyone seemed to know where they were going. Labourers pulled handcarts, samurai lugged their swords and spears to martial arts practice, and nursemaids carried babies on their backs. Children on their way to lessons balanced their desks on their heads. Maidservants carried wrapped packages for their mistresses. Even the trash collectors juggled a variety of baskets, some on poles and some at their hips. But Tsuneno carried nothing. She had only the clothes she was wearing, whatever remained of her one gold coin, and a vague idea of where she was headed.

The route from Kanda to Tsukiji led over the Nihonbashi River, the southern boundary of the main commercial district and one of Edo's busiest waterways. In the countryside, the most important thing about a river was its water: it could be slow and brown or rushing and clear; it could smell of metal or mud or rain; it could threaten to overflow or trickle through a wide silt bed. But here, even though the water made the river possible, even though it made the whole city possible – connecting to the moats of the castle, the Sumida River, and the sea – it didn't command attention. No one could hear it over the shouting of the crowds, and its glinting surface was almost entirely covered in wooden boats. Most of them were associated with the morning fish market, the biggest in Japan. They carried piles of shrimp or shellfish or eels. The river shifted uneasily, as if to dislodge them, and slumped again and again against the pilings of Nihonbashi Bridge.

Crossing Nihonbashi Bridge was like climbing a small, crowded hill. The bridge was not just a place of transit; it was also a place for commerce, begging, stealing, and urgent discussions in unfamiliar accents. Sunburned peasants stood immobile, selling the vegetables they'd carried from their villages. Otherwise, everyone was in a hurry. Few stopped to gaze out over the city, to where the shogun's castle rose in the distance, or towards the southwest, where Mt Fuji was visible on clear days, or down to the riverbanks, where warehouses turned their broad white backs to the water.

Across the bridge were commoner districts named after the groups of artisans who had been assigned those quarters when the city was first established: carpenter town, sandal town, tatami town. They'd long since become ordinary downtown neighbourhoods. To the south was Minami-denmachō, one of the oldest and most prestigious commoner quarters, where rents were high and the landholders had the onerous duty of supplying post-horses and porter services to the shogunate. The street led into the wide plaza at Kyōbashi, which used to be a firebreak and was now a place for 'temporary' stalls that had become permanent. Across Kyōbashi Bridge was the southern edge of the city, all built on landfill. It hadn't been there when Edo was established. Now it was a place where great lords had their warehouses and the True Pure Land temple complex, Tsukiji Honganji, towered above the white sails in the harbour.

Tsukiji Honganji was not a single temple but an assortment of religious institutions surrounding a great hall with a soaring peaked roof. The abbot at the main temple commanded resources that even the shogun would envy. Organizations of tens of thousands of lay believers donated eggs, candles, flowers and cash. The head of the Kyoto-based Nishi Honganji sect of True Pure Land Buddhism visited the complex the year before Tsuneno arrived. He described the main temple as if it hovered above Edo, set apart from its daily commerce. To the south, he wrote, he could see the rooftops at the post station of Shinagawa and ships coming and

going. At night, whitebait fishers set fires that made the waves
come alight. To the east, he saw the distant mountains of the Bōsō
Peninsula, to the west the peak of Mt Fuji, and to the north the
gleaming white walls of Edo Castle. But from street level, the view
was quite different. There were markets and throngs of worshippers
making their way in and out of the smaller temples clustered in
the shadow of the great hall.

Tsuneno called at one of them, a temple called Enshōji. At
the time it was an obscure place that didn't appear on most city
maps of Edo. But Tsuneno knew the temple because Giyū had
corresponded with the head priest. She presented herself as the
daughter of Rinsenji in Echigo Province and asked for assistance.
She might have hoped that the head priest's family would offer her
lodging in exchange for some light housekeeping work, the kind
she was used to from her own background in Echigo. Instead, they
suggested that she go see her aunt Mitsu in Teppozu Jikkenchō,
which was only a few blocks west. Either Tsuneno hadn't known
her aunt was there, or she'd been too embarrassed to try and visit.
But now, when the temple turned her away, she had no choice.

Tsuneno walked on to Jikkenchō, a lonely, windy strip of land
at the edge of Edo. It belonged more to the bay than to the city.
During typhoons it must have seemed as if the whole block would
be swallowed whole. Most of the people there were in the business of unloading seagoing vessels and placing the cargo on the
smaller ships that plied Edo's inland waterways. Tsuneno's uncle
Bunshichi, a householder in Jikkenchō, might have had something
to do with the shipping trade. There were barely any other stores
there, just an office where people from the outlying Izu Islands
delivered dried fish and seaweed.

Tsuneno called at her uncle Bunshichi's store, Moritaya, on the
last day of the tenth month. After nearly four weeks in Edo, she

barely resembled the person she had been. It must have been hard for Bunshichi to imagine that she could be one of his relatives. He wrote, shocked, that she was 'naked'. Tsuneno had never been to Edo, the family connection was on his wife Mitsu's side, and Mitsu was away in service in a village outside the city. So, from Bunshichi's perspective, a dishevelled woman he had never seen (and may never even have heard of) had appeared at his door telling an incredible story: she had run off with a man she barely knew, pawned all her clothes, and wandered around Edo by herself looking for work. He probably couldn't decide what to think.

In the letter he wrote to Giyū a few days later, Bunshichi's rendition of Tsuneno's story was unambiguous: she had been seduced and abandoned by a scoundrel who coveted her family's money. Chikan was 'immoral' and his relatives were all 'bad people'. Rinsenji should expect to receive letters from Minagawa-chō in Kanda, but he should ignore them: they were the nefarious work of Chikan's relatives. Certainly, Giyū should not heed any requests to redeem Tsuneno's pawned clothes. In fact, he should not send anything to Tsuneno until he received further instructions. In the meantime, Bunshichi would do his best to help Tsuneno get settled for the winter. He had consulted with Mitsu, and she had agreed to ask the family she worked for if they could arrange suitable employment.

Bunshichi was anxious for a response, but his letter didn't arrive at Rinsenji for nearly two months, which was unusual. Ordinarily, letters took around three or four weeks to cross the mountains. But as it turned out, Bunshichi's letter was headed directly into an unexpected blizzard. At the beginning of the eleventh month, when he posted the letter, only a foot of snow had accumulated in the mountains. People in Echigo were relieved, thinking that they might enjoy a reprieve after the terrible winters of the famine years. But the snow finally started falling at the end of the eleventh month, and it came all at once, in a massive storm that raged for days. By the time it stopped, everything was buried. According to the writer Suzuki Bokushi, reporting from a town just inland of Ishigami, people could barely even get in and out of their houses. Bunshichi's letter would have to wait.

*

Well before the snow started falling on Ishigami Village, Giyū was already making arrangements to deal with his wayward sister. At the end of the ninth month, when Tsuneno had been gone for nine days, he asked his secretary, Denpachi, to stop by Kōtoku's house to check on her, since she had been away longer than expected. Denpachi was shocked to find that Tsuneno had never been there at all. Kōtoku was confused, too, but then a messenger arrived bearing a letter that Tsuneno had written announcing her departure for Edo. It was addressed to Tsuneno's uncle, who had read it and forwarded it to Kōtoku, thinking he should know what had happened. (Tsuneno's uncle completely disregarded the note she had attached to the letter, which instructed him not to tell her brothers and mother anything except her address in Edo. In fact, he handed that 'confidential' note over, too.) Alarmed, Denpachi brought the correspondence back to Rinsenji and told Giyū the whole story.

Giyū was a rigid man, often disappointed in other people's behaviour, but he was also sensitive. Women left him deeply confused, but he tried to understand their motives. When he was involved in a disagreement, he sometimes wrote a thorough account of the other side of the story, as if he were obligated to some internal sense of fairness. Tsuneno's behaviour made him furious, especially since it was humiliating, and after his disastrous first marriage he was sensitive to the criticism that he could not run a household. On the other hand, he could see exactly why she had left. 'It is impossible for us to accept that she ran away with a strange priest she didn't even know,' he wrote. 'She turned her back on her family and made us lose face in front of the whole world.' But, he added, 'she was married before, and then she was divorced as a result of her selfish behaviour. It seems that she ran away without telling anyone because she didn't know what else to do.'

Giyū wanted to find Tsuneno in Edo, if only to confirm that she was there, but it was a delicate undertaking. He couldn't go all the way to the city himself. He might have thought of aunt Mitsu and uncle Bunshichi, but it seems he didn't write to them first. Instead, he asked the Rinsenji temple secretary, Denpachi, to write to one of his relatives, Isogai Yasugorō, who was in service in the Shinbashi district of Edo. Yasugorō was one of Rinsenji's parishioners. At Tsuneno's second wedding, he'd sent a gift of dried sea bream by messenger service. At her third, he was one of the guests. His mother was one of the stalwarts of the Rinsenji women's association. In other words, he was a man who could be relied on to keep the temple's secrets. Through Denpachi, Giyū asked Yasugorō to go to Minagawa-chō, check up on Tsuneno, and report back. He emphasised that this was to be done with the utmost discretion.

Meanwhile, Giyū prepared for a mortifying interview with his father's relatives, the extended Izawa family in Echigo. Ordinarily, distant relations might not have had a say in how the temple was run. But Giyū was in their debt: during the famine years, he'd borrowed two hundred gold pieces from them to keep the temple running. So he felt compelled to explain all the embarrassing details, not only that Tsuneno had run away to Edo but also that she had done so in the company of a stranger and, nearly as bad, that she had pawned all her belongings. Unsurprisingly, the Izawa family decided that Giyū should cut her off.

Giyū's letter to Tsuneno began abruptly, without even a polite inquiry about her health: 'We received the letters you wrote on the tenth.' Then he related the long story of how he learned that Tsuneno had run away, finally arriving at an indictment of her character: 'You lied and said you were going to visit Kōtoku and went to Edo instead, which is wicked in the extreme. You've cast aside your parents and siblings, which is incredibly selfish, scandalous behaviour for a woman. When I explained the situation to our relatives, they all said that if that's your true character, then we should tell you we're leaving you to fend for yourself. You should understand that you haven't just cut off this temple, but your relatives and your village as well. You've requested that we redeem the things you pawned, but that will be difficult.' By 'difficult', he meant that he had no intention of doing it: he used a verb ending common in the hybrid style, which people often used when they wanted to decline unreasonable requests. Tsuneno could understand it well enough, though she might have needed someone to read the more complicated characters out loud and arrange them in the correct order.

Giyū closed with a famous reference, quoting a well-known passage from the Confucian text *The Classic of Filial Piety*, which was one of the first things well-educated children learned to read. He rendered the sentence in blocky characters that turned sharp corners: 'Your entire body – from your hair to your toes – has been received from your parents, so you should not dare to damage it. This is the beginning of filial piety.' 'I will not speak further to someone who neglects this,' he added.

Tsuneno probably recognised the passage, but she may or may not have understood the double meaning of her brother's message.

Giyū's closing quote from *The Classic of Filial Piety* chastised her for unfilial conduct, but it also reminded her to take care of herself, to 'not dare to damage' a single hair on her head. Giyū was angry, but he was her brother, and he would never really let her go.

*

By the time the letter arrived, towards the end of the eleventh month, Tsuneno was far beyond her brother's advice. Giyū didn't know how much damage had already been done. She had given her uncle Bunshichi a confused narrative of the past weeks: the pawned clothing, Chikan's demands for 'marriage', Sōhachi's cold welcome, and Chikan's departure. But she also still insisted that Chikan had been a friend to her. It would be several months before she changed that part of her story, or before she could admit to herself what had happened.

Uncle Bunshichi had heard enough to be horrified. He prepared a set of luggage for Tsuneno, including clothing, which she desperately needed. She still had only one robe and one coat. There was one condition, though: she was not allowed to bring any of it back to her tenement room in Minagawa-chō.

Tsuneno had two choices: stay with Bunshichi, understanding that at some point he would send her home, or go back to the tenement room with nothing. By that point, she had already made one consequential decision in her life. It was more than most women – most people – ever did. They married the partners their parents had selected; they took over the family farm or business or temple. Her brothers and sisters, even the rebellious and bad-tempered ones, had stayed where they were planted, trying to hold on to what they already had. It would have been so easy for Tsuneno to cede to her uncle's superior judgement and accept his version of her story. She didn't know the city at all. It wouldn't be a failure to let her family take care of her, give her something to wear, and find something respectable for her to do until she could safely return home. It was what almost anyone else would do.

But Tsuneno had come too far, and she was too stubborn. If she went back to Echigo, they'd only try to marry her off again. She was too old to be as lucky as her sister Kiyomi and her sister-in-law Sano, both mistresses of temples, caring for their babies and tending the altars, or her little sister Toshino, living peacefully in her husband's village. Who would marry her now, knowing her history? Her options weren't any better than they were when she'd run away in the first place. In fact, they were worse.

Tsuneno had already made her choice that day on Shimogoma-chi Bridge, when Chikan offered her the city and she said yes. She had regrets – she'd risked and lost nearly everything – but she still knew what she wanted, and there was no future for her in Echigo.

Tsuneno left Tsukiji with nothing. She was still in Edo. Something else was bound to come through.

*

Left to her own devices, Tsuneno had to find work, and soon. Her cash had run out, and she was already in debt to Jinsuke, either for rent or because he had lent her money and supplies to set up her room. The problem was that she had no particular skills. She had thought that she might go into service for a great lord and 'learn the manners and customs of the upper class'. But the men around her knew better. Those positions were impossible to find on short notice. There were interviews and auditions, and the competition was fierce. In Edo's back alleys, ambitious mothers spent years planning for their daughters' future in service.

Understanding that practice and discipline could propel pretty girls from tenements to great lords' mansions, they spent their scarce coins on music, dance and calligraphy lessons. If an exhausted girl came home after a long day complaining that she was hoarse from singing or that her fingers were calloused from playing the shamisen, her mother would rush her through dinner and make her practise anyway. She would remind her daughter that a cultivated young lady wouldn't need to spend her life taking in laundry or running a tiny store in a dusty tenement. She could become a wealthy merchant's concubine or support herself as a freelance geisha. Or, in the best possible case, she could make a brilliant marriage. Even if she turned into an elegant stranger who was embarrassed by her mother's vulgar manners, all the struggle and sacrifice would be worth it.

Tsuneno couldn't compete with that kind of dedication. She was not a skilled performer, and, even worse, she had no clothes. In her most recent letter, she had begged her family to send her 'bad obi', mirror, comb, hairpin, apron and cotton-padded robe. But they weren't speaking to her, and nothing had come through. She was untalented, unfashionable and alone. Sōhachi, the rice seller, advised her to go to the local employment office and take whatever they offered.

Tsuneno went, presenting herself like any other woman in the neighbourhood. But the only job available was a position as a maid of all work in a samurai mansion a few blocks away. It was simple domestic labour, nothing glamorous. It wasn't at all what she had imagined. But when Tsuneno tried to refuse, the employment agent insisted he had nothing else. 'There wasn't anything better,' Tsuneno wrote, 'and I was so worried.'

Around the same time, Tsuneno received a surprise visitor: Yasugorō, the Rinsenji temple secretary's relative, whom Giyū had dispatched to check on her. Tsuneno knew he had left his young family behind in Ishigami Village to spend the winter in service in Edo, so as soon as she arrived in the city, she had asked her brother for his address. But she had never received an answer.

Tsuneno must have been relieved to see Yasugorō. In a city full of strangers, here, finally, was a friend. Even better, he was someone she outranked. Although he was a little older than she was and he was an established, married man, he had always deferred to her family. He understood her status and her education. He knew who she was. Maybe he would explain to the employment agent that the job he had offered was unsuitable.

If that was what Tsuneno expected, she completely miscalculated. It was true that Yasugorō was not well educated or sophisticated. He wrote in blocky, laborious script and spoke in a thick Echigo accent. In Edo, he was a common servant. But he knew the city, which gave him a different perspective on her predicament.

Yasugorō understood that the Edo labour market was unforgiving. Yes, status still counted for something. It probably showed in Tsuneno's bearing and speech. When people realised she was the daughter of a temple family, they might have used slightly elevated language and bowed a little more deeply. But even the most impeccable pedigree wasn't a skill, and it meant very little without local connections and the money to back it up. Tsuneno had neither.

Under the circumstances, Yasugorō was delighted to hear that she'd been offered respectable work. He went directly to Sōhachi and confirmed the arrangement; then he wrote to her family and announced that her fate was settled: Tsuneno would start work as a maidservant at the end of the eleventh month.

Chapter Five

SAMURAI WINTER

The eleventh month of 1839 was surprisingly mild. The days ran together, awash in weak sunlight, and the ground never froze. After spending her entire life in Echigo, it was strange for Tsuneno to walk on muddy streets, in her everyday sandals, at a time of year when she would ordinarily need snowshoes. People from her part of the country made fun of people in Edo who exclaimed over every light dusting of snow. It was easy to admire a snowfall that you didn't have to shovel. Edoites also loved their needle-thin icicles, so delicate you could snap them with a finger. Suzuki Bokushi wrote that they were 'as inconsequential as a duck fart' compared to the icicles at home.

Of course, he could afford that kind of bravado: he was a well-dressed merchant who spent the Edo winter sitting by braziers in the studios of famous writers. It was harder for a woman alone to boast about her toughness, especially as she watched the winter set in from a drafty tenement. Tsuneno knew she couldn't go home even if she wanted to: the roads back through the mountains were buried. She also didn't know when or if she would hear from her family again.

In all her thirty-six years, Tsuneno had never lived alone. She had seven siblings; she'd had three husbands. Even on the road, she'd had Chikan to keep her company. The walls of her room were thin and the alleys were crowded, so there was always the sensation of having people around, but they were all strangers. At night, she sat up, feeling sick, burning through precious ink and paper, addressing letters to family members who might not answer. 'I want to get out of this room,' she wrote, 'but unless something changes I'll never be able to escape.'

And then, every morning, she went out through the tenement gate, walked the short distance into a samurai district, and entered yet another of Edo's many new worlds.

*

Samurai and their families accounted for about half of Edo's population. They called themselves warriors, and the men among them dressed the part. They wore split trousers emblazoned with their family crests and carried paired swords at their waists. They shaved the tops of their heads and gathered the rest of their hair into glossy topknots. Ostensibly this was so that armoured helmets would fit securely, though they usually went bareheaded or wore conical sedge hats. When samurai ventured out on ceremonial occasions, they travelled in military formation: the highest-ranking member of the band went on horseback, surrounded by men on foot carrying spears, bows and banners. Even when samurai went out on ordinary errands, the more important among them tended to travel with attendants close at hand.

Not one of these men had ever fired a shot, drawn a bow or hoisted a sword in battle. The Tokugawa shogunate's Great Peace had brought the realm stability, but it had robbed samurai of the chance to prove themselves in war. They told themselves – and one another – that their ancestors had fought bravely. They had the lineages, real and fabricated, to prove it. They listened to inherited war stories and studied the martial arts in school. But it was impossible to know, really, how they would behave if they were called upon to defend the realm, their house, or their lord. So they polished their swords and kept up appearances. They aspired to an attitude of detachment from the dirty world of coins and commerce. Among strangers and in public, they tried to look as though they would draw their weapons in response to the slightest insult.

In reality, many of the samurai who walked the streets of Edo looked awkward, unfashionable, and overwhelmed. They gawked at the sights of the city and seemed uncertain when they counted out their coins to buy snacks at food stalls. These were the men from the provinces, derisively called country samurai and mocked for their naiveté. There were nearly two hundred thousand of them in Edo at any given time, comprising a fighting force five times the size of the entire British navy in 1840. They had marched into the city from all over Japan holding halberds and carrying palanquins for the domain lords, who were required to reside in Edo every other year as a show of fealty to the shogun.

These rank-and-file country samurai lived in barracks on their lords' estates and spent most of their time confined to tiny rooms. When they left on day passes for shopping or sightseeing, they were not quite sure how to behave. Even Tsuneno was more at ease in the city than they were. At least she had wanted to come to Edo, and three weeks after her arrival she already knew how to live in a tenement, pay her rent and buy what she needed. These men were just on assignment. Their lords provided everything from basic furnishings to rice rations. They did not need to learn to survive on their own in the city, which would never really be their home.

Other samurai were more self-assured. They were the shogun's own direct retainers, as opposed to the men who served domain lords, and they comprised the standing army that was supposed to defend Edo Castle against both internal and external threats. This force consisted of roughly five thousand bannermen, who were usually the descendants of men who had served the first Tokugawa shogun. Their ancestors were among the original samurai settlers of Edo, who had been apportioned good plots of land on the high ground just across the castle moat. Most still lived in the same neighbourhoods they had originally settled: Banchō, Surugadai and Koishikawa. Below them in rank were roughly twenty thousand housemen. They were also direct vassals of the shogun, but they did not enjoy the privilege of appearing before him in person at Edo Castle, and they did not qualify for the highest-ranking positions in the shogunate's administration. Their dwellings were smaller and more scattered. Together with their families and retainers, housemen and bannermen accounted for a little less than half of the city's samurai population.

Some of the bannermen had fiefdoms in nearby provinces. Typically, these weren't impressive holdings; they amounted to small collections of villages. Bannermen rarely visited their lands. If they cared to have anything to do with their territory, they employed village headmen's sons as watchmen or allowed high-status peasants to visit with greetings at the New Year. Otherwise, the land was just a source of income to them. These were urban men, Edoites born and bred.

Most bannermen, and all housemen, drew salaries from the shogun's granary in Asakusa, where row after row of low-slung warehouses jutted like sawteeth into the Sumida River. Day after day, long, flat boats docked in the granary canals and unloaded rice from the shogun's lands. Every year, it amounted to roughly five hundred thousand straw-wrapped bales. This was a flammable fortune, kept under heavy guard in the storehouse, surrounded by wells and water tanks. The highest-quality rice would be delivered to the ladies of the shogun's harem. The rest would be apportioned to the shogun's retainers: better rice for the men of highest status and worse for very low-ranking housemen.

Three times a year, the bannermen and housemen sent commoner representatives called bill stabbers to collect their salaries from the granary. These men were named after the procedure for collecting government salaries in the seventeenth century, when there had been an enormous bale of straw set outside the granary. When samurai came to receive their allotments, they had written their names on slips of paper that they tucked between bamboo skewers and stabbed into the bale. The granary workers would then collect the names and call the men to receive their portions. But it was undignified for the retainers of the shogun to sit around in front of the granary as if they were dogs waiting to be called for dinner, so they began to employ commoners to take care of this task for them. This was how the bill stabbers' business began: they collected salary rice.

But what was a samurai supposed to do with hundreds or even thousands of bales of rice wrapped in straw? There was only so much he and his household could eat (the rough calculation was that one man would eat one bale a year, though this made for meagre portions). What the samurai really needed was cash: for soy sauce, sake, charcoal, vegetables, miso, clothing, furniture, armour, and all the other large and small necessities of urban life. Separated from the land, they could not produce any of these things for themselves. So the bill stabbers, now brokers, offered a solution. They would exchange the rice for cash, collecting small commissions, and the bannermen and housemen would not have to lower themselves to commerce. Instead, on the day their rice was dispersed they would meet with the brokers at teahouses lining the riverbank, where they would receive tidy packages of gold pieces and obsequious thanks for their patronage.

Inevitably, the shogun's men outspent what they earned. This was not just a matter of samurai not knowing how to handle money; it was also a structural problem. Salaries were more or less fixed, and a man could earn more only if he received a special appointment. But the prices of most daily necessities and services were rising all the time, and the baseline value of rice drifted lower and lower as peasants learned new agricultural techniques – the use of fertilisers, crop rotations, and plant breeding – that allowed them to produce more. If the shogun's vassals wanted to maintain their fathers' standards of living, they had to take out loans. This was a service that the brokers were happy to provide. But year after year, as the salary rice yielded fewer and fewer coins, Edo's bannermen and housemen found themselves deeper in debt to men who had started as common merchants and now occupied mansions and possessed unimaginable fortunes. The moneylenders refused to meet their samurai debtors in person; instead, they remained in their guild office beside the granary gate, where they processed rice bills and spent enormous sums ordering in lunch. (Rumour had it that their monthly lunch budget was a hundred gold pieces per person – the equivalent of a low-ranking bannerman's annual salary.) The shogunate recognised the problem, and on a few occasions it issued blanket orders for loan forgiveness. Even so, during the early nineteenth century it wasn't unusual for a bannerman to owe a broker as much as three times his annual salary.

For high-ranking bannermen, there were ways to compensate. Those closest to the shogun benefited from his household's largesse. Iseki Takako, the wife of a bannerman who managed the affairs of the women in the shogun's harem, recorded such gifts in her diary: twill robes, lengths of thick white silk folded into boxes, a lacquered inkstone case, and all kinds of fish and fruits. One autumn, on the occasion of a full moon, the shogun's wife sent 'not only steamed rice with red beans and the traditional accompaniments, but also fruits, sea bream, shrimp, flounder. And persimmons and pears piled into a huge wicker hamper.'

But Iseki's household was exceptionally fortunate: the men in her family held prestigious posts at the castle, and together they collected about a thousand bales of rice a year in salary, augmented by gifts. Most bannermen drew stipends of fewer than two hundred bales a year, and housemen were even poorer. This income was still enviable to small shopkeepers and tenement dwellers, whose existence was much more precarious. Tsuneno would have been happy to have the equivalent of a low-ranking bannerman's salary; she could have set up house and even supported a husband and children. But the problem was that bannermen were heavily indebted and they were obligated to keep servants and retainers at all times. Unemployed bannermen and housemen, who were assigned to the shogun's reserve force, actually had to pay the shogunate a fee for the privilege of being allowed to do nothing.

In 1849, the wife of a middling bannerman wrote frankly about the challenges of running a household under these conditions. She told her parents, wealthy peasants who were unfamiliar with this variety of hardship: 'Even if we economise by patching and mending our old clothes, we still have to pay for our five servants. We live on a fixed salary of rice bales, so when we finish paying for all the expenses of our daily life, even if we don't eat anything at all there are only 100 or 200 small silver coins left over.' For the lowest-ranking housemen, who subsisted on only a hundred bales of rice per year, the situation was even worse. They were forced to supplement their income with handicrafts. They made calligraphy brushes, bamboo skewers, hair ties, paper lanterns and sandal thongs. Sometimes they cultivated azaleas and morning glories or raised goldfish and crickets to sell as pets. In contrast, Tsuneno's family in Echigo, which was technically of lower status, never had to resort to piecework or fish husbandry to make ends meet.

There were only two ways out of what samurai called debt hell. The first was to retrench: pawn everything that could be spared, cut staff as far as possible, plead for better rates from creditors, and economise on everything. The other was to increase the household's income. A promising son could marry a woman who could bring in some money, though this was difficult among samurai. Sometimes it was worth arranging a match with a wealthy commoner's daughter. This might have been Tsuneno's fate if she had lived closer to Edo or if her family had more friends who were samurai rather than priests. Sometimes that was a good option for a girl who wanted to leave her village and ascend to a higher social status. But the problem for bannermen was that taking a wealthy bride would yield only a one-time infusion of cash. It was far better to get promoted to a position in the shogun's administration, which would pay an appointment salary on top of the usual stipend. The best positions, those in charge of distributing jobs to other samurai or those that entailed dealings with wealthy commoners, would also provide an opportunity to receive gifts or bribes.

Promotions were not easy. Most of the shogun's vassals were underemployed, and there were far too many aspirants for every position. Even worse, there was often no way to distinguish between candidates on the basis of ability, because the jobs themselves were ceremonial: men served as attendants who stood around in the beautiful rooms of Edo Castle, as guards who rarely encountered threats, and as middle managers in a vast and usually pointless bureaucracy. In the unlikely event of a vacancy, a senior official would work behind the scenes to install his favourite. It was easy to tell who these men of influence were, because their front gates were crowded with unemployed housemen. The most desperate came at the crack of dawn every day, bearing gifts and kind words, in the hope that their discipline and consistency would make an impression. But getting a job this way was a nearly hopeless task, like 'trying to hollow out bamboo with a lantern wick'.

A few tried more creative methods. Negishi Yasumori, a bannerman known for his literary talent, started out with a miserable salary of 150 bales and rose through the ranks to an appointment as City Magistrate and a salary of a thousand bales. No one doubted that he was a man of great ability, but such a miraculous ascent demanded some kind of explanation. A later writer claimed Negishi had got his lucky break when he deliberately got drunk, staggered to a shogunal elder's mansion, and passed out in a drainage ditch. An underling found him and gave him a change of clothes, and Negishi visited every day for the next three years to express his gratitude. Ultimately, he was noticed by the master of the household and was granted a position in his service, which became the launching pad for a brilliant career.

Other bannermen and housemen, who weren't as clever or as fortunate, tried to monetise their status. Their position as samurai had given them access to the world of weapons and armour. Some worked as freelance sword appraisers, others as martial arts instructors, teaching peasants' and townsmen's sons judo and riding. Since their estates were gifts from the shogunate, they never had to pay rent, so they tried to profit by building small houses on their property and renting them out. This was officially prohibited, and it could be risky. In 1825, one bannerman got caught up in a huge scandal when it turned out that his estate housed an illegal brothel.

To solve his cash flow problems, he had constructed barracks on his property and hired a masterless samurai as their superintendent. One of the tenants turned out to be an enterprising townswoman who conspired with one of the bannerman's retainers to run a small brothel. Initially, they employed only one prostitute, but the business prospered to the extent that they were able to hire several more, and the traffic of customers coming in and out of the side exit to the bannerman's estate became impossible to ignore. At that point, the townswoman and her accomplice informed the bannerman and offered to pay him for his silence. He accepted, relieved to have the extra income. But it wasn't worth it. When the matter came to light, he was exiled to a distant island.

If being a bannerman was difficult, then being a bannerman's second or third son was far worse. With no prospect of inheriting his father's rank and salary, and no family property that could be split to give him a portion, the best a young man in this position could hope for was an advantageous adoption. Maybe there was a childless bannerman somewhere, perhaps a distant relative of the family, who wanted to take on a promising heir. Or a bannerman's daughter who needed a husband, whose parents wanted a son-in-law to take on the family name. In that case, the young groom would have to live with his in-laws, accommodate himself to the ways of a different household, answer to a new surname, and make sure he didn't anger his wife and her family. It would be a difficult few years, at least, and success wasn't guaranteed. Adopted grooms were divorced and disinherited all the time. To ease the way, it was best to bring some money into the marriage, enough to buy second and third chances. But where was the money supposed to come from?

Bannermen's sons had two things in their favour: their status as samurai and their knowledge of the city. They exploited both brazenly, relentlessly, doing anything they could to get their hands on cash. Some became notorious for extortion. In the 1850s, the second son of a bannerman perpetrated a fraud on a pawnbroker in the Kōjimachi commercial district. He appeared in the man's shop carrying a paulownia wood box wrapped in lavender silk crepe and brilliant yellow cotton. He announced that it contained a rare treasure: two living dragons, male and female, which the imperial court had bestowed upon his family in reward for his ancestors' meritorious service. These, he said, were even more valuable than the document that the shogun had issued when he granted the family its fief. But the family had recently found itself in need of cash, so he asked that their trusted neighbourhood pawnbroker accept the treasure as collateral (confidentially, of course) and issue a loan. The pawnbroker's clerk, who was not a fool, suspected that the bannerman's son was up to something, and he insisted on following the rules of his master's shop: he had to see the item before he would write out a ticket. The bannerman's son protested, 'But you see, these are living dragons – if you open the box they will surely fly away.' Nevertheless, the clerk insisted, and eventually the bannerman's son relented. When the clerk unwrapped the box and pried open the lid, two large lizards jumped out and scurried away. The bannerman's son had known this would happen, since he had starved the lizards for ten days beforehand. But he put on his most dignified face, reached for the short sword he kept at his side, and intoned, in excessively formal language, 'As I predicted, a terrible thing has come to pass. I must commit ritual suicide at this very moment.' He stood there, with the blade pressed against his stomach, until the clerk called for help and the whole household came running: the pawnshop master, the mistress and several employees and neighbours. The pawnbroker's neighbours, who were merchants themselves, knew that the shop could not survive the scandal if a bannerman's son committed suicide on the premises, and the entire block might attract the attention of the City Magistrate, possibly with unpleasant consequences. They convinced the pawnbroker to settle with the bannerman's son for the astronomical sum of five hundred gold pieces.

Another bannerman's son, Katsu Kokichi, wrote a memoir detailing his exploits. He was the same age as Tsuneno, and like her he had lived a few different lives by the time he was in his mid-thirties. As an adolescent he'd run away from home and survived for several months as a beggar wandering the highways. He'd worked as a labourer on a fishing boat and nearly been adopted by a commoner family. When he returned to Edo, he borrowed a small fortune from his brother's broker and spent a month and a half living in a brothel. Then he set himself up as a freelance sword appraiser and learned how to fence. Even after he married a respectable woman, he roamed Edo with a gang of swordsmen and supported himself through gambling and extortion.

As a man and a samurai, Katsu had advantages that Tsuneno never did. He deserted his wife for weeks at a time and wasted vast sums in brothels, but he never suffered the shame of divorce. He behaved so badly that at one point his father kept him locked in a cage for three years, but he was never disowned. On the street, his Edo accent and his martial arts training both served him well: he could talk or fight his way out of trouble. And when all else failed, he could visit a hairdresser, put on his formal split trousers, and summon the authority that was his birthright as a bannerman's son. While Tsuneno sat in her tenement in the winter of 1839, wondering if she should go into service, Katsu Kokichi was travelling the countryside on a mission to raise money for his Edo landlord, a spendthrift bannerman with no common sense. When the peasants on the bannerman's fief refused to pay,

Katsu charmed, threatened and bullied them into submission. He quickly raised the sum he required and returned to Edo a hero.

Katsu Kokichi was, by his own admission, a poor exemplar of the values the shogun's men claimed to uphold. He wasn't honest or diligent, he had no sense of loyalty or even responsibility to anyone who was supposed to be his superior, and he certainly wasn't frugal. But he was lucky. When he reached the age of forty-two and wrote his memoir, he couldn't help bragging about his good fortune: 'Although I indulged in every manner of folly and nonsense in my lifetime, Heaven seems not to have punished me as yet.'

In the winter of 1839, as Tsuneno prepared to go into service and Kokichi charmed hapless peasants, the shogun's bannermen had fewer than thirty years left. By the time their grandchildren came of age, the city would no longer belong to them. It wouldn't even be called Edo. But no one knew that yet. It would be more than two decades until they could imagine a day when the shogun did not reign from Edo Castle. In the meantime, there were other problems to attend to. Guard posts had to be staffed, swords appraised, bribes offered and taxes collected. Plans had to be made for the immediate future: a son's marriage, the late-winter cleaning, the closing of the year's accounts. And the ordinary tasks of daily life had to continue: the fires had to be lit, the water jars filled and the futons set out each night and put away in the morning. Errands had to be run. Maidservants had to be hired.

*

Tsuneno's employer was a bannerman named Matsudaira Tomo-saburō. He was either very lucky, uncommonly personable, or some combination of the two, because he was somewhere in his late teens and already commanded a stipend of two thousand bales of rice. This worked out to an enviable seven hundred gold pieces in yearly income, a fortune by most bannermen's standards. As a child, Tomosaburō had been a page to Tokugawa Iesada, the shogun's heir, who was roughly his age, and in 1839 he was promoted to the position of senior attendant. This was not an exclusive post – there were about a hundred senior attendants who supervised the young lord's stablemen, prepared his meals, arranged his hair, and laid out his clothing. Still, it was a good job with a substantial salary, and, more important, it came with the opportunity to speak directly to the shogun and gain his favour.

Most people, even most samurai, would never have that chance. For the majority of Edo's residents, the castle was a strange and mysterious space. From the commoner district where Tsuneno lived, the castle itself was nearly invisible. The main tower, which had once loomed over the city, had long ago burned down, and, citing expense, the shogunate had declined to rebuild it. In its absence, people in Tsuneno's neighbourhood, which bordered the outer moat, could see only the castle's fortifications: stone walls, heavy wooden gates, imposing watchtowers and steep, grass-covered berms. Even on commercially printed maps of Edo, the castle was almost always represented by a blank space, an absence meant as a sign of respect. A similar gap preceded mentions of the shogunate in written documents, a gesture towards the hesitation an ordinary person might feel encountering such fearsome authority.

Not everyone was overawed. When Edo Castle burned in 1838 and commoner fire brigades were allowed inside, they stole everything they could find and brought trinkets back as souvenirs. But for most, the building itself was a kind of abstraction, much like the shogun, who never appeared in public. There were rumours, but no one could say for certain what he looked like or how he sounded.

The privilege of appearing in the shogun's presence was reserved for domain lords and bannermen. On the first and fifteenth of each month, those of sufficient rank were summoned to the castle. They came in flamboyant style, riding horses, surrounded by attendants carrying spears, halberds and big, heavy boxes. Their appearance at the entrance to Ōtemon Gate was such a spectacle that it became a tourist attraction, but it was meant to impress the city, not the shogun. The men who had been summoned were required to enter the castle grounds on foot with a minimum of attendants. The horses and superfluous men would have to wait for hours in the large plaza in front of the gate, passing their time under the watch of an official from the City Magistrate's office, who was posted there in case the bored attendants started fighting.

Meanwhile, the lords and bannermen entered the main hall and took their places in order of rank, the most important among them closest to the shogun. The very existence of a suite of rooms that could hold them all was impressive. It showed that the shogun possessed Edo's ultimate luxury: space. There were dozens of tatami mats for hundreds of men, and paintings on the walls displayed sprawling landscapes of pine trees and rivers against a backdrop of gold leaf. Flocks of birds were frozen in flight, every feather and beak rendered precisely.

The men in attendance were also carefully arranged, concerned about not appearing out of place. To enter the awesome space of the castle, even a lesser room on an ordinary day, samurai had to dress with care. There were rules for everything. One could wear socks only in the winter months; if a man wished to wear socks in the summer he had to petition for an exception on the grounds that he suffered from chronically cold feet. A shaved head was required (except for one man who petitioned for an exception because he had a cold head – in reality, he was trying to hide a large, unsightly scar). A topknot was also required, which was unfortunate for those who had gone bald. They had to buy false topknots and glue them on. When the seated men bowed in the presence of the shogun, their topknots looked like rows of ink-drawn tally marks standing out against pale shaved heads.

This kind of formality and ritual was typical of Edo Castle, even on ordinary workdays. At the beginning of the eleventh month of the year, for example, there was a ceremony in which the shogun had his brazier lit for the first time that season. The event was timed to coincide with the start of winter on the calendar. If the season turned ahead of schedule, then the men were expected to endure the cold. Bathroom breaks were also a problem. On ritual occasions when men wore long-sleeved formal overskirts, it was nearly impossible to remove all the necessary layers of clothing within the confines of one of the castle's outhouses, and of course it wasn't permitted to strip down and piss in the shogun's garden. Lords, and the shogun himself, had men in attendance who carried bronze urine tubes; with only a little loosening of ties, they could be discreetly inserted into the gaps in one's robes, neatly solving the problem. But bannermen, who came to the castle without attendants, had no recourse. They would try not to drink too much in the hours before the ceremony, then grit their teeth until they could change clothes.

Matsudaira Tomosaburō, like the other men who made their careers in attendance on the shogun, was used to formal etiquette and highly complicated procedures. He knew how to bear the cold and the heat, how to bow deeply from the waist, and how to sit motionless for hours, with his knees aching and his feet going numb. Yet there were hints, here and there, of a messier reality that couldn't be contained with a show of samurai disci-pline. Occasionally, someone lost his mind and raised his voice;

very occasionally, there was a fight. Sometimes a glued-on false topknot slipped off an old man's head and fell to the floor with an embarrassing thud. And despite everyone's best efforts, the urinals in the main section of the castle were rumoured to be the most disgusting in Edo.

Tomosaburō's mansion was just outside the castle, on the other side of the Kanda Gate. His plot, which his ancestors had received from the shogunate, was rather small. It certainly didn't match up to his income or his status. But bannermen could not live where they pleased, and even looking for a new house in the same neighbourhood could require years of frustrating paperwork. Permission had to be sought from the shogunate and an appropriate parcel of land had to be found. Since Edo was so crowded, the waiting list could be a decade long. When one new spot opened up in 1824, eleven bannerman families tried to lay claim to it.

At least Tomosaburō's mansion was in a prestigious neighbourhood, Surugadai, which was home to over 250 bannermen and their families. On maps of Edo, their names appeared one after another in tiny, cramped script and the whole neighbourhood was the monochromatic white that represented samurai land. Surugadai bordered Tsuneno's neighbourhood, Kanda, but the two districts were very different. Where Kanda's blocks were crowded and noisy, Surugadai's were empty and quiet. There were no temporary stalls selling sandals or cakes, and there were far fewer noisy hawkers. Surugadai's samurai compounds were walled in, revealing little. Occasionally, a knobby tree would reach its arm over one of the walls and drop its leaves in the soil. The trunk of the tree, within the compound, belonged to the samurai who owned it. The branches, overhanging the road, were in a kind of no-man's-land, and if one fell on someone – or if someone used one to hang himself – it was an occasion for lawsuits and paperwork.

Even in Tomosaburō's relatively small compound, there was more light and air than Tsuneno could find in any of the commoner districts of Kanda. The main gate, set back a distance from the street, opened into a courtyard planted with trees. From there, a short path led to the main receiving area. This was where the bannerman handled his correspondence and entertained his guests, probably in a series of rooms that opened one into another: a luxurious expanse of tatami mats set out in groups of sixes and tens. Tsuneno had no business there. The buildings set out around the perimeter of the compound were also foreign territory: they housed Tomosaburō's retainers, including a chamberlain, common foot soldiers, and an assortment of other warrior types that Tsuneno could not have categorised. Some of them had very little money – their salaries were low – but they were still nothing like the pedlars, pieceworkers, shopkeepers and vagrants shouting across the alleys in Kanda. It wasn't just their uniforms and topknots; it was the way they deferred to one another. Their politeness. There was a kind of order in Tomosaburō's household that would have been familiar from Tsuneno's own well-run provincial home, but also a kind of strangeness: the crests and swords, the formal language spoken with an Edo accent.

Tsuneno's destination was the inner quarter of the compound, which was reached through a separate entrance. Part of it was devoted to Tomosaburō's living quarters, and the rest belonged to the women and children of the house. This was where many of the ordinary tasks of daily life were carried out: where books were read, children were scolded, kimonos and aprons were sewn, and errands and expeditions were planned. In ordinary samurai households, the men and women of the family worked along with the servants. The mistress of the house would spend most of her time on mending, weaving, spinning and doing laundry, and she might split the cooking and cleaning with one or two maidservants. Her husband and his servants and retainers would help with heavier cleaning and repairs around the house. A low-ranking samurai, even a master of his own household, didn't earn enough to exempt himself from housework. But bannermen were different, and in a family earning seven hundred gold pieces a year there was more opportunity for leisure. The women didn't have to make, or wear, homespun, and there was more money for hiring maidservants.

As a maid of all work, Tsuneno was probably not expected to cook or sew: the cooking was left to a better-paid servant, usually a man, and although Tsuneno could sew, she had not been hired as a seamstress. Instead, she was there to wait on the nine women in Tomosaburō's household – probably his mother and his wife, maybe a grandmother and one or more of his sisters, and a few attendants or higher-level servants. This ratio was not ideal. Tsuneno was used to housework, but she had always belonged to the class of people who hired servants. She had never been one herself. The women were extremely demanding, and she could barely keep up with their requests. She wrote to her brother Kōtoku: 'I wake up around six, and then I light the fire in five different rooms and prepare the bath. Then I sweep out several small rooms and clear away the nine women's sleeping mats, and then I fill the water jugs in the five rooms. Then I clear away the mistress's tray, arrange the furniture, and take care of the nine women's things and help get them ready.' It was more like running an inn than being the mistress of a peasant household or even a prosperous temple.

If Tsuneno had worked in a more modest samurai home, in some ways she might have had an easier time. Maidservants for ordinary samurai did a lot of work: in addition to light cleaning, they also cooked, did laundry, ran errands, spun thread, helped with the babies, and accompanied the ladies of the house on outings. But at least their days were varied. Tsuneno was just as busy, but at a smaller range of tasks, and she had to repeat everything nine times over. As a low-ranking maid of all work, she was responsible for everything and unable to resist her mistresses' demands. Her annual salary was relatively low: just over two gold pieces. She wasn't surprised when she learned that her predecessors in the job had all left on short notice, complaining that the employment office had deceived them about the work. Tsuneno often had to stay at Tomosaburō's mansion until midnight, freezing because she still didn't have a change of clothes or a cotton-padded robe.

She returned home to her tenement one night, exhausted, and sat up to write to Kōtoku (Giyū still wouldn't write her back): 'The work is difficult and my hands and feet go numb. When I'd been there for four or five days it was so hard that I wanted a break and asked to leave.' But she had to admit that there had also been pleasant surprises. When she finally reached a breaking point, her fellow servants had responded with sympathy. They lent her a coverlet, and her mistress gave her a futon to take back to her room. 'I came here alone,' she wrote, 'and so many people helped me get settled.' Yet this kindness caused its own problems. Every favour she accepted compounded a debt of gratitude that she had no intention of repaying. 'I'd like to ask for some time off,' she wrote, 'but I'm there to work for all of them, and they are all so nice to me that I can't do anything but continue to attend to them.' Her only option, she thought, was to emulate her predecessors and, when the time came, simply walk away.

This was a common strategy, and it wasn't hard to pull off. Servants would tell their masters that they were leaving on a pilgrimage to one of the big shrines in a different province, maybe

Ise or Konpira, then surreptitiously find another employer. One of Tsuneno's contemporaries, the Edo writer Takizawa Bakin, complained that he had gone through seven maids in one year. The situation was so dire that the shogunate, which was always concerned with promoting the virtue of loyalty, rewarded the rare Edo servants who did stay with the same masters for extended periods. The year before Tsuneno arrived in the city, the City Magistrates commended a man named Kenjirō who worked for a pharmacist near the Naitō Shinjuku post station. Kenjirō had entered service as a young boy, they wrote, and soon distinguished himself with his diligence. When the pharmacy prospered, thanks in part to his efforts, he still wore humble straw sandals every day and stayed up until midnight preparing pills for the store. When his term of service was over, he refused his payout and stayed on to care for the master's ill wife. He might have expected some consideration in return, but he displayed no resentment when his master passed him over and adopted a different heir to marry his daughter and run the store.

Kenjirō received five silver pieces for his virtue, but most Edoites had no interest in imitating his loyalty. Tsuneno was no different. She had already left behind three marriages, a family, a village and an entire province. Even as she accepted kind words and borrowed bedding, she was making other plans. Surely the bannerman could fend for himself.

*

In the end, Tsuneno spent a few weeks in service, just long enough to learn the names of her fellow servants and the preferences of the ladies of the household, long enough to recognise some of the pedlars who came with tofu and charcoal. She might have grown more accustomed to the daily rounds rearranging furniture and bedding, but she never got used to the cold early mornings. At night she walked home in the dark, arriving in Minagawa-chō long after the evening vendors had packed up their stands. The main gate to the block was shut tight and the guards were half-asleep at their posts. For a few hours her corner of the city was almost quiet. Back in the tenement room, she still had no change of clothes, so she wrapped herself in a borrowed coverlet and crawled into a borrowed futon.

On the last day of the eleventh month of the year, midwinter, it finally snowed a little. It was just a dusting, hardly even snow by Echigo standards, but people in Edo seemed to think it was an event. They commented when it stayed on the ground overnight, laying fine white traces over the courtyard pathways. The next day, the first of the twelfth month, a fierce wind whipped through the city, and that night saw the first major fire of Tsuneno's time in Edo. It started in Yotsuya, on the other side of the Edo Castle grounds. The flames never reached Kanda, but everyone was excited anyway. A few blocks away from Minagawa-chō, the ward headman Saitō Yukinari rushed to his offices to make sure everything was under control.

One day, Matsudaira Tomosaburō's mansion would burn. It was a predictable catastrophe: no one thought an Edo building would last. What would remain, they thought, was the institutional architecture of the city. It was the idea of the bannerman, if not the bannerman himself; the idea of the castle, if not the castle itself; the ability to hire another maidservant, if not the maidservant herself. It was a structure that had already endured for over two hundred years: the shogun at the centre of Edo, the samurai arrayed around the moats, the warriors at the heart of the realm.

How could they have known? The disasters that couldn't be

overcome were still waiting on the other side of the ocean, where strange men were making plans that were as inscrutable as a new maidservant's. For a little while longer, the bannermen could occupy themselves with domestic affairs, stopping every so often to remark on a winter so mild and quiet that it was barely a winter at all.

Chapter Six

COSTUMES FOR
URBAN LIFE

The first day of the New Year was auspicious; the second one was interesting. That's what people said about the start of the holiday in Edo, eagerly awaited by natives and migrants alike. The last day of the twelfth month was frantic, because, according to long-standing tradition, all the year's outstanding bills had to be settled before midnight. Stores threw their doors open and hung large signs and lanterns so that their debtors could find them. The masters sat at their desks writing out receipts, keeping other stores' clerks waiting as their own collections came in from across the city. All day long, anxious young men ran through the streets, darting into shops belonging to their masters' debtors, hurrying home to deliver cash balances, and setting out again to settle other accounts. At midnight, when the last bell sounded and the masters had given up on collecting some of what they were owed, they carried over outstanding balances and closed their books. Then it was time to complete the New Year's cleaning. It had to be finished overnight, since sweeping was unlucky after daybreak on the first – someone might unintentionally sweep out the year's good luck. When the tidying was done, just before dawn, everyone went out to the bathhouses, which stayed open late for exhausted shopkeepers and their employees. In the morning, they slept. The signs were lowered and bound with paper ties, and the doors were shut. Even the vegetable market and the fish market were closed. It was the only day all year that was a holiday for everyone.

While the merchants slept, the side streets belonged to children with animal-shaped kites and brightly painted battledores and shuttlecocks, and the main boulevards belonged to processions of warriors. The highest-ranking samurai households sent delegations in the early morning to greet the shogun at his castle. The blocks they walked through were empty, unrecognizable – the throngs of peddlers had vanished and the vendors' stalls had been cleared. Tall pine boughs bracketed the storefronts, which were hung with paper decorations on straw ropes. The streets were cleaner – they even seemed wider – and the ordinary sounds of commerce were replaced by the smack of shuttlecocks against battledores, the happy shrieks of children, and the clomping of horse hooves and wooden sandals against frozen streets.

On the second day, adults ventured out. Early in the morning, they visited crowded barbershops to get their hair oiled and set and to have their beards and foreheads shaved clean. Then they went to pay New Year's calls on their clients and neighbours, dressed in robes and jackets so stiff and new that they crackled when they moved. Mothers of servant girls ventured out of the tenements and went to big houses to pay their respects to their daughters' employers. Kabuki actors rode around the city in palanquins, visiting teahouses, patrons and teachers, asking for their renewed consideration in the New Year.

The bannerman Matsudaira Tomosaburō went to Edo Castle on the morning of the second; he had not ranked high enough to join in the first day's processions. The men and women in his household, busy preparing their master for an audience with the shogun, didn't have much time to celebrate the holiday. Even on the first day of the year, when other people were sleeping in or climbing the hill in Surugadai to see the sunrise, they were expected to demonstrate their fidelity. It was the custom in bannermen's mansions for the members of the household to assemble in the courtyard in order of rank. The retainers wore ceremonial uniforms with stiff, sleeveless overskirts, all marked with the house's crest, and the women, even the servants, wore their hair in long, segmented ponytails as they did on extremely formal occasions. They bowed in greeting, offering their continued service in the New Year.

Tsuneno, on the other side of the city, was glad she wasn't there.

*

Tsuneno was still a maidservant, but she had left the miserable room in Kanda. She had found a new master, a fantastically wealthy man, who was spending three hundred gold pieces just to renovate a suite of rooms for his new concubine, a geisha from Kyoto. Construction was still underway, but the plans were impressive. There was going to be a room dedicated to the tea ceremony, all decorated in light green. Tsuneno hadn't written to Giyū or her mother in months and she knew she had been disowned, but this was a message she couldn't contain: finally, nine weeks after reaching Edo, she'd arrived.

Tsuneno's new address, Sumiyoshi-chō, was in the heart of the theatre district. Her block had once been part of a brothel quarter; now the neighbourhood's main thoroughfare was known as Doll Street, since it was home to so many doll makers and sellers. Propped up in stores and stalls, dressed in elaborate embroidered robes, the dolls looked like expensive toys. But onstage, in Edo's popular puppet theatres, they were eerily lifelike. Guided by silent masters, their tiny carved hands opened letters and carried lanterns and their limp bodies shook with laughter and trembled in anger. When they cried, they bent their glossy black wigs to their sleeves, and their still faces seemed alive with expression.

Edo's three major kabuki theatres were just across Doll Street. They were painted garish colours, hung with strings of lanterns, and decorated with huge wooden billboards and life-sized paintings of dramatic scenes. Inside, they were hot and crowded. Dozens of lanterns hung from the ceilings, and the audience crammed onto mats below stage level and pressed into galleries on the second floor. The best seats in the house bordered a narrow wooden runway where leading actors made their entrances. They appeared at the rear of the hall, then walked through the crowds, glowing in the lantern light, close enough to touch. Onstage, they sang and danced, accompanied by drums, stringed instruments, and wailing flutes. Lions tossed manes of long white hair, arrogant young warriors stomped their feet and boasted of their strength, and heroes vanquished their enemies with graceful blows from enormous swords. Beautiful women – always played by men – flirted and danced and cried. With their painted faces, lush wigs and careful, feminine gestures, they were far more glamorous than anyone in the audience.

Offstage, the theatre district was busy until nightfall, when patrons were required to vacate the quarter and the gates were shut. On the days of big kabuki productions, the drums that called people to the theatres began to pound at four in the morning and the first shows – comic short acts and dances – started well before dawn. The plays continued, scene after scene, act after act, title after title, all day, as theatregoers and hangers-on streamed down Doll Street and pressed into the jam-packed blocks of the district.

In Sumiyoshi-chō, Tsuneno was close enough to hear the noise and the drums. The stores on her block sold products associated with the stage. There was oil to make her hair shine, powder for a snowy complexion and vermillion to paint bright-coloured lips against her face. Some packages were branded with the names of famous actors.

Tsuneno bought a few things – she couldn't resist. She sent hair oil to her sister-in-law Sano. 'The best in Edo,' she said. She sent a handkerchief for her eight-year-old nephew, Kihaku, sheets of toasted seaweed, and something more exotic for her mother: a silver coin, which she had asked for and received from her master. It was a 'Daikoku' coin, named after the laughing god of happiness who appeared on its face. But it was also an Edo inside joke, a play on words. Daikoku Jōze was the name of the official responsible for the Edo silver mint. He had nothing to do with the god, but a silver coin was a source of happiness, wasn't it?

Tsuneno had tried to clear some of her debts, at least the ones that could be settled with money. She paid her former superintendent, Jinsuke, three gold coins and gave a hundred coppers to the Rinsenji parishioner Yasugorō to compensate him for carrying her gifts and letters. But she still owed him five hundred, and living in Edo was surprisingly expensive; she had to pay for every last tea bowl and set of chopsticks herself. She had managed to buy a pillow and a pair of shoes, but she was still wearing the same black robe and coat she'd brought all the way from Echigo, and she was embarrassed whenever she met someone she knew on the street. If only her uncle would send the three gold pieces he still owed her. Then she could buy new clothes, and she might have enough money left over to enjoy her new neighbourhood.

As it was, a ticket to a play at one of the main theatres was probably out of Tsuneno's reach. A box near the stage cost one and a half gold pieces, nearly half a year's wages for an average maid-servant, and even seats in the gods at a big theatre cost roughly a month's salary. But a place near the edge of the stage, standing room, at a smaller house's summer production could be had for the price of a few bowls of noodles. And there were always perfor-mances on temple grounds and informal street shows. Sometimes they even featured the same actors.

If Tsuneno could buy a ticket, she could enter a brighter, noisier and more glamorous world, where she could stay for a few hours, entranced, until the play ended. But then the rest of Edo would be dull by comparison. The samurai Buyō Inshi said that kabuki made women lose touch with reality. 'Indeed a woman who has once seen a play becomes so besotted that she would exchange eating three meals a day for seeing it again,' he wrote. 'When young women go to the theatre, they are completely swept away.'

Luckily, there were ways to participate in the theatre that didn't cost much. Tsuneno could linger in front of the posters at bath-houses and on street corners, examining illustrations of the season's plays and looking for the names of her favourite actors among the cast. And when she heard the playbill pedlars calling in the alleys, she could run out and buy copies. Fresh off the woodblock presses, they would smell of cheap ink – a combination of fer-mented persimmon juice and rapeseed oil soot, the sharp, sour scent of the new season. She could read the playbill over and over again; she could look at the copies her neighbours passed around. If she wanted, she could paste one up on the wall, where it was the last thing she saw every night, and then she could dream of the famous actors in bold print and the up-and-comers whose stage names were rendered in tiny characters.

One of the biggest names, Hanshirō, did not appear on any of the playbills. Iwai Hanshirō V, who had become famous for playing plucky ingenues and then moved on to venomous anti-heroines, had been performing under a new stage name for years. But 'Iwai Hanshirō' had earned its place in theatre vernacular, and it was famous elsewhere in the city, too, where geisha borrowed parts of the name for their own professional monikers. Women wore clogs called Hanshirō sandals, with little notches cut into the bottom, because they resembled the shoes he wore onstage. Even people in Echigo knew the name Hanshirō if they followed the theatre; they might have seen the prints advertising his performances, where he always appeared in full costume, looking glamorous and feminine.

Before she ran away, Tsuneno might have looked at a print of Hanshirō and thought it represented everything she would never have: style, sophistication, Edo. But now it all seemed familiar and almost attainable. Now she could drop the name casually in a letter home – 'Hanshirō', without even a surname, as if he were someone she knew. And in a way, she almost did. As she proudly told her family, she was living at his house.

To be fair, it wasn't his main house and he didn't live there. Wherever Iwai Hanshirō V lived, it was someplace extraordinary. Tsuneno lived in a more modest place, Hanshirō's 'rear residence' in Sumiyoshi-chō. Hanshirō's son had been occupying the property when he died unexpectedly, and now Tsuneno's new master was renting it as a residence for his concubine. Maybe he thought it would impress her, since as a geisha she was an artist herself and she came from Kyoto, a city known for its sophistication. It did impress Tsuneno, but then again, nearly all of it did – the vast sums of money being spent, the hair oil, and especially the food.

Tsuneno thought that everything in Edo was delicious. After a lifetime in the northern countryside, she couldn't help being overwhelmed: restaurants in the city sprouted, like weeds in a rice field. In the third decade of the nineteenth century, the city's ward headmen had counted nearly seven thousand vendors of prepared foods and meals on the main streets alone. They couldn't possibly enumerate all the back-alley dives, wandering pedlars, and temporary stalls, because they were everywhere, jingling bells and singing plaintive melodies, offering steaming dumplings and cool bricks of tofu. Of the shops that the headmen did manage to count, most sold bite-sized sweets and snacks or boiled dishes to go with sake, and over seven hundred sold noodles, either udon or soba. Noodles were a long-standing speciality of Edo, and people argued vigorously about how heavily they should be sauced, how quickly they should be consumed, and even how much they should be chewed. True connoisseurs insisted that they tasted best when purchased from an anonymous 'nighthawk' vendor and slurped on the spot, in some shadowy corner, well after the ordinary stores had closed. Their discussion of sushi wasn't quite as advanced. Nigiri sushi topped with fish was invented only a few decades before Tsuneno arrived in Edo. Still, it was gaining in popularity, especially in the summer, when it was a cheap, accessible snack. Cooked shrimp and tuna cost only a few copper coins each (though egg, a delicacy, was twice as expensive).

The city's formal restaurants were far beyond Tsuneno's means, but some were probably familiar to her new employer. In private rooms and gardens, merchants, shogunal officials and lords' representatives gathered for lavish banquets, consuming course after course set out in colourful arrangements on gleaming trays. People said that chefs at the city's most fashionable establishment, Yaozen, used sweet sake just to wash radishes, and even ordinary meals of potatoes, pickles and tea were prepared according to stringent instructions. Famous chefs were every bit as dramatic and self-regarding as the swordsmen who boasted of mastering the secrets of combat. They wrote bestselling manuals with overstated titles:

Secret Digest of Exceptional Radish Dishes Throughout the Land, One Hundred Tricks with Sweet Potato and *The Digest of Secret Transmissions on Correct Food Preparation and Cutting.*

But even at celebrated restaurants, food was rarely the main attraction. There were usually geisha, who came in to sing, dance and play drinking games; this was probably how Tsuneno's master met his new concubine. Sometimes restaurant parties were the setting for a type of high-concept performance art, where famous artists and kabuki actors engaged in unusual or genre-bending displays. Calligraphers decorated dozens of paper fans, writing as quickly as they could, and actors composed poetry. Noted painters competed in frantic contests, painting with both hands at once or upside down. The elderly artist Hokusai, already very famous for his *Great Wave*, made frequent appearances, though he said he had tired of the spectacle long ago. Like everyone else, he needed the money.

Tsuneno's daily life wasn't glamorous, but it was better than her few weeks of dragging futons and filling water jugs in the bannerman's mansion. She prepared tea in her master's new tearoom, which was something she probably knew at least a little about. Though her family's inventories didn't include any tea utensils, a well-educated young woman was expected to be familiar with the basics. She also ran errands, which anyone could do, and she spent the rest of her time sewing. She even made up a robe for her master in heavy silk crepe, which was tricky. Sewing was the skill she was most proud of, and she was lucky she was good at it. Maidservants who could sew earned a lot more than women who couldn't, sometimes nearly as much as the men who attended samurai.

Tsuneno asked her mother to send a ruler from home, even though it would have been easy to acquire a new one in Edo.

Maybe it was her favourite. Maybe it was just familiar. The rituals of needlework were the same wherever she was: the pop of tiny, pricking stitches; the zip of a sharp knife through silk. Long ago she had practised with her mother and Kiyomi, filling time during the long winters as the snow piled up in the garden. She had been preparing for a different kind of life. She must have thought that, one day, she'd teach her daughter how to sew.

It hadn't worked out that way, but there were still reasons to be grateful. The drums from the theatre district. The vendors who sold vegetables already chopped up, ready to cook. The dolls nodding their little wooden heads. The elegant tearoom and the name on her address. The cold coins in her hand.

And all the unpleasant old men of Echigo, with their loud voices and thinning hair, not one of whom was her husband.

*

All through the winter and into the spring, Tsuneno was confronted with other people's laundry. On sunny days, even in midwinter, the back alleys were festooned with robes, jackets and various kinds of undergarments. The robes hung in long strips, the pieces that had been taken apart and would be reassembled, while the jackets rested on frames with their wide sleeves extended, fluttering slightly in the chilly wind. Until late spring, when the container gardens bloomed, they were the only spots of colour in the dusty alleys. Most of the laundry was cotton in striped and floral patterns, faded and worn at the edges. But there was some silk, too. Standards for clothing were rising, as a book published a decade later pointed out: 'It used to be that it was unusual for anyone in the countryside, apart from samurai, to own a coat made of patterned or striped Kaga silk. But now, even among back-alley craftsmen, there's no one who doesn't have one.' This was an exaggeration. Tsuneno, for one, did not own Kaga silk. But the hanging laundry was still an astonishing display, a series of announcements, each of which advertised the possession of a small luxury that Tsuneno still didn't have: a change of clothes to wear while the other set was being washed and dried.

Meanwhile, portraits of anonymous beautiful women and the advertisements for kabuki performances, all printed up in full colour, gave Tsuneno some idea of what the most fashionable people in the city were wearing. Of course, many of the plays had to do with historical figures, and the costumes of medieval warriors were beside the point. But other plays featured characters based on con-temporary women: geisha and shopkeepers' daughters. Tsuneno could study the shape of a print, the swoop of a collar, the precise creases of a sash or the height of a sandal and intuit what would be popular in a week or a month. Already, some stage portrayals had made fashion history: Ichikawa Danjurō V's turn as a servant girl launched 'Danjurō brown', and Sanogawa Ichimatsu's performance as a doomed young lover started a craze for the black-and-white checkerboard 'Ichimatsu pattern'. Hanshirō V had his own style, too: Hanshirō *kanoko*, a pattern that looked like an interlocking arrangement of hemp leaves. If Tsuneno looked at the prints adver-tising productions in the first month of 1840, she saw the great actor Onoe Eizaburō dressed as a geisha. He appeared huddled under a plaid coverlet in purple, orange and green, wearing a light red under-robe with a splotchy white pattern.

Tsuneno's black clothes had the advantage of not showing dirt, but she was tragically unfashionable. If she had any other robes and coats, she could have exchanged them. Even high-ranking samurai used the city's pawnshops, which offered fairly good prices for beautiful garments. Clothes that were full of holes and nearly unwearable could also find buyers. Ragmen were always walking through the alleys with their filthy, shapeless bundles, and they would take anything. Tsuneno would never want to buy from them, but they weren't selling anyway – they delivered the day's haul to stalls along the Kanda River, where rags were cleaned up and sold again. This was a bargain retail market, convenient for the casual shopper, though probably not adequate for Tsuneno, who was used to beautiful things.

In Tomizawa-chō, just blocks from Doll Street, there was a famous used-clothing market. The district was loosely named after one of the great thieves of the early seventeenth century, Tobizawa Kanzō. Apprehended and threatened with the death penalty, he struck a deal to save his life: the shogun would pardon him on the condition that he would pursue a legitimate occupation – dealing used clothing – and keep an eye on the other thieves who would inevitably be attracted to the business. His namesake market was a place where dealers who had acquired relatively high-quality clothes met brokers who bought and resold them. Some things were destined for Edo's clothing pedlars, counterparts to the ragmen, who walked around with used clothes hanging from poles across their shoulders. Other items were sold to firms based in the northeastern provinces, where peasants were eager to buy Edo castoffs. Some of Tsuneno's neighbours at home might have worn clothes that passed through Tomizawa-chō. Tsuneno had always been much better dressed than they were, but now she couldn't even afford to stay warm. She pleaded with her older brother Kōtoku: 'I don't need any of my good things. But please, please, I'm asking you to send my heavy coat and two old cotton-padded robes to keep out the cold.' She also asked her mother for an apron, as well as a mirror, a hairpin and a comb, so she could fix her hair.

At least Tsuneno's situation was temporary. The very poor suffered from a chronic shortage of clothing, and some families had fewer garments than people. The shogunate even commended virtuous daughters for going without clothes in the dead of winter so that their parents could wear their robes. Meanwhile, manual labourers, most of them men, were accustomed to working nearly naked. They couldn't afford clothes, and they worked at jobs that didn't require them. Dressed only in loincloths, they pulled handcarts, bore palanquins and ran around the city with parcels and messages. Their nudity was a marker of their low status, as obvious as the two swords that samurai wore at their waists. As if to compensate, the labourers adorned their bodies with colourful tattoos that spilled across their backs and down their thighs, cloaking their exposed skin in images of thick robes and armour, glittering fish and dragon scales, and bristling tiger fur. These markings were symbols of defiance, borrowed from the shogunate's practice of tattooing criminals, and also badges of pride for men who had survived the city long enough, and saved coins steadily enough, to visit a tattoo artist week after week for years.

Some people wore robes fashioned out of a few dozen sheets of thick paper, crumpled first to soften them, then treated with persimmon juice as a form of insulation. They smelled strange, but they could be reasonably warm. If they were made from new paper, they could be dyed any color, though they could never be laundered. There were also even cheaper garments made of used paper, which still bore the faint traces of printed characters, illustrations and ink scribbles. When they enjoyed a brief bout of popularity as kabuki costumes, people imitated them by wearing fine silk adorned with random scribbling. It was an upmarket version of street style, desperation dressed up as urban glamour.

*

In Tsuneno's neighbourhood, everyone understood the principles of costume and illusion. Producers, carpenters, doll carvers, hairdressers, painters, writers, set designers – they all made their living sustaining a dazzling artifice. But year by year, it was wearing thin. The displays of spending could still be astonishing. Rumour had it that the costumes for the three leads in the Kawarazaki Theatre's 1839 production of *The Battles of Coxinga* had cost a thousand gold pieces, far more than the annual salary of most bannermen. But there were other plays, many less successful, where actors wore costumes that looked luxurious only from a distance. The stars still wore Chinese silk embroidered with gold thread. But their costumes weren't new; they were older clothes that the theatre companies had pawned in between productions, then redeemed when it was time to put on a new play.

Leading players, including Hanshirō V, were still said to command salaries of over a thousand gold pieces a year, but the theatres were straining to pay them. They were overburdened with debt and exhausted from repeated cycles of rebuilding; with so many evening crowds and lanterns, the theatre district was prone to fire. There already had been times when one or more of the main theatres had gone dark. Though kabuki still had die-hard fans buying playbills and lining up at the narrow 'mouse gates' for admission, the general audience was dwindling. The theatre was expensive, and there were other things to see. The tent shows only cost a few copper coins, and they had exotic birds; porcupines; dead, reeking whales; and towering sculptures made entirely of brooms. Their stars were women wrestlers and snake charmers; mechanical mannequins; fantastically fat people; giants; women with scrotums; and boys covered in scales. There was also a half-barbarian child who could pluck out his own eyeballs and hand them to people. Even the best actor couldn't compete with that.

The big kabuki theatres did try to borrow some of the tent shows' allure. In the first decades of the nineteenth century, their performances featured flashy illusions and grotesque spectacles. By the time Tsuneno lived there, they set plays in the seediest corners of Edo and made lower-class city people their heroes. Samurai who sacrificed everything for their lords still appeared onstage, but they were joined by other types: abandoned children who had never known their parents; roving bandits; and hideous ghosts. Traditionalists despaired. A playwright complained that kabuki had 'hit absolute bottom'.

But the new plays captured something important about life in Edo: they drew attention to the mechanics of deception, which everyone employed, in different ways, to survive. People used their silk jackets and their money, or their paper robes and tattoos, to project an image of invulnerability, but it was never entirely convincing. Maybe, under their clothes, all the people in Edo were like the heroine of the kabuki play *Yotsuya Ghost Story*, an obedient wife who began a descent into disfigurement and madness when her greedy husband tore off her kimono and plucked out her hairpins, intending to exchange them for cash at a pawnshop. Maybe everyone in Edo was maintaining an illusion of sanity with clothes and hairpins. Or maybe they all started out as virtuous people but were transformed into monsters when they learned – over and over again – that they could never hold on to what they thought was theirs.

Early in the New Year, a package finally arrived from Tsuneno's mother: two cotton-padded robes. The Rinsenji temple secretary, Denpachi, made clear that Tsuneno was still officially cut off. These things were just an informal gift because her mother worried that she was cold. This was exactly what Tsuneno needed, and it was followed by an even better package containing unlined robes and accessories. But both parcels were addressed to her old building superintendent, Jinsuke. His wife took everything, and he refused to give Tsuneno even one unlined kimono. She still owed him money, and he probably thought he was entitled to the compensation. To Tsuneno, he was just a detestable person. If her family sent another package his way, she wrote, they should include a threatening letter.

But correspondence wouldn't solve the problem – nothing could.

Everyone in Echigo wanted Tsuneno to give up and go home. When her friend from Ishigami Village, the Rinsenji parishioner Yasugorō, still lived in Edo, before he left for the harvest in the spring, it was all he would talk about. Tsuneno was disappointed, because he was one of her only links to the village and she had hoped that he would carry news of her new life to her mother. 'I wanted to tell him about many things that I couldn't write easily in letters,' Tsuneno wrote, 'but every time I saw him all he would say was 'go home! go home!' So in the end, there was a lot I wanted to tell him that I never got to say, and I thought it was a shame.'

Now that it was summer and the roads were clear, her family agreed that it was time for her to come home. She received a letter from Denpachi, entreating her to return, and reread it several times, in tears. Giyū still wouldn't write, but maybe she hadn't lost her family and her village after all. Nevertheless, she had to disappoint them: she wouldn't leave Edo and return to her suffocating life at Rinsenji. In that regard, nothing had changed. 'I understand that you think I should come home by the 18th or 19th, but I don't agree,' she wrote. 'And no matter how terrified I am of your displeasure, I have no intention of marrying a widower.' She sounded defiant, but she worried about alienating her family. She knew how she sounded, how her disobedience might seem even more shocking when it appeared written out in her familiar hand. 'Just in the time I've been writing this letter, I've taken it up and set it aside ten or fifteen times, and still, in spite of everything, I'm shaking with embarrassment,' she admitted. But she was resolved. 'After all,' she wrote, 'whatever I've written, it all came from my heart, so please read it in that spirit.' She ended the letter with a list of things she still needed: clothing and handkerchiefs, patches of spare cloth and a ruler.

Tsuneno had one robe to cover her, self-assertion to mask her fear and a job to fill her days. It was a costume and a role, enough to get by.

*

As spring turned to summer in Edo's back alleys, 1840 was like any ordinary year. Just after the first carp streamers appeared to celebrate Boys' Day, the rainy season turned the roads to mud. Hundreds of thousands of umbrellas seemed to open all at once. Then, when the clouds parted, a million paper fans replaced the umbrellas.

On the hottest days of summer, everyone who could afford it ate eel. The daytime hours were stretched to their breaking point, and the Hour of the Mouse, which straddled midnight, practically vanished. The theatres showed cheap horror plays, and pedlars who had sold shad sushi started offering live goldfish instead.

The city gossip was full of horrifying stories of adultery and murder, as always, and the notices from the City Magistrates, posted on gates and signboards, said all the usual things. In the spring, they chastised employment agencies for not sufficiently investigating people's backgrounds. A few months later, as the summer began, a proclamation warned people not to set off fireworks in crowded places. In late summer, the magistrates lauded a virtuous hairdresser's son who had devoted himself to caring for his ageing paralysed father. The only remotely exciting proclamation commended a watchman and gate guard for their valour in disarming a disturbed man who had unsheathed a blade and threatened people on the street.

On a festival day in midsummer, crowds gathered near Ryōgoku Bridge. The plaza at the foot of the bridge was packed with noisy vendors and revellers beating drums, and there were so many lanterns that the night was as bright as day. On the river, two companies of men on barges tossed firecrackers in the air, competing to see who could put on the better show. For a moment, each brilliant explosion hung suspended above the pedlars, the drums and all of Edo, before it dissolved into smoke. Then ashes fell like snow all over the glittering river.

Tsuneno thought of Echigo. The snow country seemed closer in the summer, when the roads were clear and letters arrived more quickly, even though many of the seasonal migrants had left the city to attend to the harvest. Tsuneno had decided to stay, and so had a man named Izawa Hirosuke, who came from the village right next to Ishigami. Until she encountered him in Edo, Tsuneno hadn't seen him in twenty-four years. She'd known him when he was a child, when she was the temple daughter and he was the Kamōda Village headman's son. He used to play with her brothers. 'You were like a little brother to him,' she wrote Giyū, 'so of course you know him well.' Now, whenever she saw him, they talked about Echigo. Hirosuke still wrote home frequently, so he could bring her news about the people she knew, a kindness she appreciated all the more because Giyū had refused to write.

She and Hirosuke agreed that they would return to the province when they were old. They both wanted to die at home, surrounded by their fields and mountains, in the company of people they had known all their lives.

Like Tsuneno, Hirosuke had exchanged the security of the countryside for adventure in the city. He worked short-term jobs in service to bannermen, and when he was employed he qualified as a samurai himself. Sometimes, in his own letters and other people's, he was called a masterless samurai, a ronin. This was a technicality: his status was temporary, and his descendants wouldn't inherit it. He was only a man with pretentions to samurai status. Still, when he was employed he wore a warrior's split trousers, adorned with a household crest, and people would defer to the eminence of the family he represented. Sometimes he might even carry weapons. Since Hirosuke could read and write very well and had some of his family's resources behind him, he was a step above the ordinary men who were dispatched to barracks by labour bosses who herded them like cattle and kept a cut of their earnings. It was enough to make a life, for someone determined to stay in the city, and it was almost prestigious enough to be an acceptable option for a headman's son.

Hirosuke told Tsuneno he wanted to marry her. He was at least the ninth man to have this idea – she had three marriages and five rejected suitors behind her, and those were only the men whose names appeared on paper in the family archive. There were probably more. But Hirosuke was only the second to put the question to Tsuneno directly, without going through her parents or her older brother. The first had been Chikan, whom she had tried to refuse, nearly a year ago, when they were on the road. Hirosuke was a different case. He knew her family, and he said that he didn't want to offend them. His was a formal proposal.

There wasn't much time to decide. Hirosuke was impatient. If Tsuneno refused him, he said, he was going to go marry someone else. But Tsuneno's experience had taught her to be wary. She thought they should wait awhile, meet every so often, and get reacquainted. After twenty-four years, there was so much they didn't know. And at present, her situation in Edo was relatively stable: she liked her master, her neighbourhood, and her work. Her fellow maidservants, the women she had come to rely on for advice and borrowed clothes, assessed her situation in pragmatic terms: 'Right now you're poor, but your pay isn't too bad. And if you make your own living instead of deferring to someone else, then it doesn't matter whether you succeed or go broke. You get used to it.' Why would any woman want a husband if she could make it in the city on her own?

But the self-confidence that had propelled Tsuneno all the way to Edo faltered now that she could see her future more clearly. Her finances were precarious, and she was still in debt to the building superintendent, Jinsuke. 'As you already know,' she wrote to Giyū, 'right now, even though I'm managing to make a living, I have to buy every last chopstick and tea bowl for myself. And things are so expensive. I'm struggling, and even if I somehow manage to scrape together four gold pieces, I will have to give them to Jinsuke. It causes me so much heartache and so much worry.' Meanwhile, her misjudgement of Chikan still weighed on her. She asked Denpachi, the temple secretary, to give all her first letters from Edo to her mother for safekeeping. 'Keeping them in your office is just too embarrassing,' she wrote. She wanted to forget what she'd experienced in those weeks with Chikan. She didn't want a record of her humiliation.

Hirosuke could solve Tsuneno's financial problems by settling some of her debts. And it wasn't as if she had a better husband lined up. 'If Hirosuke and I agreed to make a go of it,' she wrote, 'then as long as I wasn't going to end up as some rich man's wife in Edo, it would be much better than staying in this situation of not knowing what to do.' Hirosuke could also put an end to one of her endless arguments with Giyū. Her brother couldn't possibly marry her off again if she already had a husband. She couldn't help making the point again: 'Even if I stayed my whole life at home, I would never have wanted to marry some widower.'

And wasn't there some satisfaction in turning the tables on Giyū? Three times, her family had told her which man they'd chosen and where she was going. They would say the name and tell her something about the family, and she would see her future unfold: temple mistress, peasant, townswoman. Now the choice was hers.

*

This time, there wouldn't be a banquet. There was no one to host and no one to invite. More important, there was no one to pay. No one would order whale meat or set out cups for sake; no one would make lists of servants or itemise a trousseau. There would be no bridal procession full of neighbours and friends and songs, no furniture to carry from one household to another. Just Tsuneno, alone, her quick mind, bad eyes and instinct for survival.

Giyū found out that Tsuneno was married when a neighbour came to Rinsenji bearing the news. The whole family was surprised and delighted, though Tsuneno's mother still hoped she would come home. Giyū, always responsible, felt obligated to warn Hirosuke about the burden he had assumed: 'As you probably know, she's a very selfish person, so please return her to us if things don't go well.' But he was also polite enough to wish the couple luck:

'We sincerely hope that, with the kindness and compassion of your family, you'll have a happy life together. You have given all of us, especially my mother, such peace of mind.'

That peace of mind was sorely needed. It had been an unhappy year. Giyū and Tsuneno's little sister Ino had died, their mother was sick and Sano was having a difficult pregnancy. The secretary, Denpachi, had an eye disease and couldn't read or write easily. Even Giyū hadn't been feeling well, and he was having trouble keeping up his correspondence. He seemed relieved to write to Hirosuke and, by implication, to his sister. He also sent Tsuneno a package: more clothes, bedding and some pieces of silk for sewing. Now she would have everything she needed.

Tsuneno knew that Hirosuke was just an ordinary man, but his willingness to call himself her husband had worked a kind of magic. She had been a source of shame and embarrassment, rejected by her family, undeserving of kindness, incompetent, untrustworthy and alone. For nearly a year, her letters home had been met with grudging help and mild insults. But with one word, 'married', her status changed. She was redeemed.

It might have been easy to resent Hirosuke for the assurance with which he transformed her life. Like Tsuneno, he was restless. He, too, had left Echigo, passed through the mountains and walked the same streets in search of work. But he moved through the city as if he was entitled to be there. And he was never vulnerable in the same way. He would not have invited the unwelcome attention of a man like Chikan, would never have faced the choice of whether to capitulate or be abandoned. And he didn't have to live with the consequences. If he had been cheated, too, if he had his own scars, then at least he didn't have to apologise for them.

On the other hand, Tsuneno had known all her life that men

and women were different. They wouldn't learn the same skills, write the same words, wear the same clothes or meet the same fate. Even rebirth in the Pure Land was harder for women than for men. Some preachers taught that women were condemned to a hell reserved for those who had polluted the earth with the blood of menstruation and childbirth. Many women repented and gave money, hoping for deliverance. Tsuneno never thought that she would grow up to be a priest like her father. She never expected to write Chinese poetry like her brother, represent the temple at village meetings, compose formal petitions to the shogun's men or calculate the payment of taxes. It would have been as ridiculous as shaving her head.

The first line of *The Greater Learning for Women* said: 'To be a woman is to grow up and leave for another household.' Tsuneno had encountered the idea as a child, either in that book or in another text for girls. They all said more or less the same thing. And for Tsuneno, who had left for Ōishida when she was only twelve, it was true. But over time, every woman learned that there was much more involved. Being a woman entailed shame and self-doubt and, above all, constraint. The trick was to learn to occupy the space one was allowed, just as women in other, faraway places taught themselves to walk on broken feet and breathe into biting stays and even, sometimes, to see the strictures as an advantage. After all, women who carried heavy loads couldn't wear corsets or bind their feet. Very poor women couldn't afford propriety, and uneducated women couldn't write letters of apology.

Tsuneno's brush traced the graceful shapes of the Japanese alphabet. She used soft, feminine language. She was angry about so many things, but she aimed her rage at people, not at abstract ideas. She was furious with her superintendent, Jinsuke, not the concept of paying rent. She resented her brother, not the institution of the patriarchal household. How could she be angry that she was a woman? She didn't know how to be anything else.

*

Backstage at the Kawarazaki Theatre, the actor Iwai Hanshirō V opened his chest of stage makeup – thick rouge made from crushed safflowers, white face powder, black ink to line his famous wide eyes, and brushes and sponges and blotting cloths in a variety of sizes. In the eleventh month of 1840, he was playing dual roles, both of them women: a streetwalker and a crone. At age sixty-five, it had been five decades since he'd first appeared onstage. He'd played princesses and arsonists, goddesses and geisha. The play he was opening in the eleventh month of 1840 was a premiere, so his characters were new. But the act of transformation was always the same.

He shaved his beard clean and blotted on cleanser. He mixed oil into his face powder to make a thick paint, then took up his largest flat brush, sweeping broad white strokes across his neck and shoulders, over his forehead and his closed eyes, down his nose and over the pink of his lips. Then stripes of the palest pink down the centre of his eyelids and across his cheeks – barely perceptible – finished with another layer of white. He dabbed vermillion on the corners of his eyes and traced his lash line in deep black; he painted vivid red lips inside the chalk white of his own. He would draw the lines a little wider for a townsman's daughter, smaller and poutier for a geisha, longer and thinner for a crone. When he played a married woman, he would paint each tooth with a black paste, just like Tsuneno.

He placed a wig on his head. He knew how to wear a woman's wardrobe, how to take small steps and pitch his voice higher, how to laugh, how to gesture, how to carry his head. But even for him, being a woman wasn't as simple as inhabiting a role and reciting one's lines, pretending until the costume and makeup came off. It was his identity, his public face. No one wanted to see prints of him as an old man in an ordinary cotton robe, the way he looked when he was at home, writing poetry. Sometimes they wanted Gonpachi the samurai, young and fierce. But more often, they wanted the beautiful woman in plum-coloured robes, with her crimson lips and masses of thick dark hair. Even in his memorial portrait, Hanshirō V would appear as a young woman.

Most people who survived in Edo had to be practised at transformation. Some, like Hanshirō, managed a public face and a private one. Others switched jobs and neighbourhoods: servants found new masters; tenants moved on. Men who sold shad roe in the spring hawked potatoes in the winter. Tenement girls practised the shamisen until they could reinvent themselves as geisha. Merchants who had failed at business rented wicker baskets and went out to pick up rubbish. Pedlars put down their poles and started shelling clams and oysters; young wives, suddenly widowed, took in piecework. And everyone changed their names. Hanshirō became Tojaku; Hanzaemon became Yakara. Kinshirō became Kagemoto; Gisuke became Gi'en.

Dressed in clothes from home, Tsuneno still looked like the person she had always been: a respectable woman from a prosperous provincial family. Giyū had finally sent her things: silk underrobes, then the cord to tie them, the padded cotton for late autumn and the obi. Every day she looked in her mirror – at last, the mirror! – and blackened her teeth, as she had since she had first married. She had been doing it so long that they were stained grey, even when they weren't painted. Her face was familiar, just older: Tsuneno, Emon's daughter and Giyū's sister, looked back at her. But in Edo, married once again, she had the chance to be someone new.

There would always be people in the city who knew Tsuneno's family and her story, but most people she met encountered an ordinary person, a married woman in her late thirties. They didn't know how she'd been cheated and betrayed, how she'd shamed her brothers. They didn't know how often, and how profoundly, she'd failed.

She discarded the name her parents had given her and started to sign her letters 'Kin'. It was short and simple, and it sounded like 'gold', which was auspicious. Giyū acknowledged the change. When he wrote to the newlyweds, he asked Hirosuke to send his regards to 'Okin', using the polite form of the new name. In his own records, Giyū would always call his sister Tsuneno, the name he was used to. But outwardly, he was willing to pretend that she had become someone new.

'Okin' sounded respectable. It was possible, wasn't it, that the dramatic part of Tsuneno's life had ended with the change of her name? Okin could live quietly in Edo for the rest of her life, and no one would need to know how she'd failed at marriage and run away. No one would know about the weeks with Chikan, or the nights shivering in the tenement, or the months she had gone without a change of clothes. Okin could be anyone. She could be a person who never made anyone worry, never argued with her brothers and never caused a problem again.

Chapter Seven

TROUBLES AT HOME

The trouble in the realm might have started in Osaka, during the desperate summer of 1837, at the height of the Tenpō famine. Osaka was the second-largest city in Japan, home to nearly four hundred thousand, dominated by noisy, boisterous merchants who were said to eat better than anyone else on the archipelago. Along with Edo and Kyoto, Osaka was the shogun's territory, as opposed to one of the domain lords' cities. The shogun had claimed it for its strategic importance. Among Japan's three great metropolises, Edo was the shogun's seat and Kyoto was the emperor's, but Osaka was the economic powerhouse that sustained them both.

The region surrounding Osaka had not suffered nearly as much as the northeast in the Tenpō famine, but rice prices were still extremely high, and the situation was exacerbated by the shogunate's policy of diverting grain to Edo to forestall riots in the capital. As a result, Osaka's poor were unable to afford basic provisions. A former shogunal official and Confucian scholar named Ōshio Heihachirō was appalled by the waste of life. Why should the poor starve while rich merchants hoarded rice and cash? Why should righteous men defer to arrogant bureaucrats who accepted bribes and spent their days and nights in dissipation? In truth, most of the shogun's men were little better than robbers, common criminals who would steal food from children in the streets. In the summer of 1837, Ōshio raised banners – 'Save the People' – and assembled an army of three hundred men. Together, they tried to wrest control of the city from the shogunate, convinced that they were delivering the judgement of heaven. But their rebellion lasted only twelve hours before it was put down, viciously, by the shogun's forces. Thousands of buildings, a whole swathe of the city, burned.

Ōshio escaped and survived briefly in hiding, but when his refuge was surrounded he lit the building on fire and perished in the flames. His co-conspirators, apprehended alive, were subjected to torture and eventually executed. Those who had died during interrogation had their bodies pickled in salt so that they could be crucified along with the others. Yet the sight of those charred, mangled and silenced bodies wasn't reassuring to the officials in power. If one of the shogun's own men could launch a rebellion in one of the realm's three greatest cities, then who knew what other kinds of violent dissent might be taking shape in other places, among men who weren't pledged to the Tokugawa house? What did that portend for the Great Peace, the shogunate's most important achievement? All over Japan, even in small, faraway villages like Ishigami, people heard and discussed news of the uprising, and they asked themselves the same questions.

In Edo, news of the rebellion in Osaka fuelled anxiety about potential unrest in the shogun's capital. The Edo City Magistrates had worked with wealthy commoner wholesalers and ward headmen to keep the city provisioned during the famine, and thanks to their efforts, the capital had narrowly avoided riots. But the economy was still fragile, and Edo's poor were still numerous, hungry and difficult to count. If they revolted, as they had in the wake of the Tenmei famine in the 1780s, they might bring down the shogunate, especially if they had the support of disgruntled samurai like Ōshio. It didn't help that ominous notices began to appear scattered in the street and pasted on walls, warning that Ōshio sympathisers in Edo were awaiting the signal to start an uprising. The City Magistrates took the unprecedented step of posting a notice condemning Ōshio at the foot of Nihonbashi Bridge. It was the first time anyone could remember that an Osaka crime had been officially acknowledged in Edo, three hundred miles away.

Later, some would argue that Ōshio's rebellion was a turning point, that the social unrest caused by the Tenpō famine was a spark that caught, burned slowly, and eventually raged into a political conflagration that consumed Japan. But others would contend that the real crisis began later, in 1839, in the city of Canton, a noisy, crowded place nearly two thousand miles away from Edo. British, French and American factories flew their flags there, Indian businessmen came to trade, and the local vernacular was a lively combination of Portuguese, Hindi, English and Cantonese. Canton was the mercantile centre of East Asia, patronised by the empires and corporations that were competing for influence in a rapidly changing economic and political order. But not one of the shogun's subjects had ever been there. They were forbidden to travel beyond the Ryūkyū Islands in the East China Sea.

It would have been surprising if Tsuneno had ever heard of Canton, though she, like most Japanese, had some vague idea about China, the source of ancient wisdom and the home of story-book heroes. While intellectuals, and especially shogunal officials posted in Nagasaki, devoured Chinese treatises, ordinary people didn't pay attention to contemporary political developments in the country across the ocean. It was enough for most to dabble in Chinese poetry or to buy silk and porcelain at special stores for 'Chinese goods', which may or may not have been Chinese. In the spring of 1839, when a Chinese official named Lin Zexu confiscated an astonishing twenty thousand chests of opium from British traders in Canton, no one in Japan heard the news for nearly a year. Tsuneno, if she ever knew, would not have cared. She would have believed, wrongly, that a conflict over opium in a faraway land had nothing to do with her.

Twenty thousand chests of opium worked out to a thousand tons and a value of $10 million. Lin had confiscated the drug because importing it was illegal and he had received an imperial commission to destroy the opium trade in Canton. More important, he had seen how opium addiction had ravaged the Chinese population and, as an official, he felt morally obligated to protect the emperor's subjects from depraved, greedy foreigners. Making a show of his determination, and his virtue, he enlisted sixty officials and five hundred labourers to break up the sticky black balls of opium, dissolve them with salt and flush them into a creek. When he had finished, he offered a prayer to the god of the sea in apology for polluting the waters.

The British merchants knew that they had been dealing in contraband, in contravention of the emperor's law, but they were also enraged that a Chinese official had washed away $10 million of their property without offering compensation. They called on the British government to avenge their losses and protect the state's interest in the opium trade. The Crown would not reimburse them for their lost cargo, but after some debate in Parliament the British dispatched a fleet of four steamships and sixteen men-of-war. They arrived in Canton in the summer of 1840, that dreamy, quiet season when Tsuneno married Hirosuke in Edo, and unleashed a military force that could be felt all the way across the ocean.

China's Qing Dynasty was completely outmatched. Its weapons had rusted; some of the guns were over two centuries old. Commanders had to lock their own men inside the forts to prevent them from fleeing. Meanwhile, the British boasted the first oceangoing iron steamship to appear in East Asia and the most powerful navy in the world. As the Chinese losses mounted, in battle after bloody battle, educated men in Japan began to take notice. With a growing sense of horror, they realised if the mighty Qing empire could be defeated, Japan had no hope of prevailing over Western gunboats if and when they arrived in Edo's harbour.

Eventually, Japanese leaders' awareness of the danger posed by both 'trouble at home' and 'threats from abroad' would come to be shared by educated peasants and even common people living in city tenements. Their foreboding would have consequences for everyone in Japan, from the shogun in his castle to the peasants in Echigo rice fields. But first, it would consume Edo.

*

In the late winter of 1840, Tokugawa Ienari, the querulous retired shogun, lay dying in Edo Castle. After reigning for fifty years and fathering dozens of children, he was still the most powerful man in the realm. His forty-seven-year-old son, Tokugawa Ieyoshi, had already succeeded him as shogun, but he was not the forceful presence his father was. For months, Ienari's samurai attendants kept his condition a secret, fearing the power vacuum that would result if it were widely understood. When he finally died on the seventh day of the first month of 1841, his attendants continued to go about their business as if he were still alive.

When the news was finally announced, it was a shock. Iseki Takako, a bannerman's wife, wrote: 'There are ordinary people who can live to be one hundred, but since he was the shogun and had everything arranged according to his wishes, you would think he would have had more time than seventy years. As shogun, he was the most influential person in the realm – he took charge of politics and so much else. The people were in awe of his vigour. But life spans are mysterious.' During the ensuing period of mourning, the men in Iseki's household were not allowed to shave their beards or the crowns of their heads for fifty days. After only three weeks, they looked like completely different people. That was the work of death: making strangers out of family.

The following summer, Tsuneno's mother died at Rinsenji. She, too, had been ill for months, and the family had not known whether she would make it through the winter. Giyū had written to Edo with updates, describing how their mother's condition had worsened since their youngest sister Ino's death. She suffered from high fevers, heart palpitations and difficulty breathing. Their brothers had gathered at the temple, taking turns watching over her during the night. Sometimes she seemed to be better, and then she would decline again. From her sickbed, she dictated a short message to Hirosuke: 'About my daughter Okin: Her essential nature isn't what one would hope, and it pains me. I'm sorry. Still, I'm so relieved that you've married her. Please, please continue to care for her in the future.'

When Tsuneno received the news that her mother had died, it wasn't a surprise. Two hundred miles from home, she and Hirosuke gathered condolences from Rinsenji parishioners. They offered incense in her memory. Tsuneno, writing home, mentioned the loss only briefly: 'It truly pains me that I was away in service when Mother passed away.' What else could she say? Her mother had sent her away three times, the first when she was only twelve, in order to make a life for her, to try to settle her in a familiar situation. But when Tsuneno left on her own terms, her mother had been distraught. Tsuneno sent her sweet, reassuring letters, with none of the fury and anguish she showed her brothers. 'I'm fine with spending money and food,' she wrote, 'and the only problem I have is clothes.' 'I'm persevering here in Edo, please don't worry about me.' 'The senior servants here are so very kind – would you please send me some of your miso-pickled radishes as a thank-you gift?' Maybe she couldn't bear to endure her mother's judgement, or maybe she was reluctant to cause more pain. She knew that as long as her mother lived, there was a person at home who would always write, who would always worry.

When Tsuneno's mother died, there were no public rituals of mourning in Edo. The temple bells didn't fall silent. The theatres didn't close. No festivals were cancelled. Samurai didn't grow beards. There were only the usual Buddhist ritual observances, the cycles of incense and offerings, the prayers at forty-nine days after the death. For as long as Tsuneno could remember, her mother had done all these things for other people. As she was a temple wife, it had been her vocation. Now, as the rest of the city moved on from mourning the retired shogun, it fell to Tsuneno to remember, to light incense and to pray.

*

The new proclamations started to appear in the summer of 1841. Sometimes they were posted on the walls by the ward gates, where the old men who staffed the guard posts sold straw sandals and goldfish. There were always notices there, stern commands from the City Magistrates aimed at instilling discipline among the people. Typically, they would take up some small, symbolic issue – the consumption of expensive, out-of-season vegetables, for example – and inveigh against it. But now the proclamations came more frequently, and their tone was unusually strident. Commoners should not wear silk crepe, even in the linings of their robes or the cuffs of their sleeves. Velvet was forbidden, and so were gold, silver and tortoiseshell hair ornaments. The lanterns for the Sannō Festival were too bright and showy. They should be smaller and dimmer. The bamboo grass and paper ornaments that townspeople hung for the Star Festival were too long. Only short ones would be allowed. People shouldn't give one another gifts for the Kanda Festival – not even pickles – because it was a useless extravagance.

These threatening notices were the opening salvo in a prolonged campaign of administrative restructuring known as the Tenpō Reforms. The campaign's architect was not the shogun himself, but his adviser, the chief councillor Mizuno Tadakuni. Mizuno believed that the shogunate needed a strong hand and a new set of policies to face the twin threats of domestic unrest and foreign aggression. Ienari hadn't been amenable to change, but Mizuno sensed an opening after the retired shogun's death, and he took advantage of the ensuing confusion to purge the former shogun's close associates, including his powerful ladies-in-waiting. He then convinced the current shogun, Ieyoshi, to announce the beginning of a reform era. This was a nod to tradition: earlier shoguns had used the same rhetoric of 'reform' when they wanted to bolster their finances and shore up their authority with regard to the domain lords.

To Mizuno, as to previous shogunal administrators, 'reform' was not only an administrative imperative. It was also a moral agenda, an insistence that the people of Japan should return to an idealised past in which commoners respected their rulers and manifested their submission through frugality and diligence. So

Mizuno – a zealous advocate for the shogun's interests – positioned himself as a moral arbiter. He hectored his subordinates in the City Magistrates' offices, demanding that they issue more and harsher notices.

The irony was that Mizuno's personal behaviour was notorious. He drank like a whale and ate like a wild dog. He collected gold and silver offerings as if he were a miraculous image of the Buddha, though his conduct wasn't remotely Buddha-like. He never helped a man who couldn't pay, and he never went out for the night without waking up in a brothel. No one had a single good thing to say about him. People in Edo joked that even his hair was terrible. They perceived that Mizuno's real, unstated goal was to consolidate power in his own grasping hands.

At first, Mizuno's pretention to civic virtue seemed to be a passing phase. After all, the city's people had seen this type of zealotry before. Fifty years earlier, in response to the Tenmei famine and the ensuing riots, the shogunate had launched a similar reform effort. The structural changes to city administration survived, but the moral reform ordinances had faded into irrelevance after only a few years. There was no reason to think that this time would be any different.

Edoites also had reason to believe that an ambitious shogunal official who seized too much power was headed for a fall. As it happened, Tsuneno's family had a tenuous personal connection to the history of doomed shogunal reformers. Tsuneno's youngest brother, Gisen, had moved to Edo to work at the venerable True Pure Land temple Tokuhonji, which was famous as the final resting place of the assassin Sano Masakoto. In the late eighteenth century, Sano had killed the son of a despised senior councillor named Tanuma Okitsugu. Like the Tenpō-era reformer Mizuno, Tanuma was loathed for his corruption and his arrogance. Commoners rejoiced when he fell from power soon after the murder of his son. The assassin Sano was forced to commit ritual suicide as punishment for his crime, but the people of Edo hailed him as a hero. They called him the Great Rectifying Spirit and placed flowers on his grave. In 1841, that grave must have seemed like a portent of Mizuno Tadakuni's downfall, though Gisen never mentioned it in his letters.

For the most part, Gisen tried to keep his distance from politics, and anything else that could be considered controversial. He wasn't close to his sister Tsuneno, whom he hadn't known well when he was growing up. He was the youngest of the Rinsenji brothers, and she left for her first marriage when he was still a small child. Years later, Tsuneno and Gisen overlapped at Rinsenji when they both divorced and returned home during the worst year of the Tenpō famine. But while Tsuneno divorced again and then languished, tormented by her failure, Gisen reinvented himself as a diligent and responsible type and went to Edo with his family's blessing.

Although Gisen was never a rebel, he shared a little of his personality with his hot-tempered sister. Unlike their older brother Giyū, who was vulnerable, self-doubting and restrained, Gisen and Tsuneno were both assertive. Perhaps it was because they were younger siblings: neither one had ever been in charge, so neither was ever required to be diplomatic. Gisen wrote beautiful letters with a sophisticated vocabulary, but if he thought someone was stupid, he wrote the word 'idiot' plainly and without apology.

Gisen saw himself as Tsuneno's surrogate guardian in Edo. It was part of the privilege and responsibility of being a man: unlike his sister, he was able to represent Rinsenji in matters of village governance and the dispersal of property. In fact, years earlier he had been sent to negotiate with Tsuneno's former husband in the wake of her second divorce. In Edo, he checked in on his sister – often bringing some kind of small gift, like ginger – and relayed information back to Giyū. At first, he was pleased to report that Tsuneno had weathered the initial months of her fourth marriage without any trouble. 'I know Hirosuke's family in the village is concerned about him,' he wrote, 'but he is making the rounds working for various people, so you don't need to worry very much. Our sister is happy and looks well.'

But in late summer, a secret report to the City Magistrates warned that an economic catastrophe was looming. The large clothing stores complained that business had fallen off: no one was buying. Carpenters grumbled that construction had come to a halt as people reconsidered their plans. Craftsmen had little work, and the entertainment districts were too quiet. The reform proclamations had turned out to be unusually harsh, suppressing consumption to such a degree that even the poorest people were worried about what might happen next.

Still, Mizuno Tadakuni forged ahead. In the autumn, the City Magistrates organised commoner headmen into groups of 'reform captains' and asked them to propose additional policies to control social disorder. Naturally, they complied.

All kinds of people are walking around with their heads and faces covered, they complained. *These strange people should be stopped, their head coverings ripped off, and their names written down. They should be detained at the guard posts if they are at all suspicious.*

Women have become accustomed to wearing men's short jackets. Some are poor women and have nothing else to wear, so they borrow their husbands' jackets to stay warm. That is acceptable. But other women wear luxurious versions of men's jackets in a misguided attempt to be fashionable. A new proclamation should be issued banning these jackets.

Women who call themselves 'singing teachers', many of whom are actually no better than illegal prostitutes, make a good living teaching music to ordinary girls. Edo parents should be ashamed of themselves for allowing their daughters to mix with such people. The girls should be embarrassed, too. The lessons should be ended immediately, and both the teachers and students should be reported to the guardhouses if they persist.

Ordinary people smoke tobacco in silver and gold pipes. This is ridiculously luxurious and should be stopped.

Maps and guidebooks have been printing the names of trifling people like sumo wrestlers, prostitutes and kabuki actors. This should be forbidden.

The list went on from there.

*

In the ninth month, the Kanda Festival went on as usual, but all the commoner women wore plain sandals and dull hairpins. Iseki Takako, the bannerman's wife, complained that the young men from samurai households wore drab coats and she missed seeing their handsome figures decked out for the occasion. It seemed to her that everything charming had been banned.

Then, only weeks later, the theatre district burned. The fire started in the Nakamura Theatre and spread to the Kawarazaki Theatre on the next block. The neighbourhood caught fire every so often – it was difficult to avoid, with all the lanterns and people packed into the wooden buildings – so at first it seemed that this particular fire wasn't a catastrophe. It merited only a brief mention by the city's most prominent diarist, who noted that the theatres would move to Asakusa, where they always set up temporarily after fires. But Mizuno Tadakuni saw the conflagration as an opportunity.

Mizuno detested the theatres and resented their place in the city. His reasoning was the argument of a samurai concerned about hereditary privilege and propriety. Famous actors were technically people of debased status, below even commoners, yet they received salaries that most bannermen would envy. They inspired the people of Edo to imitate their ridiculously expensive fashions. The women's short jackets that the headmen had complained about were actually the actors' fault. When kabuki performers picked up vulgar street style, even samurai women copied them. And the whole neighbourhood, which so charmed Tsuneno and other city women, was a nightmare of public disorder. The problem wasn't only the fires. It was the petty moneylenders hanging around on the street, who charged exorbitant interest and sent thugs to threaten people who couldn't pay. It was the teahouses where men could buy sex with pretty young 'actors'. It was the entire noisy, raucous, debauched atmosphere of the place.

Mizuno considered shutting down the theatres entirely, but in the end he was persuaded to move them to the periphery of the city. The City Magistrate delivered his verdict, and one by one, the puppet and kabuki theatres were relocated. Tsuneno's old neighbourhood was gutted. The teahouses moved, following the theatres. The doll vendors remained, but with the puppet theatres gone, they seemed incongruous. The drums were silenced. The crowds dispersed.

*

Meanwhile, more notices appeared. Dolls over nine inches tall were prohibited. Children did not need to play with such elaborate toys; they would only become accustomed to inappropriate luxuries. Women were not allowed to wear fine embroidery. Fireworks were forbidden. Expensive potted plants should not be sold. Men should not use umbrellas in the rain. The price of tofu was too high; either that, or the pieces were too small. Tofu should cost eight coppers per piece, and each block should be cut according to uniform specifications. Neighbourhood guardhouses should clarify their policies about lending out items such as sandals and lanterns and post clear lists of rules on the walls.

Women's hairdressers were forbidden to ply their trade. Even day-labouring women and maidservants had been paying to have their hair arranged, which was a 'disgraceful waste of money'. They would have to make do with messy topknots that they put up themselves. Women who did not comply, who were caught with fashionably oiled and styled hair, were arrested on the street.

Meanwhile, men gathered in the back rooms of the city's stores, in the opulent teahouses near the shogun's granary, by the wharves near Nihonbashi Bridge, and among the persimmons and grapes of Kanda Market. Their conversations were tense. Everyone who operated a business was worried. The city economy was struggling, and Mizuno's attempts to bring down prices had not succeeded as quickly as he'd hoped. There were rumours of a radical shift in policy.

The decree arrived in late autumn. The shogunate abolished the wholesaler associations, the powerful groups of shareholders in various trades that had structured the city's economy for generations. Mizuno had blamed their stranglehold on supply chains for high prices. The households belonging to the associations had been the highest-status, most prosperous merchants in Edo; the offices where they conducted their business had been marked on city maps. But with the change in policy, reform captains were dispatched to the offices with orders to confiscate and destroy the association membership registries. Even the word 'wholesaler' was forbidden, stricken from the official vocabulary and banned from display. For over a century, the greatest stores in Edo had displayed banners that announced their status in the associations. Now all the signs had to come down.

A few weeks later, dozens of female musicians who performed popular ballads were swept up in raids. In the early spring of 1842, they were found guilty of corrupting public morals and placed in manacles. Their instruments were hacked to pieces and set on fire in the magistrates' offices.

*

Tsuneno and Hirosuke heard the rumours of the relocation of the theatre district and saw the 'wholesaler' banners lowered. At first, they weathered the turmoil fairly well, but as the economy slipped further, Hirosuke began to have trouble finding consistent work, and he and Tsuneno soon ran out of money. Gisen was appalled to find his sister and her husband living in poverty, but he couldn't convince Tsuneno to leave. 'If there is some sudden crisis,' he wrote to Giyū, sounding weary, 'I'll let you know.'

Tsuneno went into service in yet another samurai's household, this time in the neighbourhood of Asakusa. She had some candles, charcoal and a lantern provided by her employer, and presumably she received the typical salary of a few gold coins. But now she had Hirosuke to support, too. She started pawning her personal effects to raise money. She even pawned a small bag with a letter still in it; she'd missed the express service deadline and had been carrying the letter around, meaning to send it, when she realised her mistake and couldn't retrieve it.

In the next letter, which did make it home, she related stories of her fellow migrants. A man named Iisuke, from a village near home, was working as a clerk. He had not been able to find a place to stay, so he was moving around the city imposing on his friends. A seventy-year-old woman had come to the city to marry and later found herself completely destitute. She had been working for a year and was practically naked; it was pitiful to see. A very fat woman named Hatsu, the mother of one of Tsuneno's acquaintances, had been coming to her house, eating their food and demanding pocket money. 'She doesn't even apologise for the trouble,' Tsuneno wrote. Meanwhile, Tsuneno knew people who were seventy gold pieces in debt. She could barely believe it. 'As for me,' she wrote, 'I've only borrowed one gold piece and two coins from the pawnshop, and look how much I've suffered for it!'

The desperation Tsuneno witnessed stood out in contrast to the wealth she saw all around her, on a scale that had been unimaginable in Echigo. 'People in the countryside have no idea what Edo is like, what the mansions are like,' she wrote. Yet even the poor were required to keep up appearances. As always, Tsuneno regarded her own lack of suitable attire as a social liability. 'I have four fellow servants,' she wrote, 'and they never talk to me except to tell me that I'm doing something wrong. They all compete with one another, and they're stubborn. Right now I have all my clothes in pawn and I'm struggling, but I think if I just manage to persevere for a little longer, it will probably get better.' And in case her brothers wouldn't understand, she added: 'It's not at all like the countryside; you can't just walk around looking terrible.'

One of the cruel ironies of the reforms, which had ostensibly meant to restrict conspicuous consumption, was that they made it impossible for struggling people to maintain a veneer of respectability. Even pawning clothes, the usual strategy of last resort when Tsuneno needed cash, wasn't working as well as it had a few years earlier. Informants to the City Magistrates' offices noted that the pawnshops were overstocked and used-clothing stores were being driven out of business: no one could get a good price for clothes, in part because no one knew what kind of clothing would be acceptable. Women had stopped wearing even cheap hair ornaments because they were afraid to stand out. Those who had more money than Tsuneno were confused; those who had less were barely dressed at all.

Meanwhile, Tsuneno had other problems. 'Hirosuke has an incredibly bad temper,' she wrote, 'and since last year he's been angry all the time. All he does is fight with me, and when he gets really angry he curses all my ancestors and tells me to go home to my family.' She hadn't expected her marriage to turn out to be so difficult. 'I know I came into this situation completely unprepared, but his relatives were all respectable, and there was absolutely no reason to believe that he'd end up in this state. Also, it wasn't as if I gave no thought to our future, but I married him out of affection, and I thought that even if we got into trouble, we'd suffer together. And then, at the end of it, when we were old, we'd go home to die.'

That vision of the future seemed like it would never come to pass, so Tsuneno had started thinking about what to do next. She had even suggested the possibility of divorce – her fourth – but Hirosuke wouldn't hear of it. 'I've told him many times that I want to split up,' she wrote, 'but of course if it comes from me it doesn't mean anything.' Technically, a divorce had to be initiated by the husband, who wrote out a divorce notice; otherwise it wouldn't have any legal force. Tsuneno asked Giyū and her other older brothers if they could intervene with Hirosuke or his family to end the marriage, but she didn't necessarily want to leave Edo. She thought she might visit home in the spring, she wrote, but she still seemed to have hope. She just had to persevere a little longer.

*

In the summer of 1842, Qing China finally capitulated to the mighty British navy. Under the terms of the Treaty of Nanjing, the Chinese agreed to pay an indemnity of $21 million, to cede the island of Hong Kong, and, most devastating, to open Chinese ports to British trade. Tariffs were fixed so that the Chinese could not change them in order to protect domestic industries, and British citizens who committed crimes on Chinese soil were granted the right to be judged by their own countrymen rather than submitting to the law of the land.

In Japan, shogunal officials and defence-minded samurai agreed that this was a grave defeat for China and, possibly, eventually, for their own country. Some hawkish intellectuals believed that the people should be informed of the problem and its urgency, including the possibility that Britain might turn its attention – and its ships – towards Japan. The shogunate demurred, preferring its ordinary policy of secrecy. But rumours flew, even among common people in Edo.

The chief councillor Mizuno made plans to strengthen Japan's defences. Shogunal troops drilled in the countryside near Edo, where they wore Western-style uniforms and took commands in Dutch. The order to fire on foreign ships was rescinded and replaced with a directive to supply them with water and firewood and send them on their way. This change in policy was not because the shogunate had determined to welcome foreigners; rather, it had become clear that provoking a vastly superior navy was a terrible, possibly suicidal, strategy.

Meanwhile, in Edo, the kabuki actor Ichikawa Ebizō V, who had often played male roles opposite Iwai Hanshirō V, was dragged out of the one major theatre that had not yet been relocated from the old district. He was placed in manacles and hauled into the City Magistrate's office to answer for his crimes. The main problem was his house, a splendid villa in Fukagawa, where his garden was strewn with great stone lanterns, the coffered ceilings gleamed with gold paint, and the elaborately carved and inlaid furniture supported a collection of exquisite dolls. For months, the magistrate had been biding his time, collecting information. He had even managed to procure and copy Ebizō's grandfather's written guidance for his descendants, which urged humility and frugality. He confronted the terrified actor: 'Not only do you subvert the law of the shogun; you disobey your own grandfather!'

In the end, the magistrate expelled Ebizō from the city. His magnificent house was razed, its treasures confiscated and collections scattered. His powerful voice would no longer echo through Edo's theatres. Ebizō would return, years later, but his heroes – those brave, beautiful young men – would never be portrayed in exactly the same style again.

*

The New Year of 1843 came and went. Edo's streets were empty and clean as always, but the decorations were less lavish. Sake was so expensive that even wealthy samurai's wives were complaining. In the spring, four commoner women in their twenties were arrested while they were out viewing the cherry blossoms. None was wearing any of the prohibited fabrics – velvet, brocade or silk – but their attire was deemed 'too showy' for the reform era. The story circulated, and people lamented the injustice: 'A heavy punishment for trifling people. All cotton – down to their linings – and not a hint of silk.'

In the third month of 1843, the shogunate delivered a more direct blow to the city's poor in the form of yet another new proclamation: 'Recently, more and more people from the countryside have come into Edo, and, since they have acclimated to the customs of the city, have no desire to return home. This is extremely troubling. We will be conducting an entirely new census, and all these people will be sent back to their villages.' The rest of the text hedged a bit, offering the possibility of leniency to those who had stores, wives and families. But the ending statement was clear: 'People who have come in recent years, who have no wives and children, who rent backroom tenements and engage in short-term labour, should be sent back to their villages immediately.'

Tsuneno had reason to worry. She and Hirosuke were married, but they had no children; they were recent arrivals; and they were not engaged in any kind of productive endeavour. Meanwhile, Hirosuke couldn't find enough work to keep up the pretence of being a low-ranking samurai. He and Tsuneno drifted across the city until they finally crashed in Shinjuku, a wilderness of inns, restaurants and brothels on Edo's western border.

Shinjuku was a way station for travellers and a gathering place for hardened, ruthless men. They were gangsters and bouncers, and worse. The neighbourhood also offered the services of 150 legal prostitutes and several times as many who were not legally recognised. They met clients in teahouses, walked out in the streets and waited behind lattice windows. Some were from Echigo, so they were almost familiar, even if they were much younger than Tsuneno and from poorer families. The geisha, both men and women, cut more intimidating and more fashionable figures, but in 1843 they were more subdued than usual. No one could forget that the entire station had been closed down during the shogun's first reform era in the early eighteenth century; the inns, brothels and restaurants had been abandoned for over five decades. Although the neighbourhood was still relatively unscathed two years into Mizuno's tenure, its luck would surely run out.

Tsuneno and Hirosuke, out of luck themselves, took refuge with Hirosuke's younger brother, Hanzaemon. He was a shady character who did odd jobs when he could talk his way into them, and he changed his name so many times that he was difficult to keep track of. Maybe that was the point. To the extent that Hanzaemon had a legitimate occupation, he was running a restaurant, the kind of generic 'food place' where a workingman could drop in for dinner on his way to a cheap brothel. At least it gave Tsuneno something to do. She had no particular experience cooking, apart from what she had learned as a daughter and then a young bride in the countryside, but her experience in service had taught her how to be polite, take orders and clear away trays.

It wasn't a successful business. Restaurants' numbers had declined during the famine, and they struggled even more in the midst of the Tenpō Reforms. Unsurprisingly, to nearly everyone except Mizuno Tadakuni, moving the theatres to Edo's outskirts, sending working people home, and forcibly lowering prices had done nothing to encourage prosperity. It might not have been Hanzaemon's fault that his restaurant was failing and it might not have been Hirosuke's fault that he and Tsuneno fought endlessly, but it was unendurable.

*

In the summer of 1843, as Tsuneno and Hirosuke struggled in Shinjuku, the shogun issued a series of notices addressed to the households of domain lords and bannermen with holdings in the region of Edo. The shogun required them to surrender their lands, effective immediately, in exchange for other territories, which would be assigned in due course. Soon lords with fiefs in the vicinity of Osaka received similar messages, and so did the lord who administered the port of Niigata in Tsuneno's home province of Echigo. In part, this was a defensive measure, one of the series of reforms aimed at augmenting the shogunate's capacity to protect Japan from a potential attack by a foreign navy. But there was also a financial motive: 'It is inappropriate that private domains should now have more high-yield land than the shogunate.'

The lords and bannermen who had been targeted were dumbfounded – this exertion of the shogun's authority, on such a grand scale, was nearly unprecedented. No one had seen anything like it for two centuries. Where would the new lands come from? And how would they be assigned? The lords might be kept waiting for years, maybe even forever, and in the meantime how would they live with their income cut off, or at least vastly reduced?

In the midst of the uproar, the Kanda Festival was abruptly canceled. Supposedly, the reason was that the shogun's twenty-third child had died in infancy. The samurai girls who lived in upscale neighbourhoods were already going to the bathhouse, arranging their hair and laying out their clothes when the news arrived: there was nothing to celebrate. The mood of the city was grim.

In mid-autumn, the shogunate finally reached a breaking point. The anger of the city's commoners, frustrated by confusing regulations and economic chaos, could be withstood, perhaps indefinitely, as long as there weren't riots. But the fury of Edo's lords and bannermen was a different matter. They would not allow their lands to be reassigned, and their intransigence made the shogun's position untenable.

The shogun, bowing to pressure, realised that he could not continue to follow his senior councillor Mizuno's lead. He dismissed

Mizuno from his position on the thirteenth day of the intercalary ninth month in 1843.

The news circulated immediately. Mizuno closed and locked the gates to his mansion, but people gathered there throughout the day, and in the evening they started shouting and cheering. They pelted the gate with small stones – so many it seemed as though a sudden hailstorm had erupted in this tiny part of the city, issuing from a dark cloud hovering over the residence of Edo's most despised man. The crowd raided the neighbourhood guardhouse, sending the samurai guardsmen running, pulled out tatami mats and furniture, and threw everything into the mansion's drainage ditch. Finally, neighbouring lords were forced to dispatch their own men to keep the peace. Hundreds of low-ranking samurai gathered carrying lanterns with their household crests, and soon it looked exactly like the scene of a big fire: furniture everywhere, people running around in the street, and men trying to contain the crowd. The samurai put an end to the revelry by morning, but young men and women still gathered to see the aftermath.

All that autumn, people in the streets played hand-clapping games and sang about the fall of the wicked councillor. Theirs was the verdict of heaven, delivered in the voice of the crowd: Mizuno Tadakuni would never impose his will on the city's people again.

*

A few days before Mizuno Tadakuni's spectacular fall, Tsuneno walked all the way across the city, passing through the bleached walls of the mazelike samurai districts, skirting the northern edge of Edo Castle's outer moat. She walked until she reached the Lord of Kaga's mansion and the red gates she'd probably passed on her first day in the city, almost exactly four years earlier. She had been with Chikan then – a bad memory. Her marriage to Hirosuke was supposed to erase that mistake and restore her reputation. But her fellow maidservants had been right when they advised her to take her chances on her own.

Tsuneno called at Kyōshōji, a temple on the edge of Shinobazu Pond. In summer dark green lotuses crowded the surface of the water, but in late autumn it was a field of straw-like stalks and shriveled flowers, with tiny ducks threading their way through. It was cold already, and dark early. Tsuneno knew the temple because her brother Gisen worked there. Although she hadn't seen or spoken to Gisen in months – she deliberately hadn't told him her new address when she and Hirosuke moved to Shinjuku – she thought she could probably use his name. It worked, of course. It always did. The combination of her respectable family and her completely disreputable appearance provoked sympathy, and the priest there said she could stay for a few days.

Kyōshōji's head priest called for Gisen, who was thoroughly embarrassed to find his older sister dressed in rags, taking refuge from yet another troubled marriage by imposing on her family's acquaintances. He decided that Tsuneno couldn't possibly stay in Edo, given the state she was in, and surprisingly, she acquiesced. Wincing at the expense, he arranged for a messenger service to escort her across the mountains. But late at night on the day before she was supposed to depart, she changed her mind. She couldn't possibly leave, she said, because her brother-in-law Hanzaemon, who ran the restaurant, would never let her go.

In theory, Hanzaemon had no claim on Tsuneno. He had provided her with a place to stay and a job, but he wasn't her husband. He had no particular status or authority. But he was intimidating. Gisen was sure that Hanzaemon was involved in some kind of illegal activity. He definitely spoke like a gangster.

When the head priest at Kyōshōji summoned Hanzaemon to ask him why he wouldn't let Tsuneno leave, his answer was shocking: 'As long as I have Tsuneno here with me, I can keep getting cash out of her family, starting with her brother, and that will do for my drinking money.' Gisen was outraged. How had Tsuneno managed to involve herself with yet another shady, unscrupulous man? It wasn't the first time her carelessness had endangered the family's reputation, and of course news of her plight would get back to their friends and family in Echigo – it always did.

Gisen was completely disgusted with Tsuneno and ready to cut ties. He hoped that Giyū would tell him that she wasn't his responsibility. She wouldn't listen to him anyway, and as far as he was concerned it was like he didn't even have a sister. 'Really,' he wrote, 'all three of them – Tsuneno, Hirosuke, and Hanzaemon – are complete idiots.'

Still, against his better judgement, Gisen made arrangements to help Tsuneno find another place to stay. He knew an acupuncturist, Yado Gisuke, who came around to treat the priests at Tokuhonji, where he used to work. Yado Gisuke was originally from Dewa Province, where Tsuneno had spent the fifteen years of her first marriage, and he felt sympathy with her as 'a fellow person from the north'. The pair of them got along fairly well, and perhaps that wasn't surprising. Tsuneno had never had a problem attracting men. Maybe they had talked about the Mogami River town, the safflowers and the white-sailed boats.

The acupuncturist didn't have much money himself, but he was willing to hire Tsuneno as a maidservant, at least for a few months, on a trial basis. She was still a married woman, but Gisen didn't stop to wonder if the acupuncturist had ulterior motives; he was just relieved to find someone who would take responsibility for his sister. 'At least now she won't be able to say we've never done anything for her,' he grumbled. He asked the priests at Tokuhonji to lend her some bedding, and then he warned her that if she got herself in trouble again he would send her home immediately. In truth, he wasn't optimistic: 'The fact is that it's hard for women to avoid getting into trouble. Even if Tsuneno manages to get rid of Hirosuke and Hanzaemon, this city is full of terrible men. She'll probably end up as some kind of roadside prostitute somewhere.'

Living with the acupuncturist Gisuke was certainly a step up from roadside prostitution, but as far as Tsuneno was concerned, it still wasn't an inviting prospect. Acupuncture tended to be the last resort of poor people, often disabled, who could find no other work. Gisuke was so broke that he didn't even have extra bedding. And it wasn't clear exactly what the job of acupuncturist's maid-servant might entail. Back in Echigo, in 1729, the authorities had issued a special commendation to a servant, Hachizō, who worked for an extremely impoverished samurai. When the samurai began to study acupuncture, desperate to make ends meet, Hachizō offered himself up as a practice patient, allowing his master to stab him with pins over and over again until his belly was swollen and red. The shogunate found this behaviour commendable, but it wasn't the kind of work that anyone would enjoy.

Luckily, Tsuneno discovered that she had a better option: the temple Tokuhonji, where she had gone to borrow bedding, was in need of a woman servant. The temple precincts in Asakusa were familiar, even though Tsuneno had never lived in that exact neigh-bourhood. The relocated theatre district was nearby, on a plot of land that had once belonged to one of Tokuhonji's samurai parish-ioners. The streets were different, but the theatres were decorated with many of the same names and faces. The atmosphere wasn't quite as lively, but at least the theatre people who had survived the purges were still in Edo, making the best of their new beginning.

For Tsuneno, the work at Tokuhonji was more like a return to the past than a fresh start. The temple was the world of her childhood, and she was diminished every time she moved through it. She had been a cherished daughter, then a daughter-in-law, then a divorced, troublesome sister, and now she was a maidservant. The winter days passed, cold and hard like beads on a rosary, as she cleaned and took orders. She barely heard from Gisen, even though he had close ties to Tokuhonji, which was the first place he'd worked in Edo. 'He's snobbish and unkind, and it makes me angry,' she complained in a letter home. 'Whenever he's around me he's condescending, and he says horrible things like "from now on I'm going to treat you like a stranger."' Hirosuke was angry at him, too, which was no surprise. Hirosuke was always angry at everyone.

Even though they were living apart, Tsuneno was still trying to provide for Hirosuke as well as she could. She wrote to Giyū: 'Here in Edo, there isn't anywhere that lends bedding to servants. So I asked Gisen, "He's my husband, can you please lend him something?" And he just ignored me, so of course Hirosuke is completely furious.'

Tsuneno stayed at Tokuhonji because it was somewhere to be: a room and a futon, a blanket, a brazier. According to Gisen, she told the people at Tokuhonji that she was there because she had been hoping that her brother might appreciate her display of diligence and redeem her clothes from the pawnshop. 'They were all thoroughly sick of her by the time she left,' he wrote.

*

Shortly after the New Year, Tsuneno left Tokuhonji and went back to Hirosuke. Unfortunately, his situation was no better. Tsuneno found yet another job in service, but it didn't pay very much.

She had tried pawning, but it was hopeless: she could barely get half of what anything was worth. She was stuck. 'People in Edo are arrogant and superior,' she complained, 'and they think I'm strange just because I come from a different province.' It didn't help that she was so poorly dressed that she really couldn't say anything in return, no matter how angry she was. She looked so bad that she was embarrassed to leave her room.

Over the next few months, Tsuneno and Hirosuke were in and out of jobs. He found a position for a few months, then lost it, and Tsuneno took in piecework to make ends meet. At one point, they were reduced to sharing a single robe. 'You'll be angry at me for saying it,' she wrote to Giyū, 'but Hirosuke is suffering, too, and I feel sorry for him.' Her letters had drastically changed in tone. For three years she had been defiant, but now she was reflective, humbled, nearly defeated. She was terrified of getting old and dying in squalor. 'Nothing has gone the way I've planned,' she wrote. 'I never intended to struggle so much.'

Meanwhile, Hirosuke seemed increasingly unstable. When they had a few coins, he spent them all gorging himself on his favourite foods. When they ran out of money, he slept all day. By the autumn, he wasn't even trying to look for work anymore.

'If I'd known even the slightest bit about his character,' Tsuneno wrote, 'I would never have married him, no matter how much he tried to convince me.' She couldn't imagine how a person could be so difficult: 'I know I have a terrible temper, too, but I've never even met anyone who is as bad tempered as he is. Really, there can't be more than one in a thousand people this bad.' He harped on other people's weaknesses, but he never seemed to notice his own failings. When his friend Masayoshi came around, the two of them berated her, telling her to get money from her rich brothers. When that failed, they taunted her for having been disinherited. They cursed Giyū. 'Priests are useless,' they said. In more ambitious moods, they plotted like a pair of highwaymen. 'We're going to take all your family's land,' they said. 'All those fields next to Ishigami Village are going to be ours.'

Tsuneno was at odds with most of her family, and had been for a long time, but Rinsenji was the place she was born. Her brothers were her blood relations; their ancestors were hers, too. Hirosuke had no right to speak of them as if they were enemies. 'I know that I fight with Giyū, and that we don't get along,' she wrote later. 'But he's still my brother! And it makes me angry when Hirosuke says terrible things about him day and night, when he himself is a complete idiot.'

'I'm fed up,' she wrote. 'Just completely and thoroughly sick of him.'

*

Over those difficult months, as Hirosuke and Tsuneno fought, he wrote out a notice of divorce six times. He would go so far as to hand it to Tsuneno, but every time he took it back. The seventh time, on the first day of the ninth month of 1844, she held on to it and walked out. The letter was short, only three and a half lines, composed in Hirosuke's clearest handwriting and stamped with his seal. It said that she was an unsatisfactory wife. But it also said that she was free.

After burning her bridges at Gisen's temple, Tokuhonji, Tsuneno knew better than to go to her youngest brother for help. Instead, she relied on Hirosuke's old friend, Fujiwara Yūzō, who lived in Hongō, near the red gates to the Lord of Kaga's mansion. He had a good job in service to a samurai, and a small room, and he agreed to look after her for a while.

With the help of an employment agent, Tsuneno found a series of temporary jobs. Her monthly salary was supposed to be one gold coin and two hundred copper coins, but she received only a little over half that sum. Meanwhile, Hirosuke was still demanding money, so she sent him five hundred copper coins every month. After she paid a commission to the employment agent, she was left with only three hundred for herself. It was less than a pedlar could clear on a single good day.

Tsuneno wrote to her brothers and confessed everything: she told them all about Hirosuke's terrible behaviour and admitted that she never should have married him. She begged them to make plans for her future. She wanted to go home. She wanted to visit her mother's grave.

Fujiwara Yūzō, who had taken custody of Tsuneno as a favour, was no happier with the situation than she was. He summoned Gisen, thinking he might feel some obligation to help his older sister, but he was completely unhelpful. Tsuneno implored Yūzō to contact Giyū instead, so he sent a letter to Rinsenji and tried to explain the situation as well as he could. He didn't know quite what had happened, just that Tsuneno and Hirosuke had divorced and that she was so poor that she barely had anything to wear. She needed cash – or at least a new set of clothes – so that she could get a better job and move out of his house.

When Yūzō's letter went unanswered after a month, he wrote another one and explained the situation again, this time in starker terms. Someone had to take responsibility for Tsuneno. Her husband had left her destitute, she was having difficulty finding consistent work, and her youngest brother had abandoned her. It was shocking, really: 'The two of them don't seem to have a sibling relationship at all.' Yūzō couldn't have a barely dressed, divorced woman living with him indefinitely. Either Giyū would have to send clothing and spending money, or he would have to arrange for an escort to take Tsuneno home to Echigo.

When the news of Tsuneno's plight finally reached Rinsenji, five weeks after Yūzō's first letter was posted, Giyū was mortified. The previous year, he had written to Gisen and told him not to worry about Tsuneno: the family simply couldn't afford to take responsibility for her. But as usual, he was ambivalent, making it clear that he'd arrived at his decision out of desperation, not a lack of concern: 'Hirosuke is supposed to be Tsuneno's guardian . . . and as you know, since we spoke of it in the spring, we are really struggling here, so even if she wanted just a little money, there's really nothing I can do. It wouldn't even matter who it was, I wouldn't be able to help, so there's no other choice but to ignore it and let her fend for herself.' Now, with desperate letters arriving from an Edo samurai he had never met, his calculation had to be different. He wrote to Yūzō, apologising profusely, and agreed to make plans to send Tsuneno home.

Giyū found an appropriate escort, a man from the Sannō Express Service, based in Echigo, and sent him all the way to Edo to meet Tsuneno. The other details of the arrangement fell to Gisen, since he was the brother in Edo. Gisen was defensive: 'After what happened with Tsuneno the last time she said she wanted to go home,' he wrote, 'I was convinced that even if I tried to talk to Yūzō it wouldn't go well.' But he followed Giyū's lead, diligently planning the trip. He even considered procuring an official pass so that Tsuneno could travel through all the checkpoints along the way home, but ultimately, after consulting with the relevant officials, he was convinced she wouldn't need one: everyone he talked to told him it was more trouble than it was worth.

By the end of the eleventh month, the escort was in Edo and Tsuneno was ready to go. But when Hirosuke found out that

Tsuneno was leaving, he was furious. Even though Hirosuke had written out the divorce notice, he had never wanted to let Tsuneno go. In fact, he had told one of Giyū's acquaintances in the city that he was refusing to return any of her possessions until she came back. Now he was desperate to keep her in Edo. Yes, they had separated, he admitted, and they hadn't spoken in a long time, but she shouldn't be able to go home without consulting him. In any case, it was a terrible time of year to try to make the trip back to Echigo – who would want to cross the mountains, and take the long way around the checkpoints, in the middle of winter?

After writing an angry letter to Giyū, Hirosuke called in his younger brother, Hanzaemon, who was working at a samurai mansion under one of his many aliases, Takeda Gorō. Hanzaemon summoned Tsuneno and enlisted one of his samurai acquaintances to help persuade her to stay. When that failed, he refused to let her leave. He even managed to detain the escort from the messenger service. But somehow, they both slipped his grasp. Hanzaemon, who was very well connected, sent men into the city to search for Tsuneno, but they came back with nothing. Hanzaemon was incensed. He went straight to Gisen's temple, intending to sue him for custody of Tsuneno, but Gisen had mysteriously vanished. Meanwhile, Tsuneno was already gone. She had left in the early morning of the sixth day of the twelfth month, without saying good-bye.

Tsuneno arrived back at Rinsenji just before the New Year in 1845, over forty years old and four times divorced. She had exchanged rice fields for row houses, temple bells for the theatre drums, her mother's pickles for nighthawk noodles. She had been a maidservant and a waitress, a masterless samurai's wife. She knew what it was like to earn money, how to budget so that she could make rent, how to calculate what percentage of her pay would go to the employment office. She had chosen her own husband – poorly, she now admitted – and gossiped with fellow servants in a bannerman's mansion. She had a past, and stories that no one at home would believe, but now she had no future.

Other people had suffered more in the turmoil of the previous five years. The famous romance writer Tamenaga Shunsui, who had been arrested and charged with obscenity at the height of the reforms, died of a broken heart, or so everyone said, after all his original woodblocks were confiscated. Others had broken under interrogation or died in jail while awaiting punishment. And thousands of people in Edo had lost their livelihoods. They had seen their art, their instruments and their life's work destroyed.

Maybe the losses would have been more meaningful if they had brought about some kind of lasting change. But instead, Japan seemed to have returned to the same untenable situation. People only knew the reforms were over when the edicts were no longer enforced, when women could start visiting the hairdresser again, when ordinary people retrieved their silk-lined robes from storage and bought them out of pawn, when the great store Echigoya stopped selling 'be careful goods' and the festivals went on as scheduled. Nothing had been accomplished, aside from the relocation of the theatre district, the detention of unlicensed prostitutes and music teachers, and the destruction of instruments and children's toys. None of the city's – or the country's – underlying problems had been solved. Edo's samurai were still impoverished; the poor were still hungry and vulnerable. Foreign gunboats still billowed steam and carried cannons, and the Japanese islands were still practically defenseless. Western merchants still delivered opium to Asian ports, now with the mighty British navy defending their interests, but even the punitive Treaty of Nanjing was less decisive than it appeared. In

China, the same parties would fight the Opium Wars all over again in just a few years.

Tsuneno, too, had returned to a situation she found intolerable. There was time to wonder what had gone wrong. Was it the political catastrophe, a threat from outside, that had destroyed her marriage? Or were the problems always there, like blight in the soil, waiting for the season to change? When she looked into the garden at Rinsenji, all she could see – all anyone could see – was snow.

Chapter Eight

IN THE OFFICE OF THE CITY MAGISTRATE

Compared to Edo, life in the countryside had a blank and muffled quality. It was all familiar: the clean sheets of snow drawn up over the fields; the dull grey ice; and the raw, smoky smell of open hearths. The mountains still loomed beyond the glassy surface of Big Pond, and the clouds still scudded in from the west. The walls were still empty, devoid of graffiti and notices – not even the 'Beware of Fire' signs that were everywhere in Edo. In a tiny farming village, most messages were delivered in person, through gossip, or passed from hand to hand on folded sheets of paper.

Tsuneno spent the winter in padded robes and coats, under bedding and blankets, behind solid walls. But only a few weeks had passed, and it was still easy to remember the exposed feeling of the city, how the cold in Edo had pierced through her thin cotton underrobe, how strangers had raked their eyes over her face, and how every sigh and snore and argument had been overheard by an anonymous person just on the other side of a wall.

At Rinsenji, there were new stone markers in the graveyard for Tsuneno's youngest sister, Ino, and her mother. Tsuneno had missed the services held at forty-nine days, but at least she could finally visit their graves. Tsuneno's other younger sister Toshino had also died, though her gravestone was with her husband's family. She had fallen ill suddenly, the previous spring, and the family had sent their older brother Kōtoku, who was a doctor, to her husband's village. He tried, but he couldn't save her. She was only twenty-seven.

Meanwhile, Giyū had settled into middle age and his wife, Sano, was as busy as ever, with several young children and a temple to look after. Kihaku, their son and heir, was twelve years old, and he went to school in Takada to learn the Chinese classics and the five sutras. Tsuneno made herself useful – an extra pair of woman's hands was always useful. She could help with the sewing and laundry, mind the babies, tend the graves and sweep the halls of the temple.

Once in a while, she would discover a remnant of her past stashed away somewhere in the house. In the spring, while the maidservant was doing the household's laundry, Tsuneno recognised a little blanket made from her childhood clothes. Her mother had pieced it together out of the things Tsuneno left behind when she went to marry the first time. She must have thought of Tsuneno as she sewed, the daughter who had married so young and lived in such a faraway place. She could have reworked Tsuneno's clothes for her younger daughters, but instead she made a half-sized blanket, the kind meant to comfort a child. Maybe it was supposed to be a gift for Tsuneno's first baby. If so, she never had the opportunity to send it.

Tsuneno grabbed the blanket from the pile. 'I'll take this,' she announced. 'It's mine.' Giyū was exasperated. His family had been using the blanket for three decades. Surely it belonged to the temple by now. But he let the matter drop. There was no use arguing with someone so stupid, he said. In reality, he must have known that he had never won an argument with Tsuneno when she really wanted something, even if that thing was just a fraying thirty-year-old blanket. It was completely worthless, anyway. Maybe it was a reminder of her mother, a symbol of the unbridgeable distance between the life Haruma had expected for her daughter and the one Tsuneno had lived. But she probably wanted it on principle. She always claimed what was hers.

*

In the spring of 1846, when Tsuneno had been home for a little more than a year, a messenger came to Rinsenji to deliver a letter from Tsuneno's former brother-in-law in Kamōda Village. It was about Hirosuke. He'd finally found a permanent job in Edo, and he wanted to send for Tsuneno. He'd asked his brother to inquire at Rinsenji: would Tsuneno marry him, again?

Tsuneno understood all Hirosuke's weaknesses: his quick temper, his lazy streak, his greed and his gullibility. He had been a truly terrible husband, and it had been barely a year and a half since their marriage had ended in disaster. Her family despised him, and who could predict whether this new, supposedly permanent job would last? She would probably end up in exactly the same situation she had left, in a cold tenement room in some dreary neighbourhood arguing over yet another visit to the pawnshop.

On the other hand, Hirosuke was still the boy from the village next door, the husband she had chosen for herself, in Edo, when she could have gone on alone. He was one of the few people who could understand both halves of her life – he, too, had traded the security of Echigo for the uncertainty of the city – and he was the only man she'd ever met with a temper to match her own.

If she didn't go back to him, she would have to stay at Rinsenji, helping Sano and the maidservants, and it wasn't clear that Giyū would tolerate her presence forever. She needed to go somewhere.

Edo wasn't the only place in the world. There were Japanese castle towns where it never snowed, where the wind smelled like clementines and the local farmers grew sweet potatoes and harvested rice three times a year. There was Kyoto, the ancient capital, where Tsuneno had travelled as a young bride, where the emperor composed poetry in his palace and weavers made luxurious brocades from safflower-dyed silk.

Beyond them, there were other cities, in foreign lands where tigers stalked through glossy jungles and red birds called across grassy plains. In their warehouses, men stacked crates of tea leaves, calico and opium; in their markets, old women traded leathery dried peppers and turquoise; in their cathedrals, families sang hymns for Easter in four-part harmony. There were places where the spring rain spattered cobblestones and glass-paned windows and women wore bell-like skirts and corsets, saris and gold bracelets, bazaar cloth and beaded headdresses, lambskin gloves with tiny buttons, bare feet and rags. Women the same age as Tsuneno bargained for curry leaves and bought boxes of chocolate truffles, tended children and washed floors, stayed at home and knit wool scarves. Some of their sisters tended clattering looms in enormous factories. Some of their brothers dug coal out of the earth.

In a few of these faraway capitals and windblown ports, men wondered about Japan. They loaded ships and drew up plans. They imagined Japanese cities and read about the shogun. They saw the 'double-bolted land' and wanted to unlock it, seeking trade, profit and glory. Like Tsuneno, who had once envisioned her own fate as a closed door, they saw Edo as the key.

As Tsuneno contemplated Hirosuke's proposal, two American warships sailed towards Edo. Their commander, a veteran of the War of 1812 named James Biddle, had just concluded the first American treaty with China, and he wanted to build on his success by signing a similar mercantile agreement with the Japanese emperor. He came to the mouth of Edo Bay, where he immediately found his vessels surrounded by Japanese barges full of samurai armed to the teeth. They took his written request to open commercial relations, and while his ships were at anchor they boarded freely and looked around. They were curious, and Biddle was happy to oblige. He was also grateful to receive supplies, including several hundred chickens, green apples and casks of clean drinking water, the best he'd had during the whole expedition. But the answer to his request, written by one of the shogun's elders, was a firm no: the Japanese would not trade with the United States – they would not trade with any foreign nations apart from Holland and China.

The message was disappointing, and the experience of receiving it was worse. Biddle boarded a Japanese boat with the intention of retrieving the letter, but he didn't alert the crew. A Japanese samurai, alarmed to see him climbing aboard, shoved him backwards, sending him tumbling back into his boat. Biddle was outraged, and for a moment his men thought he was going to command them to open up the batteries. Thankfully, he managed to keep his temper. But the incident was an embarrassment for everyone involved, and it did nothing to solve Japan's long-term problem with American ambitions in the Pacific. Commodore Biddle would never get to Edo, but the US Navy would be back.

Tsuneno's dreams couldn't range across oceans. She knew nothing of cobblestones, curry leaves or cathedrals; she had never hoisted a sail or stood lookout on a masthead, out of sight of land. Her ambitions were specific, confined to the known world, to the city she had loved and been forced to abandon. For her, there would never be anywhere else. So when Hirosuke's intermediary came to discuss his proposal in person, she didn't hesitate. Yes, she said, she wanted to go.

*

As usual, Giyū was a problem. He refused to give Tsuneno the permission she needed to marry. Why would he let his sister return to a husband who hadn't been able to support her adequately, who had tried to extort money from their family, who had pawned all her clothes? Giyū had read all her letters home from Edo; she herself said that her husband had plotted to steal her family's land and cursed her ancestors. As Giyū reminded everyone, continually, he was the one who had to pay for her travel home from Edo when Hirosuke abandoned her there in the dead of winter.

In the end, Giyū would only agree under one condition. Tsuneno would forgo all association with Rinsenji; she would never again use her family's name or ask them for money. He drew up documents so there could be no confusion. After a series of negotiations, an exchange of drafts, and a series of stamps, Tsuneno was formally expelled from the family and removed from the Ishigami Village registers.

Tsuneno was eager to leave as soon as possible, but Giyū still couldn't quite reconcile himself to the arrangement. Four days before she was supposed to depart, he told her brother-in-law that he would feel much better if she had a pass to go through the barrier at Sekikawa, even though it would take thirty days to secure it from the appropriate officials. She was incredulous – why couldn't she go around the barrier, the way everyone else did? Hirosuke, who was informed of her delay by letter, was so blindingly furious that he threatened to call off the marriage. Denpachi, the long-suffering temple secretary, had to remind Giyū that his stubbornness was counterproductive: Tsuneno had her heart set on leaving, and she had nowhere else to live. Besides, she was a foolish, selfish woman and Giyū should be happy to be rid of her. He should just swallow his pride, tell Hirosuke it had all been a misunderstanding, and let Tsuneno go.

A few days before her departure, Tsuneno met with Giyū and an intermediary to negotiate the formal financial settlement that would mark her departure from the family. They pored through the records, reaching as far back as her first marriage, tallying the expenses and transfers of property. They accounted for clothing that she had never worn and change she had been owed. They brought up the incident with Chikan, again, and the clothes she had sold on her way out of the province. They even noted the recent incident with the old blanket.

Giyū had faith in the magic of ink on paper, the rituals of copying and stamping and saving drafts. He had to believe that meticulous accounting could clear everyone's debts and settle old grudges. Otherwise, in a tiny village, how would anyone ever let them go? But that kind of record keeping was men's work, the labour of dutiful sons who had inherited their names and their houses, who had seals to darken with ink and press to the page. Tsuneno had tried making lists, in her head and in her letters, but this time she had no unfinished business and no need to keep a record.

When she finally left Echigo for the last time, Hirosuke's family went as far as Takada to see her off. It was more like her departure for her first marriage – the luggage and ceremony – than it was like her previous journey to Edo, when she'd left in secret, carrying nothing. This time, she had packed four boxes of clothes for her family to send. She travelled the familiar road through the mountains to Arai Station, where she met up with a group of eleven women travellers, and on to Kusatsu, where she stayed with a friend. The trip was easy; it only took thirteen days. But when she arrived in Edo on a windy, rainy day, she found entire neighbourhoods flooded. All the stores had put up their storm shutters, and the giant barrels under the rain gutters were overflowing. She sloshed through muddy streets, fighting the north wind and dodging umbrellas. She was home.

*

Hirosuke's new master was no ordinary, anonymous bannerman. He was one of the most famous – and busiest – men in Edo. The very sound of his title elicited awe, the 'fear and trembling' that commoners always invoked in documents. He was the great Edo City Magistrate, Tōyama Saemon no jō Kagemoto.

There were two City Magistrates, North and South, who rotated months on duty. Both were responsible for the city in its entirety, and they had a staggering portfolio of responsibilities: they judged criminal cases, took petitions, issued edicts and managed city policing and fire preparedness as well as road maintenance and waterworks. They were named after the locations of their offices, which were less than a mile apart. In 1846, Tōyama occupied the slightly grander South Magistrate's Office, near the Sukiyabashi gate to Edo Castle, facing east towards the commoner districts of Ginza and Tsukiji. He had been at his post for only a year but knew his job well, because he had served as North Magistrate during the early phase of the Tenpō Reforms. Many of the strident edicts that Tsuneno had seen posted on the city ward gates were dispatched from his office, and his men had dragged stylish young women off the streets.

Behind the scenes, Tōyama had never agreed with the reforms, and he argued bitterly with both the senior councillor Mizuno Tadakuni and his fellow City Magistrate, Torii Yōzō, over their implementation. Tōyama had no quarrel with the strict distinction between samurai and commoners. Like his more conservative colleagues, he accepted that it was his duty to impose order on the unruly people of the city, and he could be haughty and moralistic. When a woman brought a civil suit to his office in 1841, he was incredulous: 'This person – a woman – brought a complaint to my office. She is a troublemaker. Day after day, women bring complaints to my office, and I hear them, but they're all troublemakers.' Yet Tōyama also believed that he had a responsibility to protect the livelihoods of common people. When Mizuno proposed to move the theatre district, Tōyama submitted a detailed memo outlining his opposition on the grounds that it would impoverish the people who lived in that neighbourhood and destroy the property values of the area's landlords. When Mizuno issued the directive to abolish the wholesalers' associations, Tōyama stalled before circulating the edict. And when Mizuno proposed to expel migrants from the city, Tōyama opposed the order on the grounds that the newcomers were necessary to the functioning of the economy.

On each of these occasions, Tōyama's logic had been that of a samurai looking down on the city population. He came from a household that took status, and service, seriously. His father had been adopted into a family of bannermen whose low stipends matched their mediocre history. He changed their trajectory. He received one of the top scores on an exam meant to identify talented men for official positions, and he blazed a path through the highest echelons of the shogunate. He was appointed Grand Inspector, Nagasaki Magistrate and finally Finance Magistrate. He became the ideal official, much praised and frequently commended, skilled at Chinese poetry and a student of archery, horsemanship and hand-to-hand combat. He had equally high expectations for his son.

But Tōyama was never sure of his future. He was a firstborn son, but the bannerman family who had adopted his father insisted that one of their own biological children be named as the formal heir. For most of Tōyama's early adulthood, then, his path to promotion was blocked. Meanwhile, his father was often absent, travelling north to distant Hokkaido, south to Nagasaki and west to the island of Tsushima. Tōyama was left in Edo, subject to all the discipline of a high-ranking samurai household, but without an outlet for his ambition or his talent.

Perhaps this was why, years later, the townspeople told stories about Tōyama's misspent youth. They said that he had consorted with the city's thieves and gamblers, horrifying his parents. They said he frequented every brothel in town. They said that his upper body was covered in tattoos, the mark of labourers, gangsters and criminals. Maybe there was truth to this story, or maybe they were looking for an explanation for why a man who had been born and raised a bannerman displayed such sympathy for the city's poor. Either way, they constructed a legend around the man. To the people of Edo, Tōyama Kagemoto would never be the middle-aged father of eight children, a man who suffered from such terrible haemorrhoids that he had to apply for permission to ride a palanquin to Edo Castle instead of going on horseback. Instead, he was always the dashing young man they'd imagined, the one who knew their streets, played their games and spoke their language, who had somehow risen to the highest position in the city administration and now sat in judgement of them all.

The post of Edo City Magistrate was probably the most onerous in the realm, and people said that its occupants tended to work themselves to death. It was true that many of the appointees died on the job. But Tōyama, a broad, red-faced man in his fifties, was beating the odds. He was still energetic, and his loud voice rang out impressively when he questioned criminals. He had little left to prove. He had climbed even further in the shogunate's hierarchy than his extraordinarily talented father, and he had become one of the shogun's most trusted advisers. He and his wife, Okei, had been married for over thirty years, and their children had gone on to brilliant careers and marriages.

Tōyama had almost nothing in common with Hirosuke, a divorced Echigo migrant with a chequered past and only the barest pretensions to samurai status. Still, even an exalted official could understand how Hirosuke might be useful. Bannermen often hired retainers as fixers, politely termed 'subsidy assistants', to intimidate creditors and shake down the peasants who lived on their fiefs. Hirosuke could also help with the magistrate's work. Most of Tōyama's investigators were samurai with hereditary positions attached to the office, but he also had a few personal retainers who helped with enquiries. In those cases, Hirosuke's knowledge of Edo's darker corners might be helpful. And if he proved entirely incompetent, he could always be put to work accompanying the steward on errands or carrying spears and boxes.

For Hirosuke, ending up in Tōyama's service was an unbelievable stroke of fortune, a promise of security, which he had never found. Hirosuke had spent years moving between bannermen's mansions, often staying for only a month or so before he was let go. But a City Magistrate of Tōyama's reputation was unlike a regular lord or bannerman – he would need men for as long as he was in office, and he would also be able to pay them consistently. Finally, Hirosuke could afford to live with his wife. He and Tsuneno could share a room in the South Magistrate's Office, where the magistrate Tōyama and the members of his household were obliged to live during the term of his appointment.

Tsuneno's new home was one of the most fearsome places in Edo. Even its front gate was ominous, crowned with thick, dark tiles and flanked by guard posts with curving rooftops. The arrangement gave the office a menacing quality, as if it were crouched on the edge of the commoner districts, scowling under heavy black brows. When Tsuneno first arrived in the sixth month of 1846, the main doors were closed and locked, signalling that the South Magistrate was off duty, accepting no new cases or petitions, and litigants would have to go to the North Magistrate's Office instead. Of course, Tōyama was still hard at work, processing paperwork, pursuing long-term investigations, corresponding with the shogun's Grand Council regarding precedents, and attending meetings. But Tōyama's office wouldn't come to life until the following month, when the wooden doors of the main gate were thrown open to the business of the city.

When the magistrate was on duty, the great gate opened in the early morning and closed in the early evening. Beyond it, a sea of glittering black gravel was neatly bisected by a path of blue stones, which led to the office's main building. This was the grand courtyard, used for ceremonial occasions, when processions of mounted officers would stand at attention, or when the great magistrate would ride out on formal business, flanked by his attendants.

Ordinary people never used the main gate, which was mostly for show. Instead, they went through the smaller gate just to the right of it. At night, the right gate was open for urgent petitions and other emergencies; during the day, it was crowded with litigants and defendants who had come to give testimony in lawsuits. They all crammed into a tiny receiving room, where they waited for the guard in charge of summonses to call their names and cases. Typically, parties to a civil suit dreaded the tedious and time-consuming experience of waiting at the right gate, an ordeal that usually had to be repeated many times over the course of a case.

But as inconvenient as the right gate could be, it was far better than the left gate, which everyone tried as hard as they could to avoid. That entrance was reserved for the accused in criminal cases, who arrived already marked and broken after being interrogated at the city's guardhouses. Most had already confessed. For some, the sight of the torture implements kept in the guardhouses was convincing enough. Others had been bound and beaten into submission. By the time they arrived at the magistrate's office, they had no hope of exoneration. What remained for them was a series of encounters with the majesty of the shogun's authority, symbolised in the grandeur of the office and embodied in the person of Tōyama Saemon no jō Kagemoto.

The accused waited in a holding cell until their names were called; then they were escorted through a locked door, which opened with a giant key, and ushered through to a wide courtyard filled with coarse white sand. There they dropped to their knees and awaited interrogation. If they could bear to raise their eyes, they saw Tōyama and his men seated on a wooden platform above the sand, looking down at them. The proceedings were always carefully scripted: there were no surprises in the White Sands, a theatre designed to discourage improvisation. Tōyama would glance at a sheaf of documents set before him and intone questions in his booming voice: 'What is your name?' 'Where is your residence?' 'Who is your landlord?' He already knew the answers.

For the accused, trembling on the sand, each of these interrogations would be burned into memory. For Tōyama, most of the time, they were a dreary routine. He usually did not have time to review the facts of the case before the accused came to his presence. Tens of thousands of civil and criminal matters were brought before the South Magistrate's Office every year, and the details had to be handled by lesser men. But the magistrate was always required at key points in the investigation, including the initial interrogation, when the identity of the criminal was confirmed. Sometimes men and women were brought before his office late at night, after the main gate was closed, because they had been apprehended after hours. Then Tōyama would have to hurry through the halls of his residence, through a maze of offices, to the White Sands. In winter, he and his men would sit under the stars, writing by lanternlight, and Tōyama's breath would fog the air with every question. There were no braziers in the White Sands. It was not a place of comfort.

The first round of interrogation at the sands almost always ended the same way. Tōyama would make a formal announcement: 'For the duration of this inquiry, it is ordered that this person be kept in the jailhouse.' Then the accused would be hauled off to the dreaded compound at Kodenmachō, a landmark known to the outside world for its sharp, spiked fence. In its dark and crowded rooms, the accused would endure ritualised abuse from the jail bosses, especially if he didn't have friends or relatives to pay protection money. He might also face a new round of interrogation, and if he had resisted an initial confession or refused to repeat it he would be beaten with short whips or forced to kneel on grooved wooden boards while heavy stones were piled on his thighs. The only reprieve he could expect would be a return visit to the White Sands, where the interrogation would continue, or he would face his sentence.

A month after Tsuneno arrived, while she was still adjusting to the magistrate's household and waiting for her luggage to be delivered from Echigo, there was a high-profile sentencing at the South Magistrate's Office. The accused was a man named Okada Ryōmin, one of the lowly officials at Edo Castle who served food and tea. The case attracted attention because his crime had been so bold: he had attempted to steal from a castle storeroom late at night, while everyone was supposed to be asleep. Unfortunately for him, one of his coworkers heard strange noises from the vicinity of the storeroom and assembled a group to investigate. They headed down the hallway, carrying lanterns, and were shocked when the light fell on the culprit's face and they realised he was one of their own. Amazingly, he had stolen three hundred gold pieces five years earlier and got away with it, which inspired him to try again. This time he was not as lucky.

Tōyama sentenced Okada to death by beheading, followed by public display of the head, a penalty reserved for grave offences. The execution took place at the jail yard, supervised by a small group of samurai, including one who had the gruesome responsibility of swinging the blade. But the men who held Okada in place were outcasts, members of a community responsible for jobs that carried the stigma of death and pollution. When Okada's head fell to the ground, one of them was ready to retrieve it from the dust and wrap it in straw matting. Another held the body so that blood from his neck could drain into a hole dug in the ground. Then a grim procession of outcasts and patrolmen carried Okada's head to an execution ground at the edge of the city, where they jammed it on a pike beside a placard that announced the details of his crime. The rest of the corpse was left to the shogun's lead executioner and sword tester, Yamada Asaemon. If he decided Okada's body was a good candidate for 'trial cutting', he would bind it carefully with rope and then use one of the shogun's swords to hack it to pieces, taking notes so he could report on the condition of the blade. When he was finished, he would make sure to save the gallbladder for his wife, who would use it in a recipe for one of the family's proprietary medicines.

For the magistrate Tōyama, the pronouncement of a death sentence was nothing unusual. Over the years, hundreds of people had died at his command. The month Okada was executed, ten men met their deaths in the jailhouse; in busy months, it was twenty or more. When Tōyama spared a life, it was for a reason, to send a message, and the people of the city noticed. Two months before Okada was beheaded, Tōyama commuted the sentence of a man who belonged to a ring of criminals who impersonated shogunal officials and extorted money from temples. All the man's co-conspirators had died in the jailhouse while awaiting sentencing, but he was still there when a fire broke out and the gates were thrown open, presenting a perfect opportunity to escape. Yet he returned the next day and presented himself to jailhouse officials, even though he had every reason to expect that he would die in one of those dark rooms or, if not, then at the hands of the executioner. If it hadn't been for the fire, Tōyama would have sentenced him to beheading. But he took note of the man's submission and exiled him to a distant island.

Tsuneno had little to do with these cases, beyond hearing about them through the gossip among samurai who worked with her husband. She belonged to the household, not the office. Though the distance between the two realms was a matter of steps, the boundary was secured with locked doors. For once, she was on the right side. It could so easily have been the opposite. If she had been caught sneaking around the barrier at Sekikawa. If, during that terrible winter of 1844, when she had nothing to wear, she'd stolen a jacket from a woman at the public bath. Hirosuke, too, had once been poor and desperate. He might have trembled on his knees in the sand, might have been a prisoner rather than a samurai wearing two swords and an overcoat emblazoned with the magistrate's crest.

The lines were so clear – a door, a travel pass, a title, an overcoat, a marriage. On one side, abjection. On the other, safety. It wasn't Tsuneno's character, or her behaviour, that made the difference. The boundaries were distinct because they were arbitrary, the doors locked because the rooms were so close. It would take only one wrong turn, or a right one, to end up someplace you were never supposed to be.

*

The Edo City Magistrates relied on a staff of mounted officers and patrolmen to police the city. Their positions were hereditary, and they were attached to the offices: there were twenty-three mounted officers and roughly 150 patrolmen assigned to Tōyama's office, and equal numbers for his counterpart to the north. Unlike Tsuneno and Hirosuke, who were the magistrate's personal retainers and lived with him in the South Magistrate's Office, the mounted officers and patrolmen lived with their families in a crowded neighbourhood called Hatchōbori. Originally, Hatchōbori must have been the safest place in Edo, given the presence of so many lawmen. But over time the samurai started to subdivide their plots and build rental houses, and different kinds of people moved in. At first, they were doctors and Confucian scholars, an appropriate class of people to mingle with low-ranking samurai. But eventually, gamblers and pimps started to gather there, because paying rent to a landlord who belonged to the police force was the best possible form of protection.

Mounted officers were of much higher rank than patrolmen. When they appeared at the White Sands, they sat on the platform, flanking the magistrate, while patrolmen sat on the ground, with the suspects. The officers spent most of their time managing investigations, coordinating groups of patrolmen and questioning suspects and witnesses. Much of their job consisted of reducing the magistrate's workload by discouraging civil litigation. 'This is a nice settlement,' they might say. 'Why don't you take this money and give your children a nice life? Then you wouldn't have to go through all this trouble.' They received only two hundred bales a year in salary, but they had many opportunities to augment their income with bribes. Samurai paid to keep investigations quiet, and parties to civil suits offered gifts in exchange for favourable hearings.

While the mounted officers typically rode through the streets on their horses, the patrolmen made rounds of the city on foot. Immediately recognisable, even from a distance, they were unlikely fashion icons. They styled their hair in fan-shaped knots, wore overcoats adorned with the crest of the City Magistrate's office, and carried metal truncheons alongside the swords at their waists. Their main task was to conduct investigations and make arrests, but they also collected information. The highest-ranking patrolman, the 'secret inspector', was assigned to sensitive investigations and the collection of rumours about the shogun and his family. But even ordinary inspectors heard all kinds of interesting things. There might be a talking horse, or an exceptionally large infant with a mouthful of sharp teeth, a female calligraphy instructor who suddenly grew testicles, or a little girl who was possessed by a fox. There could be a sea monster in the castle moat or a foreign ship in the bay. A giant carp might return as a ghost to terrorise the heedless boys who ate it. It was important for the City Magistrates to know – rumours could breed unrest, or they might be portents. Something ominous might be coming.

Some groups of patrolmen made regular rounds of the city, dispatched in the late morning and early evening, rain or shine. A few walked irregular routes, and others were sent to inspect building sites or check for fires. They were dispatched from neighbourhood guardhouses to investigate strange occurrences, like suspicious drownings, which happened quite often. In the first year Tsuneno lived at the office, a plasterer fell off the pleasure boat he'd chartered with his friends when he got drunk and leaned over the side to urinate. A maidservant who had tried to quit her job jumped into the river after her parents forced her to go back to her master. Three lively girls, shopkeepers' daughters, were found floating in the river, tied together. A kabuki actor and a theatre usher tumbled over the side of a rowboat and drowned, apparently while trying to retrieve an errant oar. And those were only the most widely reported cases.

The patrolmen, who numbered barely two hundred, could not police such a vast city alone. They needed help with investigations and information; they needed men who knew criminals and their networks, men who weren't burdened with the crest of the City Magistrate's office and the formal restraint required of samurai. They needed men who could cross jurisdictions and find people who had gone underground. For this purpose, they employed 'fingertips', former criminals who had turned informants after a stint or two in Kodenmachō Jailhouse or a period of banishment from the city. Officially, these men were not supposed to exist. Yet there they were, accompanying the patrolmen on their rounds, wearing long workmen's trousers and wooden swords.

The fingertips existed in a strange space where the lines between criminality and bureaucratic routine were indistinct. Informants were formally appointed and could climb through the ranks to become bosses of other men. They received steady salaries from the magistrate's offices, which were financed through fines and dispersed through the patrolmen. They also held regular meetings. Every morning, the fingertips assigned to Tōyama's patrolmen gathered at the Matsuyoshi Teahouse in Kanda to discuss the business of the day. Some of it was arrests and investigations, the jobs they were being paid to do. But they also freelanced, enjoying the relative immunity that came with their position. They sponsored regular gambling games, knowing they were unlikely to be raided. They extorted protection money from petty criminals in return for promises not to report them to the magistrates. If the perpetrators were women, the fingertips sometimes coerced them into prostitution and kept the proceeds.

The people of Edo were usually terrified of the fingertips and tried to keep their distance, but this was impossible, since they circulated with the patrolmen and came back around for protection money every time they noticed that someone had opened a store. Even a shogunal elder took note. He complained that the people were more fearful of the fingertips than they were of the ward elders, who should have been the leaders of their communities. But Tōyama had always been of the opinion that his office's informants were a necessary evil, and he had once petitioned to hire more of them for the sake of maintaining order.

There were also side benefits to the organisation of city crime, at least for those who were well connected with the magistrate's office. A famous Confucian scholar paid a call on his friend, a mounted officer, after he lost a sheaf of documents to a pickpocket. The mounted officer summoned a patrolman, who contacted an informant. The scholar's purse and all its contents were returned intact by the time he and his friend finished having drinks.

Years later, people said that when Tōyama sat on the platform at the White Sands, sentencing criminals to death in his stilted language, he pulled on his sleeves, trying to hide the tattoos spilling down his arms. Was it true? Did it matter? The ink was a metaphor, and so was the City Magistrate's robe. Together, they expressed a tacit understanding: under the grandeur and formality, the straight lines and insistence on procedure, the magistrate's men followed the twisted, colourful pathways of the underworld. In the person of the City Magistrate, and in the precincts of his office, justice and crime were enmeshed so deeply they couldn't be separated. Tōyama's dark robe was draped over his body, but the ink was indelible, under the skin.

*

Now that Tsuneno was a member of the magistrate's household, she didn't have to worry much about random crime. Jinsuke, the old superintendent who had stolen her clothes, would never have tried the same stunt with a woman under Tōyama's protection. Her legal status had also changed. When Hirosuke entered the great man's service, he became a samurai, and his status was secure for as long as he was employed. His older brother in the village, who had once worried that Hirosuke would never make anything of himself, spoke in awe of his 'very important position'. Tsuneno still swept floors and carried trays, made her husband's dinner and worried about spending money, but the status and security mattered. Technically, her husband now outranked all of her brothers.

When Tsuneno chose Hirosuke over her family, she felt the loss. When she first returned to Edo, she had tried to visit Gisen, but he sent her away. He claimed that Giyū had forbidden him to speak to her. That was unlikely, since Giyū was still accepting

Tsuneno's gifts of writing paper and enquiring about the snowshoes she had left in the house. But even her correspondence with Giyū was erratic. She did try. In the spring, she sent dolls for her nieces and other girls in the village, probably thinking they would arrive in time for the Girls' Festival, but she never received an acknowledgement. She was finally succeeding in Edo, but her family was even more distant than they had been in those early years, when she sent them letter after letter from her tenement.

Then, in the autumn of 1848, Tsuneno had a strangely vivid dream. Time had somehow moved in reverse, and she was a little girl again, playing at Rinsenji with her brothers. She awoke, disoriented, thinking how extraordinary it was, and just moments later a messenger appeared with a letter from Gisen. It said that he was gravely ill, probably dying, and he wanted to see her one last time. The dream had been an omen, she thought. She hadn't heard from her little brother in two years.

Tsuneno showed the letter to Hirosuke, but he was incredulous: 'Your brother disinherited us, and now that he's sick he's writing that he wants to see his older sister? What the hell is he thinking?' Unbeknownst to her, he already knew Gisen was dying. A few days earlier, a messenger had come to him bearing an apology from Gisen's deathbed. He turned the poor man away, unleashing a tirade about how poorly Gisen had treated him and Tsuneno. Hirosuke's status had changed, but his explosive temper hadn't changed at all.

Tsuneno called for a doctor, on her own, and sent him to see Gisen. Hirosuke didn't need to know. And a few days later, as the magistrate's household was busy preparing for a visit from Tōyama's second daughter and her family, Tsuneno slipped away and walked the two and a half miles to the temple Kyōshōji, where Gisen lay dying. She had spent a miserable four days there once, in the terrible winter of 1843, seeking refuge from her husband. Now, five years later, she came directly from the magistrate's office.

Tsuneno found Gisen lying on a futon. He had been there for some time, unable to move; he had dictated his last letter to Tsuneno because he couldn't hold a brush. A priest had taken an inventory of Gisen's belongings, and the abbot at Kyōshōji had slipped the list between his blankets. Everyone knew he was dying, and this was their way of making sure his affairs were in order. He was in no position to keep track of his things. For months, as his health declined, he had been trying to make contact with Tsuneno. He had sent for their mutual friend, the acupuncturist Yado Gisuke, and even pleaded with Hirosuke's younger brother, Hanzaemon, the gangster, to intervene. Gisen had always hated Hanzaemon, but now he found himself relying on the man he had once disparaged as a 'bad sort' and an 'idiot'. Gisen had every reason to believe he would never see any of his family again.

Tsuneno knelt by Gisen's futon, and he clasped her hands. They prayed together, and then she asked if he could eat or drink. What did he want? 'Grapes,' he said, 'or pears. Maybe little clams, if you could. I'd be grateful.' The acupuncturist Yado Gisuke was also there, and he and Tsuneno both asked if there was anything else they could do for Gisen, but he didn't speak. Maybe he couldn't. He and Tsuneno never discussed their past. She didn't mention their brothers, her marriage, or their long years of estrangement. She went home feeling like she'd failed.

Back at the South Magistrate's Office, the women of the household were still preoccupied with Tōyama's daughter's visit and everyone was busy preparing for an important event. The magistrate had been summoned to Edo Castle for a formal hearing in the presence of the shogun. These hearings were rare, held every several years at most, and the stakes were high. The City Magistrates,

Temple and Shrine Magistrates and Finance Magistrates would all be in attendance, along with the various inspectors, the chamberlain and all the elders. Each magistrate would be called upon to decide two cases before the assembled officials. After these events, the magistrates would receive gifts from the shogun, usually full sets of clothing. And if a magistrate performed particularly well, he might receive a special commendation. Tōyama achieved this distinction in 1841, but he couldn't rest on his reputation. In the days before his appearance, the entire household was occupied, arranging clothing, accessories and horses and accepting gifts and wishes of good luck.

Tsuneno was so busy that when the news of Gisen's death arrived, the day after she had gone to visit him, she couldn't get away. She went to Kyōshōji at dawn the next morning. Since she was Gisen's nearest relative, she prepared his body for the funeral rites. 'When it came time to wash the body, I had trouble because the smell was horrible,' she wrote. 'I poured the water over him all by myself, and then Hanzaemon and a temple manservant helped me wash him.' Later, Gisen was dressed in a plain robe, sewn together without knots, which might bind him to the karma of his past life. His fellow priests gathered to chant sutras and write his posthumous name, and then he was placed in a coffin. At the funeral, the assembled priests and mourners sang hymns to the accompaniment of drums and bells. They gave thanks to the Buddha. Then they carried Gisen's coffin to a temple by the Kozukappara execution ground on the edge of the city, where it was set into the fire, which would leave only ash and bone.

Tsuneno had been to many funerals – as a mourner and, long ago, as a priest's wife – but this was the first time she had tended to the body of one of her relatives. Properly speaking, it should have been Giyū's job, but he was far away in Echigo. He wrote and apologised for not making the trip; he asked Hirosuke and Tsuneno to send Gisen's ashes back to Rinsenji by messenger service.

Tsuneno seemed distressed that the funerary rituals had been left to strangers, that she had to pay people she barely knew to perform the services and write out his posthumous name. Writing to Giyū, she emphasised that she had done what she could. 'I poured the water over him myself,' she wrote, 'even though I could have paid someone to do it for me, because if I had it would have been a stranger.' But she admitted that his posthumous name had to be written in a stranger's hand, that this sacred task, which her family usually performed, had been reduced to an exchange of money paid and services rendered.

As it turned out, the aftermath of Gisen's death was unpleasant. Three temples quarrelled over who would perform (and be paid for) his funeral services. Even worse, the inventory of his possessions, which the Kyōshōji abbot had stashed in his futon, had gone missing. Tsuneno and her brother-in-law Hanzaemon had good reason to think that some of Gisen's things had been stolen, but they couldn't prove it. Hanzaemon considered taking the case to the Temple and Shrine Magistrates, but the evidence was conveniently missing, and in the end he concluded that it wasn't worth it and he didn't want to disrupt the funeral. Hirosuke and Tsuneno sent Giyū an inventory of what they had recovered, along with an accounting of their expenses in arranging the service and hosting mourners. They sold most of Gisen's clothes and donated the money to the temple, but they kept a few items to place in his coffin as offerings to the Buddha.

How strange to think that Gisen, the loyal, obedient brother, who had always done exactly what his older brother had asked, would end his life this way, betrayed by priests and temples, in the shadow of a mysterious crime. How strange to think that Tsuneno would be the one to care for him in the end.

*

The City Magistrate Tōyama specialised in endings. In the months he was on duty, he sat on his platform in the White Sands and sent people to their fate: usually banishment from Edo or beheading, sometimes burning at the stake. But those were the endings of other people's stories. He wasn't as good at managing his own.

By 1848, Tōyama had overseen thousands of cases; he had shouldered the heaviest responsibilities in the realm. He had been fired and rehired, criticised and commended, and he had survived. But the tasks of his office weighed on him like the stones his men stacked on criminals during jailhouse interrogations. There was always one more, and then another. It wasn't as easy to sit in judgement for hours every day.

He began to take months off, relying on his counterpart in the North Magistrate's Office to cover for his absences. One of Tōyama's relatives, a bannerman, had been apprehended for using the magistrate's exalted name to obtain credit at the rice markets in Osaka. It was humiliating, even though he had nothing to do with the crime. He fell ill more and more often. He withdrew.

Tsuneno was a decade younger than the magistrate, but she, too, was ageing, wondering about the end of her own story. She and Hirosuke had no heirs, no one to look after them when they were old. They discussed adopting a child and they had some offers from people in Edo, but they couldn't reconcile themselves to bringing in a stranger. It would be different if the child were a relative. Hirosuke, still wary of direct contact with Tsuneno's family, asked his brother to write to Giyū with a proposal. Would he send his daughter, Otake, to Hirosuke and Tsuneno? In the wake of Gisen's death, it must have seemed like the family could mend their disagreements.

If Giyū replied, the letter didn't survive. But how could he have sent his daughter, knowing what he knew about Hirosuke? It was a desperate, impossible request.

*

Giyū died about a year later, in the eleventh month of 1849. He had lived at Rinsenji all his life, raised five children, performed countless rites, intoned the sutras. He had embodied his father's hopes and then assumed his burdens. After fifty years, he had finally grown into the role that had so little suited him as a young man, and he died knowing that his own oldest son, Kihaku, had been ordained and would carry on the household. By the standards of his family, his village and his faith, Giyū was a great success. The records of his debts, his discontent, his catastrophic first marriage and his struggles with his siblings were all buried, lost in a mountain of routine correspondence.

For Tsuneno, Giyū's death marked the end of a lifelong argument. Their roles were opposed, and so were their personalities. He was insecure, anxious and introspective; she was impulsive and strong willed. When he pushed, she resisted. When she made plans, he stood in her way. They caused each other anguish, but neither one ever let go. More than her husband, more than Gisen, and even more than her mother, Giyū had been the constant in Tsuneno's life, the person who represented home, with all its constraining, reassuring familiarity. He was the baby who was born first, a boy, and received more gifts than she did. He was the child who could run when she could only crawl, the student who learned Chinese poetry while she practised sewing. He had left to be ordained when she had left to marry, stayed home when she ran away, and remained constant when she rebelled. He told her she was outrageous, stupid, ridiculous, bad-tempered and stubborn, and then he always gave in, because she was the stronger one, more self-assured. How would she know who she was when he was gone?

There would never be an answer. No more correspondence would arrive in Edo addressed in his elegant hand. There would be no further negotiations about money, no more tirades about Tsuneno's bad behaviour. In the end, neither of them won, and neither settled.

Echigo had never been so far away.

Chapter Nine

ENDINGS AND AFTERLIVES

Commodore Matthew Calbraith Perry received a telegram from Washington in January 1852: BE READY TO COMMAND THE EAST INDIA SQUADRON. He wasn't ready at all. He had served in two American wars – the War of 1812 and the Mexican–American War – hunted pirates, had ten children, nearly died of yellow fever and received the key to New York City. He had sailed across the Atlantic, along the coast of Africa and through the Mediterranean. But he had never seen the Pacific Ocean.

At age fifty-seven, Perry still had a full head of dark hair and an iron gaze, but he was not eager for new adventures. He thought that he would rather take over the Mediterranean Squadron and cruise around Europe with his family. He was also concerned that the navy had abolished flogging. How was he to maintain discipline? And he was suspicious of what he might be asked to do. Was he being dispatched to open trade with Japan, as the politicians in Washington had suggested? Or was he being sent as an ambassador of democracy, with the ultimate aim of changing the Japanese system of government? Perry was sceptical of the American zeal to convert old monarchies to new republics, which

223

had only heightened after the European revolutions of 1848. He thought that his countrymen should 'learn to let our neighbours' affairs alone, and look out for our own.'

He did, however, understand the importance of the mission. He had spent the previous four years on shore duty supervising the construction of new steamships at the Brooklyn Navy Yard. These state-of-the-art vessels were supposed to project American might into the world, but they could not make the trip across the Pacific to the treaty ports of China without taking on coal. The American secretary of state, Daniel Webster, was concerned for both commerce and war, and he expressed the national interest in creating a refuelling station as a matter of divine entitlement. Coal, he wrote, was 'a gift of Providence, deposited by the Creator of all things, in the depths of the Japanese islands, for the benefit of the human family.' Perry was less prone to hyperbole, but he could grasp the stakes, especially for the military. The US Navy could build all the steam warships it could afford, but without Japanese coal the United States would not be able to compete with the British in the East.

Perry asked for assurances. He wanted to choose his favourite officers to accompany him, and he wanted to be certain that he wouldn't meet the same ignominious fate as his old friend Biddle, pushed aside by an anonymous samurai. Perry also needed to know that he was authorised to use force if necessary. He wasn't going to go all the way across the world only to be politely rebuffed and sent on his way with a supply of drinking water and chickens.

Assurances granted, the old commodore prepared to set out to sea one more time. At first, the navy offered him the command of the *Princeton*, supposedly the latest in steam technology, but Perry was sceptical: the construction was terrible, the boiler unreliable. He chose, instead, his old favourite, the *Mississippi*, which had served him well in the Mexican–American War. She was a beautiful ship, a side-wheel steamer, and he had overseen her construction himself. She was graceful, powerful, with tall masts and modern eight-inch guns, capable of travelling at speeds of over seven knots, sure to make an impression on the Japanese.

Perry travelled from his home in New York City to Annapolis, where President Millard Fillmore boarded the *Mississippi* to wish the mission well. The ship took on coal, then travelled to Norfolk, Virginia, a town of six thousand, enslaved and free, the small, industrious suburb to a city of masts. There Perry oversaw the last stages of provisioning his ship, making sure he had everything: casks of water, fresh fruit and vegetables, hammocks, grog, instruments, pens and ink. And gifts for the Japanese, assembled over several months: agricultural tools and books, bolts of machine-woven cotton cloth and weapons from Samuel Colt. The most important piece of cargo was a letter from the President of the United States to the Emperor of Japan, rendered in English, Dutch and Chinese. It was a request for 'friendship' and 'commerce', specifically the provisioning of American vessels and the accommodation of shipwrecked American sailors. It touted the wealth of the new state of California – 'sixty million dollars of gold every year' – and boasted that American steamships could reach Japan in just eighteen days. The missive's appearance was equally confident and overbearing. It was a large parchment bound in blue silk velvet, resting in a rosewood case alongside the seal of the United States, which was fitted into its own solid gold box.

Finally, with the letter signed and ship provisioned, Commodore Perry was as prepared as he would ever be. At the command of the overloaded *Mississippi*, riding three feet deeper in the water than usual, he left Norfolk on 24 November 1852. He was going to Edo.

*

Tsuneno and Hirosuke were in service with yet another new master: Honda Suketoshi, the Lord of Iiyama Domain. His mansion was only a block away from where Tsuneno's first Edo employer, the bannerman Matsudaira Tomosaburō, had lived. It was a very short walk to Minagawa-chō, where she had spent her first miserable weeks in a tenement. But it wasn't exactly as if she had returned to where she started. Now she was married, with years in service to samurai households behind her. It had been nearly fifteen years since those early, disorientating days in the city, when she had stayed up past midnight in a cold tenement, burning through lamp oil and paper, writing letters to the family she was desperate not to lose. She was forty-eight, and nearly all her old correspondents had died. She hadn't been back to Echigo in nine years, and her connections to the countryside had worn thin. She still worked, she still struggled, and she could count her losses in faraway gravestones and in letters that never arrived. But she knew where she belonged. She could claim at least one small, hard-won victory: she was an Edoite at last.

Early in 1853, Tsuneno fell ill. She had been sick many times before – anyone who reached middle age in the nineteenth century was a survivor. But this time was different. It was one of the 'cold sicknesses', clearly: a fever and chills. Decades later, it might have been diagnosed more precisely as typhus, malaria or influenza. The weeks wore on, and she didn't improve. Hirosuke called a doctor, who sold them medicine, but the pills seemed to have no effect. He consulted another doctor, who offered a different medication, but Tsuneno refused to take it. 'I'm not changing now,' she said, and Hirosuke realised there was nothing to be done. She was as stubborn as always. Eventually, she recovered enough to drink a little sake, but she still seemed to be seriously ill. Hirosuke asked for leave from their employer. He insisted that he was doing everything he could: 'I'm looking after her all by myself,' he wrote in a shaky hand, sounding like the querulous old man he was.

Hirosuke wrote to Kihaku, Tsuneno's nephew, the child to whom she had once sent copper coins. 'He must be so big now!' she'd written in one of her letters to Giyū. That was years ago. Now he was ordained, the twenty-one-year-old head priest at Rinsenji. He hadn't seen his aunt since he was a boy. He wrote a polite message back and enclosed two small gold coins. He claimed he was embarrassed to send so little.

*

When Tsuneno came down with her fever, Commodore Perry and his men were in Mauritius, a sugar-producing island well east of Madagascar. Over the previous months, their ships had crossed the Atlantic and then rounded the Cape of Good Hope. Mauritius was of particular interest, and not only because the port facilities were in perfect order (Perry wanted to make a report to the US Lighthouse Board – they could learn a thing or two). It was also a place where Perry, no doubt thinking of political debates in the United States, could observe the consequences of the British Empire's abolition of slavery. Enslaved Africans had been replaced by Indian labourers, and the commodore wrote that he was favourably impressed, because the planters still managed to profit.

In the spring, as Tsuneno drifted through weeks of aches and chills, the ships made their steady progress across the Indian Ocean to Ceylon, through the Strait of Singapore, and on to Canton. Perry was disappointed with the legendary port city, full of 'wretched, half-clad people', 'poverty and filth'. The teenage purser's clerk aboard the *Mississippi*, who managed to disembark and spend a few days sightseeing, had a better time. He learned how to bargain, ate a few good meals and set off fireworks in the streets with his friends: 'the Chinamen must have thought that we were a set of demons just let loose'!

*

Tsuneno died a few weeks later. She had been sick for nearly three months by then; the days must have run together. She might not even have recognised the time of year – the very beginning of Edo summer, the season for wisteria and cuckoo calls, paper fans and mosquito nets, pedlars selling duck eggs and the doll market at Nihonbashi.

Someone knew the exact date and conveyed it to her family: it was the sixth day of the fourth month of Ka'ei 6. Tsuneno had always said that she wanted to go home when she was old. She had wanted to be near her family when she died. But she had chosen Hirosuke – and Edo – and she no longer belonged in Ishigami Village, at the temple near Big Pond.

When she left for Edo the first time, as a much younger woman, she had started a set of calculations in her head and then on the page. She recorded the coins she had left with her uncle and the clothes she had left at the pawnshop, the salaries she had earned at her various jobs, the rent money she owed to her superintendent, and the interest that accrued on her loans. Among these lists and calculations, she wrote of the gains and losses that couldn't be quantified. Her desire to see the city, finally fulfilled on a brilliant late-autumn day. Her humiliation, later, when she was forced to confront the truth about her travelling companion and what he had done to her. Her exhaustion and frustration at her first job; her delight in the food and hair oil and silver coins and famous names in the theatre district. Her hope in the husband she had chosen herself and then her rage at his failures. Her indignation when Gisen repudiated her and then her regret when he died. In the final calculation, she had gained a city and lost a province; gained a husband and lost a family; gained a measure of independence and lost the chance to have children of her own.

Maybe, by the time she put down her brush for the last time, she thought it was worth it.

*

To Perry and his men, the day Tsuneno died was Friday, 13 May 1853. They were stuck in Shanghai, where the commodore transferred his command from his beloved *Mississippi* to the more spacious *Susquehanna*. He would bring both ships to Japan; along the way, he would also meet up with the *Saratoga* and the *Plymouth*. That would give him a total of four vessels, more than enough to intimidate the Japanese.

In Shanghai, Perry had time to survey the political situation in East Asia. China was in turmoil from the Taiping Rebellion. 'It is not extravagant to suppose that these internal commotions are but the beginning of some great change in the condition of the eastern nations, and in connection with the extraordinary advances of the Anglo-Saxon race,' he wrote. While he had previously expressed reservations about messianic republicanism, he couldn't help predicting 'some mighty revolution which is to prostrate the despotic power which is now in the ascendant, and rear up in its place forms of government more consonant to the spirit and intelligence of the age.' When he went to Japan, he thought, he would hasten the work of time, dragging a left-behind country into the present.

He would spend the next day and much of the following night taking on coal, and then his ships would depart for the Japanese archipelago at last.

*

In the days after Tsuneno's death, someone had to handle the correspondence, the funeral and all the mundane routines of mourning. The rites might have been carried out at Tokuhonji or Kyōshōji, the temples where Tsuneno had the closest connections, but neither Hirosuke nor Kihaku was as diligent a record keeper or correspondent as Tsuneno and Giyū had been. Gisen's death, five years earlier, had been marked by lists and letters, but Tsuneno's was barely recorded at all. There was only a small slip of paper in the Rinsenji archive, a note of Tsuneno's date of death, her age and her posthumous name. In the afterlife, she would be known as 'Wise, Brilliant, Skillful, Obedient Woman'. 'Obedient.' It was her last transformation.

Hirosuke might have lived for thirty more years. He could have married again; he could have ended his life in the service of some other family or all alone in a tenement. He may even have returned to Echigo in the end, just as he'd always promised Tsuneno they would. He might have had another life or he might have died soon after she did, but none of it left a trace.

While Tsuneno still lived, her existence pulled Hirosuke to the page, brush in hand, to write to her brothers and leave something of himself behind. She conjured him in the lines of her letters: he schemed and plotted, slept and ate. He cajoled her with charming lines and irritated her with terrible ideas. He had altered the course of her life, and in exchange, she wrote his name and he lived, too. In the archives at Rinsenji, Hirosuke was a person, fully realised, Tsuneno's husband.

But when she died, she left him stranded on some distant shore of history. There was so much to mourn that he might not have understood: without her, he would be forgotten.

*

Tsuneno's forty-ninth-day memorial service was at the height of summer: 1 July, according to the Western calendar. Someone in Edo, or maybe in Echigo, said prayers and sang hymns as her spirit hovered between this realm and the next. There is no record.

Commodore Perry and his men were also in ambiguous territory. They had landed in the Ryūkyū Kingdom, a tributary state of Qing China that was militarily dominated by Japan. Perry understood that the islands were 'Japanese dependencies', and he was dogged at every turn by Japanese spies. After much insistence and negotiation, he managed to meet with the Ryūkyūan Queen Dowager's regent at her palace. He was impressed with the landscape and the food, but not the tea ('quite weak, and without sugar or milk') or the people ('deceitful and unscrupulous of truth'). He was much more taken with the Bonin Islands, due east, which reminded him of the Atlantic vineyard island, Madeira. But his men liked the people they encountered and were stunned by Ryūkyū's natural beauty. When the divers went under to check the ships, they found themselves in an underwater garden, full of live coral and bright, darting fish.

On 2 July, the day when Tsuneno's spirit was fully pacified and released into the Pure Land, Perry's ships departed Ryūkyū and headed for Edo. They steamed up the coast for the next five days, through a thick fog, which parted briefly to reveal a stunning view of Mt Fuji. Then, on 8 July, they dropped anchor at Uraga, about twenty-four miles from Edo, where the Japanese were expecting them. Immediately Perry's fleet was surrounded by boats. On one of them, a man held up a written proclamation in French demanding that the squadron leave. Perry refused, of course, and the purser's clerk aboard the *Mississippi*, watching the Japanese men gesture frantically, thought 'they must have all come to the opinion that we were a queer sort of people'.

He was right. News of the ships' arrival reached Edo immediately. By 1853, books about the Opium War were circulating widely and even some literate commoners understood the threat presented by black ships belching a noxious fog. City gossip turned from the usual chatter about fights and bathhouse fires to a tense discussion of the foreign ships and the fate of the Uraga Harbour Magistrate. Soon more boats started to appear around the fleet: ordinary people, hoping for a look.

Perry, who had not yet found an appropriate official to take receipt of his letter, threatened to deliver it himself. He turned his four ships and headed inland. By then, his vessels were surrounded by a hundred Japanese ships, most containing armed men, samurai. The *Mississippi* blew its steam whistle, an ear splitter screaming across the water. Some of the men in the junks abruptly stopped rowing, stood up and stared, dumbfounded, as if they had no idea what might happen next. Others beat a path towards shore.

The Americans' display of force had its intended effect. The next day, the Japanese arranged a place for Perry to deliver his message. On 14 July, he went to shore on a barge along with roughly four hundred men, including a brass band playing 'Hail Columbia', a slow passage punctuated by blasts of the *Mississippi*'s steam whistle. The young purser's clerk, who was on the barge, said it made the blood thrill in his veins, but he saw that the men onshore looked as if their last day had come. Perry, accompanied by two African-American bodyguards, was received by a large complement of shogunal officials. For more than a mile around the meeting site, the shore was lined with thousands of samurai. Two handsome cabin boys stepped forward to deliver Perry's missive in its wood and gold case. Perry said he would allow the Japanese a year to deliberate and then he would return. He exited the meeting to the strains of 'Yankee Doodle'.

In Edo, the mood was grim. The very centre of the city, Nihonbashi, was abandoned: no people carrying luggage across the bridge, no samurai out on errands and not a single boat on the river. The shops and stalls along the banks were all closed; the fish market was empty. A doctor who had been out for a walk wrote to his relatives in the provinces: 'It was deserted and lonely – truly disheartening. On blocks where on an ordinary day there would be crowds out on the streets past midnight, I could walk five or six blocks and only meet two or three people.'

The rank-and-file samurai in the city prepared for the ships to return, buying weapons and horse gear and practising gunmanship. Meanwhile, high-ranking officials of the shogunate planned, worried and sent around a memorandum asking the domain lords for advice. The emperor, Kōmei, opposed any treaty with foreigners that would allow them to invade his sacred islands. He fulminated in Kyoto; his opposition was well-known. But ultimately, the shogun's men believed they had no choice: they had seen the black ships and the guns. They could fire round after round of gunfire at Japanese coastal cities and burn them to the ground. They could blockade Uraga Harbour and doom Edo to starvation. When Perry returned, the shogun's men would negotiate a treaty.

Perry's return in the early spring of 1854 was an event. Commoners in Edo said that they were going on pilgrimage and snuck out to see the ships, which now numbered eight; some even hired fishing boats so that they could sail out and go aboard. For those who couldn't see the spectacle for themselves, artists produced broadsheets featuring illustrations of the belching ships and their extraordinary men. There was Perry, looking fat and droopy eyed; the American translator, looking pinched and scholarly; musicians with their instruments; and African-American sailors, dressed very poorly, flying through the rigging.

The two sides held a summit in a field near the village of Yokohama on 8 March. The commoner headmen in Edo had all been warned: they would hear loud noises, celebratory gunshots, but they should tell the townspeople not to panic. The Americans brought a contingent of over five hundred, including three different bands. People in Edo were interested in the menu, news of which had been leaked: it included an assortment of chicken wings, sashimi, pickled and fresh vegetables, several preparations of fish, two kinds of tea and, of course, sake. Rumour had it that the meals cost three gold pieces per American. The Perry expedition's artist, who sampled some of the food, was pleased but perplexed: the dishes defied description. There was no bread, and in its place there seemed to be some sort of very mild cheese. (It was tofu.)

The main event at the summit was the negotiation of the Treaty of Kanagawa, which opened two ports to American ships: Shimoda, just south of Edo, and Hakodate, on the northern island of Hokkaido. It also provided for an American consul to take up residence in Japan, with the ultimate aim of negotiating another, more extensive, commercial treaty. The Americans left satisfied with their progress. In the end, a man who accompanied the mission observed, 'It cannot be said that Japan ever really yearned to be "opened" any more than an oyster does; yet when that time came, she yielded as gracefully as any oyster I ever had the pleasure of meeting.'

There was only one major disappointment: Perry had wanted to anchor at Edo, so that he could see the city before he departed, but he was dissuaded by the high-ranking samurai who had negotiated the treaty. They explained that the appearance of Perry's squadron so close to the city was likely to cause a mass panic. If he persisted, they said, they would be held responsible and they would have no choice but to kill themselves. In the end, Perry brought his ships part of the way into the bay, to demonstrate that he could, and then turned them back. None of the men on Perry's mission saw Edo.

*

Perry returned a hero and spent the last years of his life burnishing his reputation: he had opened Japan. The textbooks would all tell the story of how he and his ships had played a part in making the modern world. They would not spare a word for Tsuneno. It was understandable. Why would they? She was an insignificant person who died before Perry arrived, and even if she hadn't, he would never have encountered anyone like her. He met with samurai, diplomats, men who mattered. Years later, they would get their mentions, too, names and dates neatly arrayed in dictionaries and encyclopaedias. To Perry – to all of them – women were not even background players in the drama of foreign relations. At best, they were stagehands, silently bringing props, then retreating to wherever they belonged.

Perry's ship was a world of men, and so was the negotiating table. Someone somewhere on dry land had attached each one of the eighteen buttons to the commodore's coat, had threaded a needle again and again to sew the fringe on his epaulets. But he didn't need to think about it. He couldn't be bothered with the person who polished the silver and scrubbed the floors at the naval commandant's house in Brooklyn or the person who was, at that very minute, caring for his grandchildren, ensuring that his name and his family would survive in the world.

When the samurai returned from their outing to Yokohama, someone would wash their clothes, too, and receive the gifts and enquiries from their neighbours, and check on the lessons for the children and the medicine for their parents. That night, and for all the nights afterwards, someone would clear away their trays and pour their tea and set out their futons and carry their water and light their lanterns and hold their babies and give directions to their servants and lie awake worrying over their coats and snowshoes and firewood and head colds and weddings and fortune-tellers and writing paper and copper coins. And each one of those women had her own motives, her reasons for staying or her plans for leaving, her ambitions and ideas, a thousand things to remember and even more that she would never write down.

Tsuneno couldn't have seen her life in heroic terms, as contributing to the building or opening of nations or the emergence of a new era. She was one person, an individual, a woman who made choices and – as she might have seen it – left very little behind. No children, no legacy. Just letters.

But if women like her hadn't come in from the countryside, Edo wouldn't have grown. If they hadn't washed floors, sold charcoal, kept the books, done laundry and served food, its economy could not have functioned. And if they hadn't bought theatre tickets, hairpins, bolts of cloth and bowls of noodles, the shogun's great city wouldn't have been a city at all. It would have been a dusty military outpost full of men, one of a thousand, not worth all the effort.

Tsuneno's legacy was the great city of Edo: her ambition, her life's work. Her aspiration for a different kind of existence propelled her from home, and she might have said that the experience of Edo changed her. But she also shaped the city. Every well she waited at; every copper coin she spent. Every piece of clothing she pawned or mended. Every tray she carried. The big decision to migrate and every tiny choice she made later, in the days and years that followed. They made households function and sent the pedlars on their rounds; they made it possible for the City Magistrate to issue his edicts; they sent the peasants out to the safflower fields in Dewa Province and the wholesalers to market in Kanda; they lit the lanterns in the Nakamura Theatre; they built the great stores at Nihonbashi. The city wasn't just a backdrop to Tsuneno's life. It was a place she created, day by day. And when she died, other women, other unknown people, would take up her work.

*

The year after Perry's ships departed, late at night on the second day of the tenth month, an earthquake struck Edo. Walls crumbled. Roofs collapsed. The shogun fled the interior of his castle and took refuge in the garden. The fire watchmen swayed in their towers. Braziers and lanterns overturned, and dry straw mats and floorboards ignited. In the dark hours of the early morning, lords dressed in firefighting garb rode through the streets to Edo Castle, navigating the rubble and dodging flames. They had to pay their respects, to make their concern known, to show that they were ready.

The earthquake discriminated – low-lying commoner districts were hit the hardest, places like Tsukiji, where Tsuneno's uncle Bunshichi had lived, and the crowded neighbourhood near Kanda

Myōjin. Surugadai, where Tsuneno had been in service, occupied high land that was more stable. But the fires that came amid the aftershocks tore through tenements and mansions alike. On Lords' Row, not a single compound was spared. The South Magistrate's Office was miraculously untouched, but the lords' mansions surrounding it burned. Part of the problem was that the lords had been stockpiling firearms in the aftermath of Perry's mission and when the flames breached their storehouses they exploded. In the Lord of Aizu's residence alone, 130 men and thirteen horses perished.

In the entire city, roughly seven thousand died and fifteen thousand buildings were destroyed in the earthquake and its aftermath. For months, people squatted in temporary shelters. Although the bathhouses and barber shops managed to reopen within days, the provisioning of the city had been so thoroughly disrupted that not a single pedlar could make the rounds. Miso, salt and pickles were in short supply, and there were reports that samurai in some of the bannermen's households had resorted to digging out and eating the grains of rice that had been plastered into the barrack walls as adhesive. If there had been an ordinary fire, then some of the city would have been spared and it would have been easier to return to normal. But in this case, all of Edo was struck and people across the city suffered.

Perry didn't cause the earthquake, but the people of Edo imagined that the black ships and the shaking of the earth were related catastrophes. A folk belief held that earthquakes were caused by a giant subterranean catfish. When the fish thrashed, the ground trembled. In over four hundred anonymous broadsheets issued after the disaster, artists portrayed the catfish, his victims and his beneficiaries: the carpenters, plasterers and roof tile merchants who made money rebuilding. In one print, the black catfish appeared as a black steamship, belching coins in place of steam, promising foreign trade and profit. In another, the catfish and Perry engaged in an intense match of tug-of-war, with an Edo plasterer as the referee. 'Stop this useless talk of trade!' the catfish yells. 'What are you talking about, you stupid catfish?' Perry replies. 'Mine is the country of benevolence and compassion.' The lines connecting the earthquake and the foreign threat weren't clear, and people weren't entirely certain whether the catfish was a tormentor or a saviour. But they sensed that the ground they stood on was unstable.

Other, long-term reverberations of Perry's mission were intense and destructive. The shogunate signed commercial treaties with all the great Western powers, not only the United States. In 1858, a series of agreements called the Ansei Treaties stipulated that the United States, Russia, the United Kingdom, France and the Netherlands would all be allowed to appoint consuls and come to trade at Japan's designated open ports. They would also pay fixed tariffs, which meant that the Japanese could not set their own rates. Emperor Kōmei, who had continued to oppose the agreements, served as a rallying point for opposition to the shogun's policies. Soon radical samurai issued calls to heed the emperor's wishes and eject the foreigners: 'revere the emperor and expel the barbarian!' In 1863, the shogun, whose predecessors hadn't left Edo in hundreds of years, went all the way to Kyoto to be received by the emperor. He was trying to forestall a rebellion.

Tsuneno's first, brief employer, the bannerman Matusdaira Tomosaburō, was caught in the middle of the political turmoil. Well before Tsuneno died, he was adopted by the Lord of Kameyama Domain, near Kyoto, and became the new lord himself, assuming the name Nobuyoshi. Still ambitious and talented, he became a shogunal elder and was appointed as emissary to the foreign powers. This was a prestigious position but a thankless one. The shogunate's negotiating position was always fairly weak, and dealing with foreigners on the shogun's behalf made him a target for xenophobic radicals.

Tomosaburō suffered his worst crisis in 1862, when samurai from the powerful southwestern domain of Satsuma murdered a British trader who had wandered into their lord's retinue on the Tōkaidō Highway. In truth, some of the British man's compatriots thought he had it coming: he was often drunk, loud and obnoxious. But the British couldn't ignore the insult, and they demanded that the shogunate execute the men responsible and pay an indemnity. It was a staggering sum, a third of the shogun's annual income. It fell to Tomosaburō to help negotiate the agreement, which radicals vehemently opposed. They were armed, increasingly well-organised, and dangerous, but they were not Tomosaburō's main concern. He was afraid that the British might bombard Edo if their demands were not met. He made plans to evacuate the shogun's ladies from Edo Castle and issued an order to temporarily change the course of the Tōkaidō Highway to protect it from an attack from the sea. He also devised a strategy to calm the city when the townspeople panicked and started hoarding food. In 1839, when he was the young, up-and-coming bannerman who hired Tsuneno, none of it would have seemed possible.

Edo escaped bombardment, but the shogunate had to pay the indemnity and offer apologies, which further inflamed its domestic critics. Meanwhile, beginning in 1859, European and American merchants came to trade at the open port of Yokohama. There weren't that many of them – roughly one or two hundred by the 1860s – but they made their presence known, buying up silk thread, drinking like fiends, butchering cattle and racing their horses through people's rice fields. Japanese merchants flocked to the port, selling silk and cows, offering services and changing currency. Foreigners buying up gold coins caused massive inflation in Edo; the cost of living rose 50 percent. The city withered as trade began to head directly to Yokohama, bypassing the old Edo wholesalers. Then, in 1862, hundreds of thousands of samurai left after the shogun relaxed the requirement that lords spend one year of every two in his capital. Between 1862 and 1868, Edo lost half its population.

The city was already on its knees when it received the final blow: an uprising led by samurai from the southwest, whose calls to 'revere the emperor' were now accompanied by a more ominous phrase, 'topple the shogunate'. They took Kyoto and then advanced on Edo. The last Tokugawa shogun had already resigned his office. Unlike all of his predecessors, he had never lived in Edo Castle; he had spent the entirety of his short reign in the vicinity of Kyoto, trying to placate the emperor and his allies. When he realised that the rebels intended to abolish the shogunate and seize his lands, he fled by ship, back to Edo, to raise the resistance. But by then he was powerless.

The defence of the city was left in the charge of an Edo native, a bannerman's son. His father was Katsu Kokichi, the feckless samurai who had lied, stolen and gambled his way through the city in the years when Tsuneno was working as a maidservant. Kokichi's son turned out to be his opposite in temperament: 'serious', 'frugal' and 'never wasteful'. As a young adult, he became famous for his study of Western military technology and his (then iconoclastic) opinion that the shogunate needed to build a modern navy. Like nearly everyone else in Edo, he, too, changed his name, choosing 'Kaishū,' using the characters for 'sea' and 'ship'.

In 1860, ten years after his father's death, Kaishū became the captain of the *Kanrin Maru*, the first Japanese vessel to sail to the United States. He spent months in San Francisco and then went overland to New York, where his group paraded down Broadway in a scene immortalised by Walt Whitman: 'Courteous, the Princes of Asia, swart-cheek'd princes, / First-comers, guests, two-sworded princes, / Lesson-giving princes, leaning back in their open barouches, bare-headed, impassive, / This day they ride through Manhattan.' Back at home, Kaishū paired his straw sandals and split-toed socks with a pair of Western-style trousers. He wore his short sword tucked into his belt as if it were a pistol in a holster. He had inherited his father's Edo swagger, if not his personality.

When the loyalist forces reached Edo, on a dismal spring day in 1868, Kaishū negotiated the surrender of the castle. He could see the end coming, and he wanted to spare Japan a bloody civil war that would make it vulnerable to foreign domination. In his account of the negotiations over the surrender, written much later, he recalled that he had told the leader of the invading army, 'If you are bent on threatening weak people with brutal force, we shall not shrink from accepting the challenge. Even as it is, we are making ourselves the laughing stock of foreign nations. If you will spare the city, I will be personally and officially grateful even unto death.' This posture earned him the criticism of his fellow shogunal officials and more than one attempted assassination. But it worked. He handed over the castle, and his city – his father's city, Tsuneno's city – didn't burn.

Still, Edo was a ghost of what it had been and only the barest shadow of what it would become. It had been fifteen years, barely a moment, since Tsuneno had died and Perry's ships had anchored at Uraga. But the world she had known, the bannermen in their ranks, the City Magistrate in his office, the shogun in his castle, the retainers in their barracks, it was over.

*

If Tsuneno had lived a little longer, she would have seen a new city, Tokyo, emerge from the destruction. The rebirth wouldn't have surprised her: the Edo she knew had survived fires, earthquakes, a famine and Mizuno Tadakuni's disastrous reforms. But other changes would have been astounding. Women of her generation witnessed things they never would have imagined.

Matsuo Taseko, a poet born into a rural family in 1811, was roughly the same age as Tsuneno's little sisters. In her fifties, she became a loyalist political activist. In the third month of 1869, she was in Kyoto to see the emperor she still venerated leave his capital for the last time. He rode in an enclosed palanquin, surrounded by a procession of warriors and courtiers. The imperial court had been in Kyoto since its founding, nearly eleven hundred years earlier. Now the emperor would reign from Edo Castle. It was a drastic shift, the end of an era. Before the shogun fell, none of the Japanese emperors had ever been to Edo. They had never even seen Mt Fuji. But the architects of the new regime argued that the move was necessary, both for the sake of the nation and for the shogun's former capital. Kyoto had traditional arts and history, and Osaka had commerce. Without the national government, they feared, Tokyo had nothing.

But Tokyo thrived beyond their wildest imaginings once it was firmly established as Japan's imperial capital. The places Tsuneno had known were thoroughly transformed. Tsukiji, where the great Honganji temple looked out to sea, became a foreign quarter in the 1860s. Its centrepiece was a new famous place of the capital: the

Hoterukan, also known to foreigners as the Yedo T'skege Hotel, a massive building with a curved gate and bright red shutters, crowned by an incongruous weather vane festooned with bronze bells. A grassy area nearby became known as Navy Field because it was home to naval schools and training facilities, but it was still empty enough that children went there in the summer to catch grasshoppers. It was only in the twentieth century that Tsukiji became synonymous with the greatest fish market in the world.

Minagawa-chō, the obscure neighbourhood in Kanda where Tsuneno had rented a tenement, was almost as unknown in the 1880s and 1890s as it had been when Tsuneno lived there fifty years earlier. But its neighbour, Mikawa-chō, became famous for its overcrowded dosshouses, pawnshops, cheap restaurants and cholera outbreaks. It was featured several times in a muckraking book called *In Darkest Tokyo*. Tsuneno, who had spent some of the darkest months in her life in that part of the city, would have recognised the portrayal of boarding houses full of desperate men, many of them migrants. But she was blessedly ignorant of cholera, which was first introduced to the city in 1858 by the same foreign ships that brought so much else from the outside world.

Sumiyoshi-chō, where Tsuneno had worked at Iwai Han-shirō V's rear residence, was incorporated into the larger neighbourhood of Doll Town. In the first years of the new era, a popular shrine relocated to the area and took over the role the kabuki and puppet theatres had once played in attracting revellers. For a time, it was the most prosperous shopping district in all of Tokyo, and a print of the neighbourhood in the 1880s depicted its crowning glory: a towering brick chimney, blowing smoke over throngs of shoppers.

Ginza, where Tsuneno's favourite employer worked, went through a more dramatic transformation. It burned down in 1872, in a conflagration that also destroyed the Tsukiji Hotel. Carrying on the grand tradition of Edo urban redevelopment, the new government used the disaster as an excuse for a new round of city planning. Ginza became a neighbourhood of brick buildings, glass windows and gas lamps, with wide streets and paved sidewalks. Woodblock print artists loved the idea – another new famous place! – and they depicted it as a bustling district of horse-drawn carriages and rickshaws, full of stylish men who accessorised their kimonos with black umbrellas and bowler hats. In fact, few people wanted to live in the new 'bricktown', since the buildings were stuffy and damp. For decades, even the celebrated wide streets looked slightly awkward, with scrappy little trees planted directly in the road. Still, it was an important symbol of what modern Tokyo might become, someday.

Echigo changed, too. Ishigami Village merged with its neighbours to become a new entity, Meiji Village, named after the emperor. Kihaku applied to the new local government for a permit to brew sake, and he donated fourteen yen for the construction of a public elementary school. The next generation, boys and girls, would study the same subjects, side by side. When Kihaku was young, he had learned what his father and grandfather had learned before him. He had been taught to identify himself by his village and province. But his grandchildren would learn to say that they were Japanese, from Niigata Prefecture.

In 1886 a train station opened in Takada, and by 1894 there were six departures a day through the mountains to Nagano. The days of women travelling around the barrier at Sekikawa, or sneaking through the dog door, were long gone. Within only a few decades, the journeys that had taken Tsuneno ten days, and which cost her so much sorrow, took only one very long day of travel, including a transfer, and cost about two yen. The train arrived in Tokyo at the new Ueno Station, near Kyōshōji, where she had once visited her dying brother.

Tsuneno might have lived to see all of it. Matsuo Taseko, the loyalist activist, died in 1894. She survived to see her grandchildren marry and begin lives of their own. The girls of that generation, born around the time of the fall of the shogunate and the restoration of the emperor in 1868, inherited a different world. On the surface, most led lives much like their mothers' and grandmothers', preoccupied with running households, tending to babies, labouring on farms, working as maids, washing laundry and making dinner. But their aspirations shifted: new things were possible. Some of them were the first to travel abroad, the first to go to universities, the first to publish autobiographies and go on lecture tours. One member of that generation, the daughter of an Echigo samurai, became a celebrated American writer. She was born in the snow country in 1874, in a castle town much like Takada, a place Tsuneno would have recognised. She died in 1950, in New York City, where she taught the Japanese language at Columbia University. She felt like she'd lived hundreds of years in one generation.

*

But Tsuneno didn't live, and she had no children. She would never welcome a granddaughter home from elementary school, tug on the edges of the bow in her hair, set her books aside and ask about what she'd learned: the emperor on his white horse, the countries of the world, the magic of a telegraph, the technology of a postage stamp. She would never lean across a low table, cradling an imported teacup between her stiff fingers, and listen to the little girl chatter about the boy in her class who teased her or the friend who spilled her ink across the desk.

If Tsuneno's life had gone just a little differently – if Giyū had sent her his daughter, Otake; if she'd survived the spring of 1853 to see Perry's ships arrive in Uraga; if she'd managed to endure the fires and earthquakes and epidemics of the subsequent decades, as so many others did, what then? What would she have said, if she had the chance, sitting in a little room in a city called Tokyo, if the girl was tired and, wanting to avoid her homework, asked her grandmother for a story?

If Tsuneno had lived, she might have been guarded, reluctant to tell a story that included so much heartbreak, so many choices that wouldn't make sense to a younger woman who grew up in a different age. She might have been a difficult, short-tempered grandmother the way she was always a difficult, short-tempered wife. She might not have had time for stories. She might have wished that Giyū had burned her letters.

But maybe she would set the cup down and let her tea get cold. Maybe she would want to tell her story, her side of it, at last. It would be better than her brothers' story and certainly better than a historian's, full of 'maybes' and 'might haves'. If Tsuneno spoke, and kept speaking, her voice might fill the room. She would sound like her mother and her sisters, with the Echigo accent she had never lost.

'Oh, it was so long ago,' she might say. And then time would run backwards – the emperor would retreat into the shadows of his Kyoto palace; the bricks of Ginza would dissolve into the earth. The signals would vanish from the telegraph wires, and the rickshaws would turn back into palanquins. The train line from Takada would sink into the dust, and the snow would settle in the mountain passes. Tokyo, a dot on a map of the world, would lose its shape; its edges would run and bleed. As the tall buildings fell to earth, the old wooden fire towers would climb and the alleys

would expand, mazelike. The pedlars would appear, singing all
the old songs, the patrolmen and fingertips would come by on
their rounds, and the women gathered by the well would scrounge
for old copper coins. The boats would gather for the fish market
at Nihonbashi; the samurai would proceed in ranks through Ōtemon Gate. Edo's morning glories would bloom on their trellises,
the last great City Magistrate would ascend his platform in the
White Sands, and Hanshirō V would make his entrance from the
back of the theatre, gliding across the catwalk on his high clogs,
black eyes shining.

The city would be endless, again, and her story would begin.

EPILOGUE

A hundred and eighty years after Tsuneno walked into Edo, I brought my younger son to Tokyo. It was the same season – a bright day somewhere between late autumn and early winter, with not a trace of snow in the air. We came from the airport via the Narita Express, a train that opened to much fanfare in the early 1990s, the height of the 'bubble era', when it seemed as if Japan might take over the world. We sped past tiny rice fields and through the wilds of suburban pachinko parlours and entertainment complexes. Then we dove into a tunnel and were delivered into the heart of what is, once again, the largest city in the world.

That night, my four-year-old son sat by the window of our hotel room on the thirty-seventh floor, watching the trains come and go from Tokyo Station. They looked like toys: grass green and vivid orange. Over the following days, he fell in love with the machines that sucked his subway tickets from his fingers and spit them back half a second later. He stood mesmerised in front of the vending machines, staring at the strange array of bottles; he was shocked by the rows of roasted whole fish in the department store food hall. He went to a contemporary art museum and danced under a waterfall of streaming neon lights. To him, that was Tokyo: a child's city, where everything was new.

I saw the city I had known for more than twenty years, a grey tangle of steel and concrete stretching from the bay to the mountains. Thirteen subway lines and thirty-six rail and monorail lines, swirling around the green space of the Imperial Palace. Thirty-eight million people – in business suits and kimonos, gauzy tutus, skinny jeans, school uniforms, prairie dresses – riding escalators, waiting in line for pastries, reading paperback novels, drinking coffee and staring at their phones. An infinite city, the backdrop to so many years and summers of study – a second home.

But after following Tsuneno's life for nearly a decade, I could also see the barest outlines of a different, older, city: the one she knew, where the skyscrapers were rickety fire towers and the sound of traffic was the clomping of wooden clogs on dirt, where the grounds of the Imperial Palace were the precincts of Edo Castle. Somewhere among the glass and steel towers in Shinjuku, Tsuneno and Hirosuke had tried to run a restaurant; near the monuments in Ueno Park, she knelt by her younger brother's deathbed and said good-bye. A short walk from the grand department stores and luxury boutiques in Ginza, she passed through the long hallways of the South Magistrate's Office.

Most of the physical landscape of Tsuneno's city is gone, levelled by earthquakes, fires and firebombs. There are a few exceptions: one of the red gates to the Lord of Kaga's mansion, which Tsuneno might have passed on her way into the city, still stands at the entrance to the main campus of Tokyo University, and the Fujimi watchtower of Edo Castle still looks out over the city from its base of heavy grey stones. But most of Edo dwells in the realm of collective memory. It lives under glass at museums and in a corner of every bookstore, in the shopping arcades of working-class neighbourhoods, and in the kitchens of old restaurants devoted to eel or noodles. One of the newest Tokyo subway lines is called the Great Edo Line, which seems fitting: the old city still runs just beneath the surface of the new one, moving to its own subterranean rhythm. But you have to know where it is, how to feel its presence.

At home, if I mention Edo in a seminar room, or at an airport, or at a school bus stop, the word meets with blank stares, even among people who would instantly recognise Tokyo. Important elements of Edo's popular culture – kabuki, geisha and woodblock prints – are presented as generically Japanese and timeless. Hokusai's *Great Wave* is an icon, spraying its foam across shopping bags and coffee mugs, but the city that produced his work, where he sat in restaurants and dashed off paintings for adoring crowds, has disappeared. Where there should be a living, noisy, chaotic place called Edo, there is blankness or, at best, a refined and static culture, something foreign and out of reach.

But Edo is knowable, and so are its people, even the ones who did not leave great names or achievements in their wake. They couldn't see what was coming, that their city would be renamed, that the shogunate would fall, that their old wooden neighbourhoods would be replaced by brick and stone, then steel and concrete. They couldn't foresee how quickly and catastrophically their world would expand, that their own endless city would become one global capital among many, another dot on the map. But these people left their stories for us to find, not as representatives of Japan or a vanished traditional culture, but as the lifeblood of a great, vibrant city, people who walked on muddy streets, had trouble sleeping when their neighbours were noisy, and spent their money on ink and paper so they could write letters home. Their voices, which reach us from 170 years and half a world away, can seem startlingly familiar. They tell us about the noise and crush of cities, the aspiration, the energy, the costs. As long as their writings survive, Tsuneno's world, which seems so far from our own, isn't quite lost yet.

ACKNOWLEDGEMENTS

Japanese archivists work creatively and tirelessly to conserve materials and educate the public, including foreign researchers like me. During the course of my research, the entire staff of the Niigata Prefectural Archives was enormously helpful; they marked up finding aids (back when they were still on paper), showed me the basement storage area where they keep the Edo period weapons, and, on one memorable occasion, confirmed Tsuneno's birth date when I discovered it scrawled on the back of a document. I owe special thanks to Tamiya Minako, Minagawa Kazuya and Ozaki Noriko. At the Tokyo Metropolitan Archives, the head archivist, Nishiki Kōichi, and Hirose Sanae were thoughtful and generous guides to the material. At the Ōishida History Museum and Archives, Ōtani Toshitsugu patiently explained the history of the town. Other archivists and public historians created the comprehensive city, village and prefectural histories that I referred to constantly. Their work made this book possible.

Other Japanese scholars were extraordinarily generous with their time and expertise. The historian Asakura Yūko at Jōetsu Kyōiku Daigaku took me on a tour of the area where Tsuneno grew up, and shared her deep knowledge of the region. The great historian of Edo, Yoshida Nobuyuki, wrote much of the scholarship that informs my portrait of the city. He and Yoshida Yuriko helped me interpret two of my most difficult documents, even reading one of them off my tiny phone screen while riding in the back of a taxi. I'm also grateful to Yokoyama Yuriko for sharing her rigorous analysis of women's and gender history and Waka Hirokawa for insights into the history of medicine. Finally, my first Japanese mentor, Yabuta Yutaka, will recognise his influence in these pages. He gave me my first paleography dictionary, and he will be gratified to know I've used it so much that it has completely fallen apart.

Reading the documents for this project often felt like an impossible task, and sometimes the handwriting was beyond my ability to decipher. My friend and colleague Murayama Kōtarō helped me read the first of the documents and get some sense of how Tsuneno's writing worked. Laura Moretti and Yamasaki Yoshiro shared their expertise when I hit a wall. Yamagata Takashi was a wonderful reader and explainer of documents. I couldn't have completed the project without his transcriptions of some of Giyū's and Gisen's correspondence.

While writing this book, I was lucky to receive generous funding from the National Endowment for the Humanities, the Japan-US Friendship Commission, the Alice Kaplan Institute for the Humanities and the Weinberg College of Arts and Sciences at Northwestern University. My scholarly community also offered invaluable support. Fabian Drixler and Satoko Shimazaki read chapters and offered brilliant commentary, and Andrew Leong helped with tricky readings. Evan Young introduced me to Iseki Takako's diary. Daniel Botsman, David Howell, Luke Roberts, Anne Walthall, Sarah Maza, Deborah Cohen, Tom Gaubatz and Laura Hein read through the entire manuscript and offered comments at a book workshop sponsored by the Northwestern History Department – they improved the book immensely. I'm especially grateful to Dani for enduring years of email about this project. I also thank my long-distance Japanese history writing group – David Spafford, Morgan Pitelka and Maren Ehlers – for their encouragement.

In Evanston, thanks to Youjia Li, Rajeev Kinra, Melissa Macauley, Peter Carroll, Haydon Cherry, Peter Hayes, Caitlin Fitz, Ed Muir, Daniel Immerwahr, Ken Alder, Edward Gibson and Adrian Randolph; to my original leave-year writing group: Kevin Boyle, Susan Pearson, Geraldo Cadava, Helen Tilley and Michael Allen; to Annerys Cano, Susan Delrahim, Eric West, Tricia Liu and Jasmine Bomer. Elsewhere, I'm also grateful to Andrew Gordon, Deborah Baker, Scott Brown and Janice Nimura for their advice and support at various points in the project.

An amazing group of women brought this book into the world. Jill Kneerim and Lucy Cleland saw the potential in this project about an obscure woman in a faraway place. Kathy Belden was a brilliant editor and champion, as was Becky Hardie at Chatto & Windus in the UK.

Thank you to my friends: Deborah Cohen, my first and most indispensable reader; Laura Brueck and Sarah Jacoby, my writing squad at Waysmeet; the Amagais of Tokyo and the American Midwest; and the Strong Female Protagonists: Liz Marsham, Jennie Connery and Jessica Jackson, fighting patriarchy while evenly distributed across US time zones.

And finally, thank you to my family: John and Barbara Stanley; Kate Stanley, Doug Hopek and their family; all the Zakarins; and especially my two little boys, Sam and Henry. My husband, Brad, can make me laugh in almost any situation – he really is the love of my life.

NOTES

Prologue

xvii 1801: In the West, 1801, not 1800, was recognised as the first year of the new century.

xvii President John Adams opened: Emerson and Magnus, *The Nineteenth Century and After*, 77.

xvii Napoléon: Schwartz, *Century's End*, 144.

xvii the French republican calendar: Shaw, *Time and the French Revolution*, 103–4.

xvii 'a greater change': *The Messenger* (New Haven, CT), January 1, 1801. Similarly, *The American Citizen and General Advertiser* predicted 'a new era commencing in which principle, talents, and republican character will become triumphant over villainy, ignorance and personal vice' and peace and happiness would extend to the 'friends of liberty in every part of the world.' *The American Citizen and General Advertiser*, January 1, 1801.

xviii 1.2 million: on estimates of the population, Takeuchi, *Edo shakaishi no kenkyū*, 17–19.

xviii One of the bills: Rinsenji monjo #587. I use short form citations for the Rinsenji monjo. For the full titles, authors and dates of each document, please refer to the searchable online finding aid at the Niigata Prefectural Archives (https://www.pref-lib.niigata.niigata .jp/?page_id=569). The reference number for the Rinsenji monjo is E9806.

xix Emon's neighbours had already mended: Suzuki, *Snow Country Tales*, 9–21.

257

xix curving pathways and small canals: Rinsenji monjo #1452.

xix Emon's family: Niigata kenritsu bunshokan, ed., 'Shozō monjo annai.'

xix Takeda Shingen, the Tiger of Kai: Sato, *Legends of the Samurai*, 204–31.

xix Japan's new military hegemon, the forerunner to the shogun, sorted: Berry, *Hideyoshi*.

xx every corner of his daily life: Howell, *Geographies of Identity in Nineteenth-Century Japan*.

xxi difficult year: 'Ōgata daiakusaku ni tsuki sho haishaku nado gansho,' in Ōgata chōshi hensan iinkai, ed., *Ōgata chōshi, shiryō-hen*, 219–20.

xxi boxes full of paper: these items, now removed from their boxes and neatly filed, comprise the Rinsenji monjo (E9806), kept at the Niigata Prefectural Archive in Niigata City.

xxi astonishing number: the estimation of one in five is based on Tone Keizaburō's study of school attendance in farming villages in the Kantō region, where people were relatively well educated. Rubinger, *Popular Literacy in Early Modern Japan*, 131.

xxiii on a website: https://www.pref-lib.niigata.niigata.jp/?page_id=569.

Chapter One: **Faraway Places**

1 Baby gifts: Rinsenji monjo #1012.

1 didn't have a name: Bacon, *Japanese Girls and Women*, 2–3.

1 didn't survive: Somewhere around 40 percent of infant deaths occurred during the first month of life. Drixler, *Mabiki*, 252.

1 customary: See a similar example in Ōguchi, *Edojō ōoku o mezasu mura no musume*, 27–28.

2 midwives: The Rinsenji birth records always listed the names of at least two village women as midwives, whom they paid with gold coins. On the tasks of midwives, see Yonemoto, *The Problem of Women*, 247, n. 41.

2 nappies: Horikiri, *The Stories Clothes Tell*, 16–17.

3 country songs: Tamanoi, 'Songs as Weapons.'

4 half the land: *Kubiki sonshi: tsūshi-hen*, 398.

4 Yamadas of Hyakukenmachi: *Kubiki sonshi: tsūshi-hen*, 402.

4 spent money freely: See the examples in Takahashi, *Mura no tenarai-juku*, 16–17.

5 Shinran: Dobbins, *Letters of the Nun Eshinni*.

5 'This is truly a sect': Teeuwen and Nakai, eds., *Lust, Commerce, and Corruption*, 164.

5 tended to raise large families, believing that infanticide . . . was a sin: Drixler, *Mabiki*, 42–43.

5 'all the treasures that fill three thousand worlds': Tokuryū (1772–1858), *Bōmori kyōkai kikigaki*, translated and quoted in Starling, 'Domestic Religion in Late Edo-Period Sermons,' 281.

6 something even a toddler could say: There was some debate over whether toddlers could be saved. See Drixler, *Mabiki*, 54.

6 local accent: We know this from how she writes words in her letters. 'Ido' for 'Edo,' or 'maeru' for 'mairu.' For a discussion of women's use of dialect in their writings, see Yabuta, *Joseishi to shite no kinsei*, 275–91.

6 'paddle' through powdery snow: Suzuki, *Snow Country Tales*, 13–16, 149, 168.

6 Kōtoku: The family called him Izawa Kōtoku, and he was a doctor in Takada. See Rinsenji monjo #2111. Tsuneno called him 'older brother.' Rinsenji monjo #1709.

7 By midwinter, it was so high: Suzuki, *Snow Country Tales*, 13–16.

7 'What enjoyment is there': Suzuki, *Snow Country Tales*, 9.

7 'freezing from equinox to equinox': *Kubiki sonshi: tsūshi-hen*, 53.

8 Big Pond and Little Pond: *Kubiki sonshi: tsūshi-hen*, 336.

8 brightly coloured maps: Rinsenji monjo #1451, Rinsenji monjo #1452.

8 Inō Tadataka: Wigen, *A Malleable Map*, 93–97; Frumer, *Making Time*, 94–101.

8 surveyor's diary: Sakuma, ed., *Inō Tadataka Sokuryō nikki*, 69.

8 map of southern Echigo: Inō, 'Echigo: Echigo, Tagiri, Takada, Tonami' [map], in *Dai-Nihon enkai yochi zenzu*, vol. 80 (1821), accessed through National Diet Library Digital Collection, http://dl.ndl.go.jp/info:ndljp/pid/1286631?tocOpened=1.

9 Japanese natural scientists: Marcon, *The Knowledge of Nature and the Nature of Knowledge in Early Modern Japan*, 256–59.

9 seven or eight: For examples of girls beginning education at that age, see Takai, *Tenpōki, shōnen shōjo no kyōyō keisei katei no kenkyū*, 21; Etsu Inagaki Sugimoto, a samurai daughter from Echigo, refers to an 'after the sixth-birthday school,' *Daughter of the Samurai*, 17. On girls' school attendance and education in general see Rubinger, *Popular Literacy in Early Modern Japan*, 120–24, 133–36; Kornicki, 'Women, Education, and Literacy,' in Kornicki, Patessio, and Rowley, eds., *The Female as Subject: Reading and Writing in Early Modern Japan*, 7–38; and Corbett, *Cultivating Femininity*, 37–41.

10 forced to apologise: Kornicki, 'Women, Education, and Literacy,' 12.

10 A sophisticated girl: Takai, *Tenpōki, shōnen shōjo no kyōyō keisei katei no kenkyū*, 24–25; Yabuta, 'Nishitani Saku and Her Mother: "Writing" in

the Lives of Edo Period Women,' in Kornicki, Patessio and Rowley, eds., *The Female as Subject*, 141–50.

10 village school: On schooling, see Rubinger, *Popular Literacy in Early Modern Japan*, 127–36; Takai gives an example of a female teacher in Kiryū who took both female and male students, *Tenpōki, shōnen shōjo no kyōyō keisei katei no kenkyū*, 20–24. Giyū's son Kihaku (later Gien) would study with a local teacher for instruction in the 'four Chinese classics and the five sutras,' Rinsenji monjo #1645.

10 *Primer on Names*: (*Nagashiraji tsukushi*) Takahashi, *Mura no tenaraijuku*, 29–30.

10 counties of Echigo: These textbooks were compiled at a very local level, so that a school in Kubiki would have its own *Village Primer* (*Murana*) with a list of nearby villages, mountains, et cetera. There was a separate primer for the names of all the provinces. Koizumi Yoshinaga, 'Learning to Read and Write: A Study of Tenaraibon,' in Hayek and Horiuchi, eds., *Listen, Copy, Read*, 100; Takahashi, *Mura no tenaraijuku*, 30.

11 He came to know, vaguely, that he lived in the land of the gods: On the various Shintō gods, Buddhas, and their relationship in popular religion, see Hardacre, *Shintō: A History*, chapter 9.

11 some of them were more amenable: On the lords' performance of submission, see Roberts, *Performing the Great Peace*.

12 convenient manual: Takai, *Tenpōki, shōnen shōjo no kyōyō keisei katei no kenkyū*, 31–34.

12 He bound his compositions in a book: Rinsenji monjo #1521.

13 Giyū quoted: Rinsenji monjo #1726.

13 most famous were reissued: Yonemoto, *Problem of Women*, 6.

13 'The only qualities that befit a woman': *The Greater Learning for Women*, translated in Chamberlain, *Things Japanese*, 455.

13 *Women's Amazing Library*: 'Onna manzai takarabako' (1784), in Emori, ed., *Edo jidai josei seikatsu ezu daijiten*, vol. 4, 174.

13 pages of pictures: Yabuta, '*Onna daigaku* no naka no "Chūgoku,"' in Cho and Suda, eds., *Hikakushtikeki ni mita kinsei Nihon*, 141–62.

14 'To be a woman': *The Treasure Chest of the Greater Learning for Women*, author's copy.

15 making up an unlined kimono: Dalby, *Kimono*, 20–21, 70; also see the diagrams reprinted from instruction manuals in Emori, ed., *Edo jidai josei seikatsu ezu daijiten*, vol. 4, 109–14.

15 right way and a wrong way: On lessons in self-cultivation and feminine comportment, see Yonemoto, *Problem of Women*, chapter 2, for an overview (51–92), and for specific examples, Sugimoto, *Daughter of*

the Samurai, 24; Takai, *Tenpōki, shōnen shōjo no kyōyō keisei katei no kenkyū*, 42–44.

15 'Of the many skills': quoted in Yonemoto, *Problem of Women*, 67.

15 'I was bad at sewing and calligraphy': quoted in Gordon, *Fabricating Consumers*, 70.

15 right way to sew: 'Onna manzai takara bunko' (1784), in Emori, ed., *Edo jidai josei seikatsu ezu daijiten*, vol. 4, 112–13.

16 Needles: Guth, 'Theorizing the Hari Kuyō.'

16 would be displayed: Lindsey, *Fertility and Pleasure*, 82–83, 181–82.

18 dozens of pieces of clothing: Rinsenji monjo #1680.

18 they all owed their existence to an era of global trade: Fujita, 'Japan Indianized.'

20 halted the export of silver . . . copper followed in 1865: Jansen, *China in the Tokugawa World*, 40.

20 curtailed silk imports: Wigen, *The Making of a Japanese Periphery*, 97–98; Morris-Suzuki, *The Technological Transformation of Japan*, 29.

20 Nankin stripes, Santome stripes: Rinsenji monjo #1680.

20 the word 'stripes': Fujita, 'Japan Indianized,' 190–91.

20 clocks: Frumer, 'Translating Time'; Jansen, *China in the Tokugawa World*, 36–37.

20 eyeglasses, magnifying glasses, telescopes: Screech, *The Lens Within the Heart*, 182–83.

21 Engelbert Kaempfer . . . 'closed empire': Bodart-Bailey, ed., *Kaempfer's Japan*, 29.

21 opium: Spence, *The Search for Modern China*, 131–32.

21 Canoes travelled . . . clubbed them to death: Igler, *The Great Ocean*.

22 convicts: Anderson, 'Convict Passages in the Indian Ocean.'

22 people in Hitachi Province: Howell, 'Foreign Encounters and Informal Diplomacy in Early Modern Japan,' 302.

22 'If that double-bolted land': Melville, *Moby-Dick*, 127.

22 Russians circumnavigating: Krusenstern, *Voyage Round the World in the Years 1803, 1804, 1805 and 1806*, 210–50.

23 few whalers: Howell, 'Foreign Encounters,' 304–8.

23 Japanese sailors: Miyachi, *Bakumatsu ishin henkaku-shi: jō*, 77–94. Also thanks to Anne Walthall for alerting me to Saitō Yoshiyuki's unpublished work on this subject.

23 Honda Toshiaki: Keene, *The Japanese Discovery of Europe*, 91–112.

24 The ship sailed directly . . . gravity of his error: Wilson, *Defensive Positions*, 113–21.

24 Russians, spurned: Shmagin, 'Diplomacy and Force, Borders and Borderlands,' 100–34.

24 *Diana*: Golownin, *Narrative of My Captivity in Japan.*

25 'disease boats': Igler, *The Great Ocean*, 65.

25 'white men with horrible looks': Olaudah Equiano, quoted in Rediker, *The Slave Ship*, 108.

25 Umeka: Rinsenji monjo #1015, Rinsenji monjo #1016.

26 black demons: Suzuki, *Snow Country Tales*, 151–52.

26 naked young carpenters: Suzuki, *Snow Country Tales*, 132.

26 those who returned: Tsukamoto, *Chiisa na rekishi to ooki na rekishi*, 144.

27 Emon had been there: Rinsenji monjo #1072.

27 Giyū went: Rinsenji monjo #935.

27 Tsuneno's uncle: Rinsenji monjo #859.

27 'Edo style': Iwabuchi, 'Edo kinban bushi ga mita "Edo" to kunimoto,' 63.

27 entertaining story: Suzuki, *Snow Country Tales*, 151–52.

28 impossible standard: Takai, *Tenpōki, shōnen shōjo no kyōyō keisei katei no kenkyū*, 61–75.

28 Miyo: 'Aiwatase mōsu issatsu no koto,' Kansei 10.7, Hasegawa-ke monjo, Niigata Prefectural Archives.

28 Riyo: Katakura, 'Bakumatsu ishinki no toshi kazoku to joshi rōdō,' 87.

28 Taki: Saitō, *Shichiyashi no kenkyū*, 155–206.

28 Sumi: Hayashi, 'Kasama jōkamachi ni okeru joseizō,' in Kinsei joseishi kenyūkai, ed., *Edo jidai no joseitachi*, 262–66. A few months later, Sumi ended up as a prostitute in Itabashi Station, but her brother bought out her contract and transferred her to the custody of a used-clothing dealer in Asakusa.

28 Michi: Walthall, 'Fille de paysan, épouse de samourai'; Masuda, 'Yoshino Michi no shōgai,' in Kinsei joseishi kenkyūkai, ed., *Edo jidai no joseitachi*, 115–46.

28 long and broad tradition: Stanley, 'Maidservants' Tales.'

29 'come from her father': quoted in Hubbard, *City Women*, 22.

29 Finnish girl: Moring, 'Migration, Servanthood, and Assimilation in a New Environment,' in Fauve-Chamoux, ed., *Domestic Service and the Formation of European Identity*, 49–50.

29 Marie-Anne Lafarge: Maza, *Servants and Masters in Eighteenth-Century France*, 41.

29 Annushka: Martin, *Enlightened Metropolis*, 249–50.

30 'I wanted to go to Edo': Rinsenji monjo #1716. Tsuneno repeated a similar sentiment in Rinsenji monjo #1710 and her uncle reports her saying the same thing in #1697.

Chapter Two: **Half a Lifetime in the Countryside**

31 In 1816: Calculating backwards from the 'fifteen years' she had been married when she was sent home in 1831, see Rinsenji monjo #1777.

31 'The months and days': Matsuo, *The Narrow Road to Oku*, 19.

32 Every girl did: Cornell, 'Why Are There No Spinsters in Japan?'; Walthall, 'The Lifecycle of Farm Women.'

32 At twelve, Tsuneno was young: Tsuneno's parents admitted that she was young and later thanked Jōganji for taking her in at that age. Rinsenji monjo #1777. On average, the demographer Hayami Akira estimated that in the mid-to-late nineteenth century Echigo girls probably married around nineteen, but in northern provinces he found marriages of girls as young as ten in the early eighteenth century. Hayami, 'Another Fossa Magna: Proportion Marrying and Age at Marriage in Late Nineteenth-Century Japan.'

32 her aunt Chisato had been a thirteen-year-old bride: Rinsenji monjo #906.

32 At twelve, most girls weren't even menstruating: menarche was later in pre-industrial societies; this is one of the assumptions in Drixler, *Mabiki*.

32 a girl under the age of fourteen or so could be too young: See an example in Stanley, *Selling Women*, chapter 6, in which a fourteen-year-old prostitute was considered 'too young.'

33 correspondents for generations: See the envelope in Rinsenji monjo #1978, addressed by Tsuneno's grandfather, who was staying at Jōganji. The contents are actually different – a letter from Tsuneno's brother Girin.

33 a thousand people: Ōishida kyōiku iinkai, *Ōishida chōritsu rekishi minzoku shiryōkan shiryōshū*, vol. 7: *Shūmon ninbetsuchō.*

33 safflowers: Kikuchi, 'Benibana emaki o yomu.'

33 Bashō visited: Bashō, *The Narrow Road to Oku*, 103.

33 'I too want to go': Nishiyama, *Edo Culture*, 105.

33 Marriage did that for women: Nagano, 'Nihon kinsei nōson ni okeru maskyurinitī no kōchika to jendā.'

35 miso bucket: Rinsenji monjo #1767.

35 how much they paid labourers: Rinsenji monjo #1763.

35 Kiyomi had a sharp tongue, and her husband complained: Rinsenji monjo #1764.

35 'Kiyomi is acting like a criminal': Rinsenji monjo #1939.

35 a difficult lord: Kasaya, *Shukun 'oshikome' no kōzō*.

35 Cages were in courtyards: Yamakawa, *Women of the Mito Domain*, 184–89.

36 Giyū's transition to married life: The following story, in its entirety, comes from the account Giyū wrote, 'Nairan ichijō.' Rinsenji monjo #2758.

36 he had been the head of the household and the head priest for five years: Rinsenji monjo #2852.

39 'Girin's misconduct in the fifth month': Rinsenji monjo #2758.

39 Giyū remarried: Rinsenji monjo #1823.

39 When she died in 1859: Rinsenji monjo #1039. On posthumous names, Williams, *The Other Side of Zen*, 26–29.

39 Women at Rinsenji talked: Giyū complained that his mother and Kiyomi slandered him in the aftermath of his failed marriage. Rinsenji monjo #2758.

39 Sano was already twenty-five: Sano's age is calculated from Rinsenji monjo #911.

39 five babies: Rinsenji monjo #911.

40 warm letters: Rinsenji monjo #1699; Rinsenji monjo #1725; Rinsenji monjo #1712.

40 they should love him back: Rinsenji monjo #2758.

40 No matter how much she argued with Giyū: Rinsenji monjo #2049.

40 Girin arrived in Ōishida: Rinsenji monjo #2758.

41 trip to Kyoto: Rinsenji monjo #981.

41 wrote home to Rinsenji: Rinsenji monjo #1978.

41 fire: Nagai, *Ōishida chōshi*, 203; the date is Tenpō 1.3.19; the 'temple next door' is Jōsenji.

41 lost its entire collection: Seki, 'Shihon chakushoku "Ōishida kashi ezu" ni tsuite,' 43–44, 48.

42 notice of divorce followed: Rinsenji monjo #1777.

42 Hundreds of people: estimated from the population registers in which families were entered as Jōganji parishioners. Ōishida kyōiku iinkai, *Ōishida chōritsu rekishi minzoku shiryōkan shiryōshū*, vol. 7: *Shūmon ninbetsuchō*, 6–13, 36–43.

42 'My parents are devastated': Rinsenji monjo #1777.

43 nearly half of women: Kurosu, 'Divorce in Early Modern Rural Japan,'

126, 135; on the ubiquity of divorce, also see Kurosu, 'Remarriage in a Stem Family System'; Fuess, *Divorce in Japan*.

44 Women who divorced in their twenties: Kurosu, 'Remarriage in a Stem Family System,' 432.

44 Her father worried: Rinsenji monjo #1777.

44 They were farmers: Rinsenji monjo #1675; Rinsenji monjo #1674.

44 contents would be displayed: Lindsey, *Fertility and Pleasure*, 79–88.

44 'Should this unlined kimono': Risnenji monjo #1694.

44 bill: Rinsenji monjo #1678.

45 Toshino: Rinsenji monjo #2107.

45 gratefully accepted: Rinsenji monjo #1678.

45 hosted a party: The details here are in Rinsenji monjo #1675; Rinsenji monjo #1674.

45 expected alms: Ehlers, *Give and Take*, 86–89.

45 people lined the road: *Ōshima sonshi*, 774.

46 If an official message: *Niigata kenshi tsūshi-hen*, vol. 5: *kinsei* 3, 705.

46 many of Ōshima's young people: *Ōshima sonshi*, 430, 432.

46 Some went for years: *Ōshima sonshi*, 431.

46 villagers pooled their money: *Ōshima sonshi*, 439.

46 Everyone in her household: Walthall, 'The Lifecycle of Farm Women.'

47 which strain to plant: on the process of planning and planting, see *Kubiki sonshi*, 382–85, 388.

47 almanacs and manuals: On calculating farming families in other parts of Japan, see Smith, *The Agrarian Origins of Modern Japan*.

47 in 1833, the year Tsuneno arrived: The following description of the Tenpō famine in the region of Ōshima is cobbled together from a number of sources, including *Kubiki sonshi*, 439; *Ōshima sonshi*, 417–19; *Niigata kenshi tsūshi* 5: *kinsei* 3, 17–22; *Jōetsu shishi: tsūshi-hen* 3, *kinsei* 1, 267–73; and 'Kisai tomegaki,' Tenpō 9 in *Niigata kenshi shiryō-hen* 6: *kinsei* 1: *Jōetsu*, 854; and *Matsudai chōshi*, vol. 1, 553–57.

49 the headman in Mine Village panicked: *Ōshima sonshi*, 418.

49 Murono: 'Kisai tomegaki,' in *Niigata kenshi shiryō hen*, vol. 5: *kinsei* 1: *Jōetsu*, 854.

49 in the area as a whole: *Jōetsu shishi, tsūshi-hen* 3, *kinsei* 1, 272; Kikuchi, *Nihon no rekishi saigai*, 151 (chart showing Takada).

49 'the worst of all time': 'Kisai tomegaki' in *Niigata kenshi shiryō hen*, vol. 5: *kinsei* 1: *Jōetsu*, 854.

50 sold off a stand of woods: Rinsenji monjo #441.

50 wrote to a correspondent: Rinsenji monjo #450.

50 reported that the formerly prosperous town was devastated: Rinsenji monjo #1737.

50 lost over 10 percent: Janetta, 'Famine Mortality in Japan,' 431. Statistics include outmigration; the region here is Hida.

50 There were wild reports . . . to continue their work: Kikuchi, *Kinsei no kikin*, 200–5. Domain here is Akita.

51 sending away daughters-in-law: *Ōshima sonshi*, 418.

51 vulnerable people were disappearing: See the story of Kimi in *Ōshima sonshi*, 436–437; *Matsudai chōshi jōkan*, 556.

51 birth to a healthy girl: Rinsenji monjo #2109.

51 People did it all the time: Yonemoto, 'Adoption and the Maintenance of the Early Modern Elite.'

51 heard about the divorce from his uncle: Rinsenji monjo #1682.

51 'Nothing especially bad has happened': Rinsenji monjo #1686.

51 agreed that Giyū could keep: Rinsenji monjo #1674.

52 temple's death register: Rinsenji monjo #1275.

52 He died in early fall: Rinsenji monjo #1876.

52 'This year Tsuneno, Girin, and Gisen all divorced': Rinsenji monjo #1876.

53 four potential husbands: Gotō, *Essa josei*, 399–402.

53 area as a whole: *Jōetsu shishi*, vol. 3, *kinsei* 1, 132, 141.

53 Initially, Tsuneno agreed: Rinsenji monjo #1677; Gotō, *Essa josei*, 399–400.

53 an entirely new match: Gotō, *Essa josei*, 401. The details of this third wedding and its aftermath are in Rinsenji monjo #1673.

54 Inada-machi: *Jōetsu shishi tsūshi-hen* 4, 293. Map of Takada in ibid., 314.

54 Takada felt alive: Sugimoto Etsu described the winter this way in Nagaoka, a similar snow country castle town. *Daughter of the Samurai*, 1–2.

54 Barely six weeks after the wedding: Rinsenji monjo #1673.

55 she had intended to die: Rinsenji monjo #2049.

55 'She was married': Rinsenji monjo #1714.

55 Perhaps there was a widower: We know that Tsuneno was supposed to marry a widower because she said so, in Rinsenji monjo #1710 and Rinsenji monjo #2049. In fact, this was Giyū's original plan when her first marriage failed. Rinsenji monjo #1777.

55 'If I stayed at home,' 'I understood that my own unacceptable conduct,' 'When I wasn't brave': Rinsenji monjo #1710.

56 wooden door reinforced with metal: *kanado*, Rinsenji monjo #1710.

56 Tsuneno had told her parents: Rinsenji monjo #1697.

56 She also told her uncle: Rinsenji monjo #1716.

56 Tsuneno told Giyū and her mother: Rinsenji monjo #1704.

57 She sold many of the items: Rinsenji monjo #2096.

57 left three gold pieces: Rinsenji monjo #2049.

57 She already knew him: Giyū wrote that Chikan had visited the temple on 9.22 and Tsuneno left home two days later. Rinsenji monjo #1726.

57 At the time, she had told him: Rinsenji monjo #1716.

57 When Tsuneno met Chikan: Rinsenji monjo #1716.

Chapter Three: **To Edo**

59 At first, the process of planning to leave appeared to be ordinary: The reconstruction of Tsuneno's last day in Takada comes from her letters, especially Rinsenji monjo #1700 and Rinsenji monjo #1716.

59 Giyū had always thought: Rinsenji monjo #2758.

60 One of her younger brothers: Rinsenji monjo #2758.

60 a well-known story: *Ōshima sonshi,* 452–53.

62 'By the way, as I've been telling everyone': Rinsenji monjo #1700.

62 There Tsuneno wrote another letter: Rinsenji monjo #1711

63 Later, she would claim: Rinsenji monjo #1716.

63 Sekikawa Barrier: Vaporis, *Breaking Barriers,* 122–23; Asakura, 'Kinsei ni okeru onna tegata no hatsugyō to Takada-han,' 193; Shiba, *Kinsei onna no tabi nikki,* 102–4. On the logic of the checkpoint system and its history, see Vaporis, *Breaking Barriers,* 99–134.

63 would have been enough: Seeking a cure at a hot spring and visiting a temple were two common reasons to procure passes. Vaporis, *Breaking Barriers,* 121; Asakura, 'Kinsei ni okeru onna tegata,' 193.

63 It was easier to bypass: On the experience of passing through this barrier, see Kanamori, *Sekisho nuke: Edo no onnatachi no bōken,* 89–97.

64 dog door: Shiba, *Kinsei onna no tabi nikki,* 111.

64 cost a few dozen copper coins: Shiba, *Kinsei onna tabi nikki,* 111–12; Vaporis, *Breaking Barriers,* 190–91.

64 grey starlings: Haga, *Edo jōhōbunkashi kenkyū,* 85, cited in Moriyama, *Crossing Boundaries in Tokugawa Society,* 23.

64 stone mortars: Kitahara, *Hyakuman toshi Edo no seikatsu,* 46–47.

65 'On the way, Chikan started saying': Tsuneno, quoted in her uncle's letter, Rinsenji monjo #1697.

65 'impure intentions'; 'After all': Rinsenji monjo #1710.

65 legal definition: The term was *gōkan* or *oshite fugi*, both of which implied force. Stanley, 'Adultery, Punishment, and Reconciliation.'

67 a tall Chinese hackberry tree: Tōkyō-to Itabashi-ku, ed., *Itabashi kushi*, 368–72.

69 'The shogunal inspectors do not have any documentation': 'Shubiki-uchi' in *Kokushi daijiten*. Also 'Edo no han'i.' Tokyo Metropolitan Archives, http://www.soumu.metro.tokyo.jp/01soumu /archives/0712edo_hanni.htm. The map, 'Edo shubiki zu' (1818), is held at the Tokyo Metropolitan Archives.

69 stacked three storeys high: See the illustration in Saitō, *Edo meisho zue*. On the slightly tired atmosphere of the station, *Itabashi kushi*, 328–29.

70 relief kitchen . . . people he had buried: *Itabashi kushi*, 366–67; Kiku-chi, *Nihon no rekishi saigai*, 147.

71 weren't even marked: See Fujiya, *Bansei on-Edo ezu* [map], 1854. Also see the Nakasendō's path in Kodama, *Fukugen Ōedo jōhō chizu*, 16–17, 32–33, 46–47, 58.

71 residents were mostly farmers: Yoshida examines the population regis-ters from an outlying chō and finds that most were farmers or sellers of produce. *Dentō toshi Edo*, 114.

71 brilliant red gates: At the time, the complex had three red gates. The biggest was the gate constructed in 1827, later known as the Tōdai Akamon, the main entrance to the University of Tokyo. Miyazaki, *Daimyō yashiki to Edo iseki*, 15.

72 the Mouse: Vaporis, *Tour of Duty*, 158; 'Nezumi kozō,' *Kokushi daijiten*.

72 the rooms on the perimeter: Miyazaki, *Daimyō yashiki to Edo iseki*, 19–20; Yoshida, *Toshi Edo ni ikiru*, 104.

73 little dolls: See the collection of Shinryū'in (1787–1870), wife of Maeda Narinaga (1782–1824) and, in Tsuneno's time, the Maeda dowager. Shinryū'in's collection is held at the Seisonkaku Museum in Ken-rokuen Garden in Kanazawa City, Ishikawa Prefecture.

73 how much it all cost: Isoda, *Bushi no kakeibō*, 41–44.

73 Hongō: Takeuchi, *Edo shakashi no kenkyū*, 62–74.

74 'milky fragrant powder': Groemer, *Street Performers and Society*, 276.

75 flooded the streets with drums and banners: Utagawa, *Kanda Matsuri dashizukushi* (1859).

75 bright and dry: This and all subsequent information on Edo weather on particular days is from *Saitō Gesshin nikki* or *Fujiokaya nikki*.

75 oxcart drivers: Yoshida, *Toshi Edo ni ikiru*, 222–24.

76 Yatsukōji: Saitō, *Edo meisho zue.*

76 the city burned: On the culture of fires see Wills, 'Fires and Fights.'

77 The year before Tsuneno arrived: Chiyoda-ku, ed., *Chiyoda kushi,* vol. 1, 650–51.

77 Merchants were setting out: Shimizu, 'Eating Edo,' 54.

77 prices: *Fujiokaya nikki,* vol. 1, 114.

77 Kanda was a wholesale market: Shimizu, 'Eating Edo.'

78 They had estimated: Fujita, *Tōyama Kinshirō no jidai,* 152.

79 1843 ranking: 'Shinban Ō-Edo mochimaru chōja kagami' (1846).

79 high-end clothier: There is a householder, Ichibei, in Mikawa-chō who appears on a list of luxury dealers in Edo compiled by shogunal officials in Tenpō 12. *Shichū torishimari ruishū,* vol. 1, 280.

79 undistinguished shopkeepers: Nakagawa and Hanasaka, eds., *Edo kaimono hitori annai,* 44, 66, 127, 145, 204, 220. Two other luxury dealers from the first block of Mikawa-chō appear in the Tenpo 12 list, a landlord named Sōbei and a renter, Kinbei. Tōkyō Daigaku Shiryō Hensanjo, ed., *Shichū torishimari ruishū,* vol. 1, 263, 292.

79 second block of Minagawa-chō: 'Minagawa-chō' in *Nihon rekishi chimei taikei.*

80 confused it: Rinsenji's correspondents did this. For example, Rinsenji monjo #1697; Rinsenji monjo #1698.

80 Sōhachi: Yasugorō mentioned that Sōhachi's father was in Echigo. Rinsenji monjo #1698. Tsuneno wrote that he ran a rice shop (*tsuki-gomeya*). Rinsenji monjo #1711.

80 sweaty, undignified labour: On labour in rice shops, see Katakura, *Tenmei no Edo uchikowashi,* 115–16.

81 During the severe Tenmei famine: Katakura, *Tenmei no Edo uchiko-washi,* 11, 14–15.

81 Two years later, in Paris: Garrioch, 'The Everyday Lives of Parisian Women and the October Days of 1789.'

82 After the city was pacified: Walthall, 'The Edo Riots,' in McClain, Merriman, and Ugawa, eds., *Edo and Paris,* 417–19.

82 city savings association: Katō, 'Governing Edo,' in McClain, Merriman, and Ugawa, eds., *Edo and Paris,* 62–63.

82 wealthy commoners in Edo braced for riots: Fujita, *Tōyama Kinshirō no jidai,* 203.

82 When tenants stopped paying: There were three main waves of unrest during the Tenpō famine years, each of which inspired charitable donations by elite merchant households. See Yoshida, *Kinsei kyodai toshi no shakai kōzō,* 207–19.

82 shogun's men worked feverishly: Yoshida, *Kinsei kyodai toshi no shakai kōzō*, 19–24.

82 For three years: Things went back to normal a few weeks after Tsuneno arrived. *Edo machibure shūsei*, vol. 13, 325–26.

82 Still, stores like Sōhachi's: Yoshida, *Kinsei kyodai toshi no shakai kōzō*, 208.

82 a good day's work: *Fujiokaya nikki*, vol. 1, 114. Edoites measured rice prices not by how much money a fixed amount of rice would cost, but by the more practical, and depressing, measure of how much rice a fixed amount of money would buy. This is calculating from Mitamura Engyō's assumption that a pedlar made about four hundred mon per day – see the discussion in Mega, *Buke ni totsuida josei no tegami*, 163.

83 'Even when we're looking': *Fujiokaya nikki*, vol. 1, 118.

83 He was furious: Rinsenji monjo #1697.

84 The men in the barracks: All these are activities described in Iwabuchi, 'Edo kinban bushi ga mita "Edo" to kunimoto.'

85 merchants responsible: Shimizu, 'Eating Edo,' 115–17.

85 The ward headman, a famous writer named Saitō Yukinari, scribbled: *Saitō Gesshin nikki*, vol. 1, 189.

85 remarking on the warm start: *Fujiokaya nikki*, vol. 1, 114.

85 'I struggled so much': Rinsenji monjo #1716.

Chapter Four: **A View from a Tenement**

87 pathways so narrow: See, for example, the diagrams of chō plots (*machiyashiki, kakaeyashiki*) in Katakura, *Edo jūtaku jijō*, 20, 23, and 27, which show narrow alleyways and right angles and the locations of toilets and wells. A map of the fourth block of Mikawa-chō, right in Tsuneno's neighbourhood, shows four outhouses for about two dozen rental units and suggests that the area had a high building-to-land ratio (23–25). Also see the illustrated reconstructions in Sasama, *Ō-Edo fukugen zukan: shomin-hen*, and the picture of an alley gate in Shikitei Sanba, *Ukiyodoko* (1813–1814), in Gaubatz, 'Urban Fictions of Early Modern Japan,' 207.

88 guarantor: Tsukamoto, 'Kariya ukenin.'

89 Jinsuke: On the superintendent's name and the dates Tsuneno stayed in his room, see Rinsenji monjo #1699.

89 the tenement superintendent: Nishizaka, 'Yamori.'

89 surrogate parents: One popular ditty went: 'The *ōya* (*yamori*) are like

parents [*oya*]; the tenants [*tanako*] are like children [*ko*]. Sasama, *Ō-Edo fukugen zukan: shomin-hen*, 52.

89 Tsuneno disliked him: Rinsenji monjo #1715.

89 'three-mat': Tsuneno called it a *sanjōshiki*. Rinsenji monjo #1716. Later, *sanjō yashiki* would become Tokyo slang for the type of place where poor people lived.

90 'They say that someone': Shikitei Sanba, *Ukiyodoko* (1813–1814), translated in Gaubatz, unpublished manuscript.

90 The only light: There were corner units, but a three-mat, rented cheaply and on short notice, probably wasn't one of them.

90 tiny, wooden-floored space: See the illustration of a typical tenement kitchen in Sasama, *Ō-Edo fukugen zukan: shomin-hen*, 55.

91 could barely describe her situation: Rinsenji monjo #1716.

91 her neighbours: Most of these are occupations mentioned in the Meiji population record for Mikawa-chō. Katakura, *Edo jūtaku jijō*, 25. See another list of occupations for *uradana* tenants in two other neighbourhoods in Yoshida, *Dentō toshi Edo*, 113–14.

92 chatted across the alleys: Edo fiction is full of these imagined conversations, particularly in the work of Shikitei Sanba. See Joel Cohn's wonderful translation of part of *Ningen banji uso bakkari* ('In the World of Men, Nothing but Lies'), in Jones and Watanabe, eds., *An Edo Anthology*, 349–63.

92 'get together with the other wives': Teeuwen and Nakai, eds., *Lust, Commerce, and Corruption*, 365.

93 Most Kanda tenement rooms: This is also an estimate derived from the Meiji-era population record for the fourth block of Mikawa-chō. Katakura, *Edo jūtaku jijō*, 25.

93 gate guard: Yoshida, *Dentō toshi no Edo*, 253–54; Minami, *Edo no machi bugyō*, 162.

94 a short note: Rinsenji monjo #1705.

94 another, longer letter: Rinsenji monjo #1706.

94 'It's snowy there': Rinsenji monjo #1706.

94 'As for the money': Rinsenji monjo #1707.

95 'At some point': Rinsenji monjo #1707.

95 Chikan left: Rinsenji monjo #1716.

96 a lot of money: Calculating from Tenpō 14 exchange rates, 1 bu equaled 1,575 mon. Isoda, *Bushi no kakeibō*, 55. One pedlar could clear about four or five hundred mon per day (Mega Atsuko, *Buke ni totsuida josei no tegami*, 163). One bu was also the take-home pay for Echigo seasonal labourers, who stayed on for three months during the winter,

also receiving room and board. Kishii, *Edo no higoyomi*, vol. 2, 178. A robe would cost more, judging from what clothing pawned for in Edo in Tenpō 14. Isoda, *Bushi no kakeibō*, 63.

97 Mitsui Echigoya: On the number of clerks, see the graph on pg. 39 of Nishizaka, *Mitsui Echigoya hōkōnin no kenkyū*; Yoshida, *Kinsei kyodai toshi no shakai kōzō*, 232; on the lifestyle of clerks at a similar store see Aburai, *Edo hōkōnin no kokoroechō*; Sakurai, 'Perpetual Dependency.'

99 different type of commerce: On the street scene at Nihonbashi, see the early-nineteenth-century scroll 'Kidai shōran' as it is rendered and described in Asano and Yoshida, eds., *Ōedo Nihonbashi emaki ezu: 'Kidai shōran' no sekai.*

100 used paper: Yoshida, *Dentō toshi Edo*, 261–63.

101 commanded resources: Teeuwen and Nakai, eds., *Lust, Commerce, and Corruption*, 164.

101 The head of the Kyoto-based Nishi Honganji sect . . . clustered in the shadow of the great hall: Fujioto, ed., *Tsukiji Betsuin-shi*, 206.

102 Giyū had corresponded: Giyū wrote Enshōji after he knew Tsuneno had visited, and the letter was not an introduction but seemingly part of a larger correspondence. Rinsenji monjo #1714.

102 a lonely, windy strip: 'Jikkenchō,' in *Nihon rekishi chimei taikei*, accessed through JapanKnowledge. https://japanknowledge.com/library/.

102 Tsuneno called at her uncle Bunshichi's store: Rinsenji monjo #1697.

103 'naked': Rinsenji monjo #1697.

103 letter he wrote to Giyū: Rinsenji monjo #1697.

103 around three or four weeks: The letters Tsuneno wrote in Minagawa-chō on 10/10 were delivered within four weeks. We know this because Giyū writes that he received them in Rinsenji monjo #1726, which he dated 11/9.

104 Suzuki Bokushi, reporting: Suzuki, *Snow Country Tales*, 198. I converted the date from the translation, which had changed the Japanese date to a Western one.

104 Giyū was already making arrangements: Rinsenji monjo #1726.

104 a letter that Tsuneno had written: Rinsenji monjo #1700.

104 note she had attached to the letter: Rinsenji monjo #1701. This explains why letters from Tsuneno to other people, including Kōtoku and her uncle Kyūhachirō, survive in the Rinsenji collection.

104 thorough account: See, for example, Rinsenji monjo #2758 on his first marriage or Rinsenji monjo #939 on Tsuneno's second departure from Echigo.

105 'It is impossible for us': Rinsenji monjo #1714.

105 sent a gift of dried sea bream: Rinsenji monjo #1674.

105 he was one of the guests: Rinsenji monjo #1673.

105 stalwarts of the Rinsenji women's association: Rinsenji monjo #1165.

105 Through Denpachi, Giyū: Rinsenji monjo #1726. A few days later, Denpachi dispatched a messenger to Jienji in Koyasu Village, the temple Chikan said he was affiliated with, to look into his background. He must have found out that Chikan was who he said he was, because the matter of his identity was never mentioned again.

105 borrowed two hundred gold pieces: He explained this in a letter to Hirosuke later. Rinsenji monjo #1722.

106 'We received the letters you wrote': Rinsenji monjo #1726.

107 He prepared a set of luggage: Rinsenji monjo #1718. Rather than calling her uncle or his family by name, she referred to the entire household as 'Tsukiji.' Naming people after their place of residence was customary in all the correspondence relating to Tsuneno. Giyū's correspondents referred to him as Rinsenji, after the temple, and everyone called Tsuneno's uncle Kyūhachirō's family 'the new house' or 'Iimuro' after their village. Tsuneno signed some of her own letters 'Tsuneno in Kanda' (Kanda nite Tsuneno), and many of the correspondents wrote 'Kanda' when they were referring to Sōhachi.

108 in debt to Jinsuke: Rinsenji monjo #1699.

108 'learn the manners and customs': Rinsenji monjo #1708.

108 ambitious mothers spent years: Yonemoto, *The Problem of Women in Early Modern Japan*, 81.

109 most recent letter: Rinsenji monjo #1708.

109 Sōhachi, the rice seller, advised her: Rinsenji monjo #1716.

109 'There wasn't anything better': Rinsenji monjo #1716.

110 asked her brother: Rinsenji monjo #1707.

110 blocky, laborious script: Rinsenji monjo #1698.

110 he wrote to her family: Rinsenji monjo #1698.

Chapter Five: **Samurai Winter**

111 'as inconsequential as a duck fart': Suzuki, *Snow Country Tales*, 128.

112 'I want to get out of this room': Rinsenji monjo #1718.

113 men from the provinces: See the discussions in Iwabuchi, 'Edo kinban bushi ga mita "Edo" to kunimoto,' and Constantine Vaporis, *Tour of Duty*, chapter 6.

113 the size of the entire British navy: Ferguson, *Empire: How Britain Made the Modern World*, 138.

114 employed village headmen's sons: Chiyoda-ku, ed., *Shinpen Chiyoda kushi: tsūshi-hen*, 435.

114 Edoites born and bred: Totman, *Politics in the Tokugawa Bakufu*, 139, 152.

114 shogun's granary in Asakusa: Ujiie, *Hatamoto gokenin: odoroki no bakushin shakai no shinjitsu*, 94.

116 lunch budget: Teeuwen and Nakai, eds., *Lust, Commerce and Corruption*, 246.

116 wasn't unusual for a bannerman to owe: Mega, *Buke ni totsuida josei no tegami*, 50.

117 recorded such gifts: Fukasawa, *Hatamoto fujin ga mita Edo no tasogare*, 34–35.

117 'not only steamed rice': Fukasawa, *Hatamoto fujin ga mita Edo no tasogare*, 37.

117 Iseki's household: Fukasawa, *Hatamoto fujin ga mita Edo no tasogare*, 20.

117 stipends of fewer than: This is calculated as of Kansei 10 (1798). See Ogawa, *Tokugawa bakufu no shōshin seido*, 29.

117 'Even if we economise': Mega, *Buke ni totsuida josei no tegami*, 53 (small coins = *monme* in this translation).

117 forced to supplement their income with handicrafts: Ujiie, *Hatamoto gokenin*, 96.

118 cultivated azaleas and morning glories or raised goldfish and crickets: Takiguchi, 'Kashin yashiki to Edo shakai,' 80.

118 Most of the shogun's vassals were underemployed: Totman, *Politics in the Tokugawa Bakufu*, 141–52.

119 'trying to hollow out bamboo with a lantern wick': Ujiie, *Hatamoto gokenin*, 96.

119 Negishi Yasumori: Ujiie, *Hatamoto gokenin*, 107–8.

119 huge scandal: Miyamoto, 'Kakushi baijo to hatamoto keiei.'

121 fraud on a pawnbroker: Ujiie, *Hatamoto gokenin*, 51–53.

122 Katsu Kokichi: Katsu, *Musui's Story*; Ōguchi, 'The Reality Behind *Musui Dokugen*: The World of the *Hatamoto* and *Gokenin*.'

123 'Although I indulged': Katsu, *Musui's Story*, 156.

123 Matsudaira Tomosaburō: This and subsequent information on his status and income from Ogawa, ed., *Kansei-fu ikō hatamoto-ke hyakka jiten*, vol. 5, 2574.

124 seven hundred gold pieces: Converting from Mega Atsuko's calculations in *Buke ni totsuida josei no tegami*, 50.

124 would never have that chance: Walthall, 'Hiding the Shoguns.'

124 When Edo Castle burned: Fukasawa, *Hatamoto fujin ga mita Edo no tasogare*, 199–200.

125 appearance at the entrance to Ōtemon Gate: Sasama, *Fukugen Edo seikatsu zukan*, 46–47; Vaporis, *Tour of Duty*, 7.

125 suite of rooms: Fukai, *Zukai Edojō o yomu*, 22–25; Sasama, *Fukugen Edo seikatsu zukan*, 25–27.

125 rules for everything: Ujiie, *Hatamoto gokenin*, 23–30.

126 ceremony: Tokyo Metropolitan Archives, 'Edojō no fuyu shitaku: hibachi.'

126 Bathroom breaks: Ogawa, *Edojō no toire*, 27–31.

127 most disgusting in Edo: Tokyo Metropolitan Archives, 'Edo jidai no zumen o yomu (2): toire no iroiro.'

127 Tomosaburō's mansion: marked on the 'Surugadai' map in *Edo kiriezu* (1849–1862).

127 When one new spot opened: *Shinpen Chiyoda kushi: tsūshi-hen*, 451–52.

127 over 250: *Shinpen Chiyoda kushi: tsūshi-hen*, 434.

127 empty and quiet: *Shinpen Chiyoda kushi: tsūshi-hen*, 495.

127 trunk of the tree: *Shinpen Chiyoda kushi: tsūshi-hen*, 459.

128 relatively small compound: description of the space from examples in Hirai, ed., *Zusetsu Edo 2: daimyō to hatamoto no kurashi*, 68-69.

128 men and women of the family worked along with the servants: Yoshida, *Kinsei no ie to josei*, 158, 170–73.

129 'I wake up': Rinsenji monjo #1716.

129 Maidservants for ordinary samurai: Yoshida, *Kinsei no ie to josei*, 173–74.

130 just over two gold pieces: This seems to have been the standard pay for a bannerman's maidservant in the Tenpō era. It was exactly what the bannerman's wife Itō Maki paid her maidservant. Mega, *Buke ni totsuida josei no tegami*, 50.

130 'The work is difficult': Rinsenji monjo #1716.

130 Servants would tell their masters: Tōkyō Daigaku Shiryō Hensanjo, ed., *Shichū torishimari ruishū*, vol. 1, 270.

131 Takizawa Bakin: Saitō, *Shōka no sekai, uradana no sekai*, 71.

131 Kenjirō: *Edo machibure shūsei*, vol. 13, 304–5.

132 major fire: *Saitō Gesshin nikki*, 198; *Fujiokaya nikki*, vol. 2, 119.

Chapter Six: Costumes for Urban Life

135 The first day: This description of the various customs of the New Year in Edo is drawn from Kishii, *Edo no higoyomi: jō*, 28–85.

136 so stiff and new that they crackled: Asaoka, *Furugi*, 49.

137 had found a new master: Rinsenji monjo #1699.

139 sold products associated with the stage: 'Sumiyoshi-chō' in *Nihon rekishi chimei taikei*. Some actors had their own stores in other neighbourhoods; see Taguchi, *Edo jidai no kabuki yakusha*, 233–38.

139 'The best in Edo': Rinsenji monjo #1699.

139 silver mint: Tsuneno's master may have had some connection there; she called him her 'master from Ginza' (*Ginza no danna*), though 'Ginza' was just as likely to refer to the neighbourhood near Nihonbashi. In Tsuneno's time, the mint was right next to Sumiyoshi-chō. On Daikoku Jōze, see 'Daikoku Jōze' in *Kokushi daijiten*.

139 tried to clear some of her debts: Rinsenji monjo #1699.

139 surprisingly expensive: Rinsenji monjo #2049.

139 buy a pillow and a pair of shoes: Rinsenji monjo #1710.

139 embarrassed: Rinsenji monjo #1699.

139 box near the stage: Teeuwen and Nakai, eds., *Lust, Commerce, and Corruption*, 336.

140 a month's salary: Ten or twenty silver pieces, which worked out to somewhere between a quarter and a third of a ryō. Taguchi, *Edo jidai no kabuki yakusha*, 67–69.

140 a place near the edge of the stage: Shimazaki, *Edo Kabuki in Transition*, 89.

140 Sometimes they even featured the same actors: Yoshida, *Mibunteki shūen to shakai*, 125.

140 'Indeed a woman': Teeuwen and Nakai, eds., *Lust, Commerce, and Corruption*, 336.

140 Tsuneno could linger: This passage on the print culture surrounding kabuki draws from Shimazaki, *Edo Kabuki in Transition*.

140 Iwai Hanshirō V: The most recent Hanshirō, Hanshirō V's son, Hanshirō VI, had died in 1837. On the Hanshirō actors and the femme fatale figure, see Durham, 'The Scandalous Love of Osome and Hisamitsu,' 64–66. Tsuneno does not specify that 'Hanshirō' refers to the kabuki actor, but I am making the connection based on the fact that the Hanshirō lineage had property in Sumiyoshi-chō. Iwai Hanshirō VIII was born there in 1829. Nojima, *Kabuki jinmei jiten*, 143.

141 geisha borrowed: Tōkyō Daigaku Shiryō Hensanjo, ed., *Shichū torishimari ruishū*, vol. 1, 44.

141 Hanshirō sandals: 'Hanshirō geta' in *Nihon kokugo daijiten*.

141 proudly told her family: Rinsenji monjo #1699.

141 Hanshirō's son had been occupying the property: Ihara, *Kinsei nihon engekishi*, 470.

141 everything in Edo was delicious: Rinsenji monjo #1699.

141 city's ward headmen had counted: Yoshida, *Dentō toshi Edo*, 274–76.

142 people argued vigorously: Terado Seiken, 'An Account of the Prosperity of Edo' (*Edo hanjōki*), trans. Andrew Markus, in Jones, ed., *An Edo Anthology*, 491.

142 Nigiri sushi: Nishiyama, *Edo Culture*, 171.

142 People said that chefs: Nishiyama, *Edo Culture*, 167–69.

142 bestselling manuals: Rath, *Food and Fantasy in Early Modern Japan*, 176–78; Nishiyama, *Edo Culture*, 150.

143 high-concept performance art: Clark, 'What is Ukiyo-e Painting?'

143 She prepared tea: Rinsenji monjo #1699.

143 expected to be familiar with the basics: Corbett, *Cultivating Femininity*, 98–121.

143 also ran errands: Rinsenji monjo #1699.

143 Maidservants who could sew: Ogawa Kendō, *Chirizuka dan* (1814), quoted in *Edo fūzoku shi*, 57.

144 already chopped: Harada, *Edo no shoku seikatsu*, 27.

144 'It used to be': Shiga Shinobu, 'Sanseiroku kōhen' (1856), vol. 1, folio 13, in *Edo jidai josei bunkō*, vol. 52.

145 stage portrayals had made fashion history: Kikuchi, *Edo oshare zue*, 102–3. Buyō Inshi mentions other examples in Teeuwen and Nakai, eds., *Lust, Commerce, and Corruption*, 336.

145 Hanshirō V had his own style: 'Hanshirō kanoko' in *Nihon kokugo daijiten*.

145 prints advertising productions: For the date of the production, Unknown artist, 'Tsuji banzuke for Ume saku ya wakakiba Soga at the Kawarazaki Theater,' Tenpō 11.1; for the print itself, Utagawa Kunisada, 'Onoe Kikugorō no Omatsuri Sashichi, Onoe Eizaburō no Geisha Koito,' Tenpō 11. Sometimes scenes were added later, so this print might have appeared after the first production of the play.

145 Even high-ranking samurai: For example, see Isoda, *Bushi no kakeibō*, 63.

146 Ragmen: Yoshida, *Dentō toshi no Edo*, 259–60.

146 Tomizawa-chō: 'Tomizawa-chō' in *Nihon rekishi chimei taikei*; Sugimori, 'Furugi no shōnin.'

146 clothing pedlars: Yoshida, *Dentō toshi no Edo*, 258–59.

146 'I don't need any of my good things': Rinsenji monjo #1716.

146 asked her mother for an apron: Rinsenji monjo #1699.

147 commended virtuous daughters: *Fujiokaya nikki*, vol. 2, 136; *Edo machibure shū*, vol. 13, 182.

147 manual labourers: Teeuwen and Nakai, eds., *Lust, Commerce, and Corruption*, 303.

147 marker of their low status: Makihara, *Bunmeikoku o mezashite*, 14–16.

147 tattoos: on the shogun's practice of tattooing, Botsman, *Punishment and Power*, 27.

147 robes fashioned out of a few dozen sheets: Maruyama, *Edo no kimono to iseikatsu*, 65.

148 costumes for the three leads: Taguchi, *Edo jidai no kabuki yakusha*, 213–14; see the discussion of this incident in Yoshida, ed., *Edo kabuki hōrei shūsei*, 347–48.

148 looked luxurious only from a distance: Tōkyō Daigaku Shiryō Hensanjo, ed., *Shichū torishimari ruishū*, vol. 1, 229; Fujita, *Toyama Kinshirō no jidai*, 81. Another report made the same observation that kabuki theatres were not investing in new gold and silver costumes but repurposing old ones. *Shichū torishimari ruishū*, vol. 1, 220.

148 tent shows: Markus, 'The Carnival of Edo.'

148 half-barbarian child: Fukasawa, *Hatamoto fujin ga mita Edo no tasogare*, 64–66.

149 The big kabuki theatres did try to borrow: Shimazaki, *Edo Kabuki in Transition*, 226–27.

149 'hit absolute bottom': *Juami hikki* c. 1840, quoted in Shimazaki, *Edo Kabuki in Transition*, 101.

149 the heroine of the kabuki play *Yotsuya Ghost Story*: See the discussion in Shimazaki, *Edo Kabuki in Transition*, 111–19.

149 package finally arrived: Rinsenji monjo #1698.

150 even better package: Tsuneno mentions it in Rinsenji monjo #1710.

150 His wife took everything: Rinsenji monjo #1715.

150 he left for the harvest: Rinsenji monjo #1717.

150 'I wanted to tell him': Rinsenji monjo #1699.

150 'I understand that you think': Rinsenji monjo #1710.

151 the notices from the City Magistrates: *Edo machibure shū*, vol. 13, 329–37.

152 crowds gathered: Fukasawa, *Hatamoto fujin ga mita Edo no tasogare*, 57–59.

152 Until she encountered him in Edo: Rinsenji monjo #2049.

152 'You were like a little brother to him': Rinsenji monjo #2049.

153 when he was employed, he qualified: Botsman, *Punishment and Power*, 75–77.

153 labour bosses: Yoshida, 'Hitoyado.'

153 Hirosuke told Tsuneno he wanted to marry her: Rinsenji monjo #2049.
154 'Right now you're poor': Rinsenji monjo #2049.
154 'As you already know': Rinsenji monjo #2049.
154 'Keeping them in your office': Rinsenji monjo #1710.
155 'If Hirosuke and I agreed to make a go of it': Rinsenji monjo #2049.
155 'Even if I stayed my whole life at home': Rinsenji monjo #2049.
155 Giyū found out: Rinsenji monjo #1722.
155 'As you probably know': Rinsenji monjo #1722.
156 unhappy year: Rinsenji monjo #1722.
157 Some preachers taught: Williams, *The Other Side of Zen*, 50–58, 125–28.
158 playing dual roles: Utagawa Kunisada I, *Actors Sawamura Tosshō I as Takeda Katsuyori, Iwai Shijaku I as Emon no Mae, and Iwai Tojaku I as Streetwalker Okimi, and Ichiwa Ebizō V as Boatman Sangorō*; Utagawa Kuniyoshi, *Actors Ichikawa Ebizō V as Yokozō, Iwai Tojaku I as Kansuke's Mother Miyuki, and Sawamura Tosshō I as Jihizō*.
158 He shaved his beard clean: This description of putting on kabuki makeup is drawn from Nagatani, *Kabuki no keshō*.
159 Even in his memorial portrait: Utagawa Kunisada I, *Memorial Portrait of Actor Iwai Tojaku I, with Iwai Kumesaburō III*. Thank you to Satoko Shimazaki for this insight.
159 Merchants who had failed: Yoshida, *Nijūisseki no Edo*, 89–91.
160 Giyū acknowledged: Rinsenji monjo #1723. Meanwhile, in his own records, he'd continue to call her Tsuneno for the rest of his life.

Chapter Seven: Troubles at Home

161 nearly four hundred thousand: There is much debate about the size of Osaka's population in the Edo period. See Yabuta, *Bushi no machi Ōsaka*, 1–28.
161 Ōshio Heihachirō: Bolitho, 'The Tempō Crisis,' in *The Cambridge History of Japan*, vol. 5: *The Nineteenth Century*, ed. Marius Jansen, 8–9; Jansen, *The Making of Modern Japan*, 248–51; Najita, 'Ōshio Heihachirō.'
163 City Magistrates took the unprecedented step: Fujita, *Tenpō no kaikaku*, 19–20.
163 Canton: Platt, *Imperial Twilight*, xviii.
163 idea about China: On the complicated place of China, Chinese knowledge, and 'Chinese things,' see Jansen, *China in the Tokugawa World*, and Suzuki, 'The Making of Tōjin.'

164 Lin Zexu confiscated: Platt, *Imperial Twilight*, 350–81.

164 no one in Japan heard the news: News of the conflict finally reached Japan via Dutch ships in 1840. Fujita, *Tenpō no kaikaku*, 186.

165 China's Qing Dynasty was completely outmatched: Platt, *Imperial Twilight*, 412, 421–22.

165 educated men in Japan began to take notice: Fujita, *Tenpō no kaikaku*, 185–94.

165 would come to be shared: Walthall, *The Weak Body of a Useless Woman*; William Steele, *Alternative Narratives in Modern Japanese History*, 32–60.

165 Tokugawa Ienari, the querulous retired shogun, lay dying: Fukasawa, *Hatamoto fujin ga mita Edo no tasogare*, 168–69.

165 'There are ordinary people who can live': Fukasawa, *Hatamoto fujin ga mita Edo no tasogare*, 170.

166 not allowed to shave: Fukasawa, *Hatamoto fujin ga mita Edo no tasogare*, 170. It was seven days for commoner headmen. Tōkyō komonjo-kan, ed., *Edo: 1838–1841*, 12.

166 Tsuneno's mother died: Rinsenji monjo #2054.

166 Giyū had written: Rinsenji monjo #1723.

166 'About my daughter': Rinsenji monjo #1723.

166 gathered condolences: Rinsenji monjo #2054.

166 'It truly pains me': Rinsenji monjo #2064.

167 'I'm fine with spending money': Rinsenji monjo #1699.

167 'I'm persevering here in Edo': Rinsenji monjo #1712.

167 'The senior servants': Rinsenji monjo #1713.

168 Commoners should not wear: *Edo machibure shū*, vol. 13, 380.

168 lanterns for the Sannō Festival: *Edo machibure shū*, vol. 13, 381.

168 bamboo grass: *Fujiokaya nikki*, vol. 2, 200; *Edo machibure shū*, vol. 14, 392.

168 gifts for the Kanda Festival: *Edo machibure shū*, vol. 14, 404.

169 personal behaviour was notorious: Bolitho, 'The Tempō Crisis,' 40–41.

169 No one had a single good thing to say: *Fujiokaya nikki*, vol. 2, 193.

169 Gisen, had moved to Edo: Rinsenji monjo #2047.

169 Sano Masakoto: Hall, *Tanuma Okitsugu*, 133–35.

170 he wrote the word 'idiot': Rinsenji monjo #2042.

170 he had been sent to negotiate: Rinsenji monjo #1674.

171 ginger: Rinsenji monjo #2064.

171 'I know Hirosuke's family': Rinsenji monjo #2067.

171 a secret report: *Shichū torishimari ruishū*, vol. 1, 215.

171 *All kinds of people*: Yoshida, ed., *Edo kabuki hōrei shūsei*, 356.

172 Iseki Takako: Fukasawa, *Hatamoto fujin ga mito Edo no tasogare*, 55.

172 a brief mention: *Fuikokaya nikki*, vol. 2, 216.

173 women's short jackets: Yoshida, ed., *Edo kabuki hōrei shūsei*, 354; *STR*, vol. 1, 239.

173 petty moneylenders: Yoshida, ed., *Edo kabuki hōrei shūsei*, 353.

173 teahouses where men: Pflugfelder, *Cartographies of Desire*, 155–157.

173 The City Magistrate delivered his verdict: Yoshida, ed., *Edo kabuki hōrei shūsei*, 373–77.

173 Dolls over nine inches: *Fujiokaya nikki*, vol. 2, 222–23.

173 Women were not allowed . . . umbrellas in the rain: *Fujiokaya nikki*, vol. 2, 228.

174 Tofu: *Edo machibure shū*, vol. 14, 30–31.

174 guardhouses: *Edo machibure shū*, vol. 14, 71–72.

174 hairdressers: *Fujiokaya nikki*, vol. 2, 260.

174 wholesaler associations: Katakura, *Ōedo happyaku hatchō to machi nanushi*, 199–200.

175 female musicians: *Fujiokaya nikki*, vol. 2, 231.

175 At first, they weathered the turmoil: Rinsenji monjo #2059.

175 'If there is some sudden crisis': Rinsenji monjo #2063.

175 Tsuneno went into service . . . couldn't retrieve it: Rinsenji monjo #2051.

176 'She doesn't even apologise for the trouble': Rinsenji monjo #2051.

176 'As for me': Rinsenji monjo #2051.

176 'People in the countryside': Rinsenji monjo #2051.

176 'I have four fellow servants': Rinsenji monjo #2051.

177 pawnshops were overstocked: *Shichū torishimari ruishū*, vol. 1, 306–7.

177 cheap hair ornaments: *Shichū torishimari ruishū*, vol. 1, 318.

177 'Hirosuke has an incredibly bad temper': Rinsenji monjo #2051.

177 'I've told him many times': Rinsenji monjo #2051.

177 Technically, a divorce had to be initiated: Fuess, *Divorce in Japan*, 78–79.

178 shogunal officials and defence-minded samurai agreed . . . took commands in Dutch: Fujita, *Tenpō no kaikaku*, 197–201.

178 The order to fire: Fujita, *Tenpō no kaikaku*, 207–10.

178 the kabuki actor Ichikawa Ebizō V: *Fujiokaya nikki*, vol. 2, 277–78.

179 'Not only do you subvert the law of the shogun': Matsuoka, *Torii Yōzō*, 25–26.

179 the magistrate expelled: *Fujiokaya nikki*, vol. 2, 278.

179 Sake was so expensive: Fukasawa, *Hatamoto fujin ga mita Edo no tasogare*, 42.

179 'A heavy punishment': *Fujiokaya nikki*, vol. 2, 323.

180 'Recently, more and more people': *Edo machibure shū*, vol. 14, 321–25.

180 gathering place for hardened, ruthless men: Yoshida, *Mibunteki shūen to shakai: bunka kōzō*, 453.

180 prostitutes: Yoshihara, *Naitō Shinjuku*, 95–101.

180 No one could forget: Yoshihara, *Naitō Shinjuku*, 170–71.

181 took refuge with Hirosuke's younger brother: Rinsenji monjo #2042. Hanzaemon was a common name, and it's impossible to confirm that this Hanzaemon was the same one as Tsuneno's brother-in-law, but it seems very likely.

181 Restaurants' numbers: Yoshida, *Dentō toshi Edo*, 276.

181 fought endlessly: Rinsenji monjo #2042.

181 the shogun issued a series of notices: Bolitho, 'The Tenpō Crisis,' 39–40.

182 'It is inappropriate': Bolitho, 'The Tenpō Crisis,' 40.

182 the Kanda Festival: Fujisawa, *Hatamoto fujin ga mita Edo no tasogare*, 56.

182 the shogunate finally reached a breaking point: Bolitho, 'The Tenpō Crisis.'

182 He dismissed Mizuno . . . see the aftermath: *Fujiokaya nikki*, vol. 2, 375.

183 hand-clapping games: *Fujiokaya nikki*, vol. 2, 383–85.

184 Tsuneno called at Kyōshōji: Rinsenji monjo #2042.

185 'As long as I have Tsuneno': Rinsenji monjo #2042.

185 'Really': Rinsenji monjo #2042

185 Gisen made arrangements: Rinsenji monjo #2041.

185 'a fellow person': Rinsenji monjo #2041.

185 'At least now': Rinsenji monjo #2041.

186 'The fact is': Rinsenji monjo #2041.

186 didn't even have extra bedding: Rinsenji monjo #2041.

186 Back in Echigo, in 1729: Sugano, *Edo jidai no kōkōmono*, 122–24.

186 Tsuneno discovered that she had a better option: Rinsenji monjo #2034.

186 relocated theatre district was nearby: Rinsenji monjo #2047.

187 'He's snobbish and unkind': Rinsenji monjo #2035.

187 'Here in Edo, there isn't anywhere that lends bedding': Rinsenji monjo #2035.

187 Tsuneno stayed at Tokuhonji because: Rinsenji monjo #2031.

187 'They were all thoroughly sick of her': Rinsenji monjo #2031.

187 Tsuneno left Tokuhonji and went back: Rinsenji monjo #2031.

187 Tsuneno found yet another job in service, but it didn't pay: Rinsenji monjo #2044.

188 'People in Edo are arrogant and superior': Rinsenji monjo #2044.

188 She looked so bad that she was embarrassed: Rinsenji monjo #2044.

188 sharing a single robe: Rinsenji monjo #2044.

188 'You'll be angry at me': Rinsenji monjo #2044.

188 'Nothing has gone': Rinsenji monjo #2044.

188 Hirosuke seemed increasingly unstable: Rinsenji monjo #2027.

188 'If I'd known even the slightest bit': Rinsenji monjo #2027.

188 'I know I have a terrible temper': Rinsenji monjo #2027.

189 'Priests are useless': Rinsenji monjo #2027.

189 'We're going to take': Rinsenji monjo #2027.

189 'I know that I fight': Rinsenji monjo #2027.

189 'I'm fed up': Rinsenji monjo #2027.

189 he wrote out a notice of divorce six times: Rinsenji monjo #2027.

189 The letter was short: Rinsenji monjo #2009.

189 she relied on Hirosuke's old friend: Rinsenji monjo #2003; on Hirosuke and Yūzō's association, Rinsenji monjo #2006.

190 Her monthly salary was supposed to be: Rinsenji monjo #2027.

190 less than a pedlar could clear: Mega, *Buke ni totsuida josei no tegami*, 163.

190 Tsuneno wrote to her brothers and confessed: Rinsenji monjo #2027.

190 Fujiwara Yūzō, who had taken custody of Tsuneno as a favour, was no happier: Rinsenji monjo #2003.

190 he wrote another one: Rinsenji monjo #2005.

190 'the two of them don't seem to have': Rinsenji monjo #2005.

191 Giyū was mortified: Rinsenji monjo #2004.

191 'Hirosuke is supposed to be': Rinsenji monjo #2043.

191 He wrote to Yūzō: Rinsenji monjo #2004.

191 'After what happened with Tsuneno': Rinsenji monjo #2006.

191 when Hirosuke found out: Rinsenji monjo #2011.

192 he had told one of Giyū's acquaintances: Rinsenji monjo #2127.

192 Yes, they had separated, he admitted . . . in the middle of winter?: Rinsenji monjo #2011.

192 Hirosuke called in his younger brother, Hanzaemon: Rinsenji monjo #2014, Rinsenji monjo #2017. Gorō was actually Takeda Yakara, aka Hanzaemon. Tsuneno calls Yakara Gorō in Rinsenji monjo #2009.

192 Hanzaemon summoned Tsuneno . . . Tsuneno was already gone: Rinsenji monjo #2017.

192 Tsuneno arrived back at Rinsenji just before the New Year: Rinsenji monjo #2018.

193 Tamenaga Shunsui: Shirane, *An Early Modern Anthology*, 388–92.

193 'be careful goods': Tōkyō Daigaku Shiryō Hensanjo, ed., *Shichū tori-shimari ruishū*, vol. 1, 492.

Chapter Eight: In the Office of the City Magistrate

196 Toshino: Rinsenji monjo #2114, Rinsenji monjo #2111, Rinsenji monjo #2112.

196 Kihaku: Rinsenji monjo #1645.

196 while the maidservant . . . someone so stupid, he said: Rinsenji monjo #637. Half-sized blanket here *hanbuton*.

197 a messenger came: Rinsenji monjo #637.

198 it wasn't clear that Giyū would tolerate: Denpachi made the point to Giyū that Tsuneno had nowhere else to live if she didn't go to Edo. Rinsenji monjo #637.

199 James Biddle: Long, *Sailor-Diplomat*, 209–16.

200 Yes, she said: Rinsenji monjo #637.

200 Giyū was a problem: Rinsenji monjo #637.

200 drew up documents: Rinsenji monjo #2026.

200 Tsuneno was eager to leave: Rinsenji monjo #637.

200 Giyū still couldn't quite reconcile himself . . . incident with the old blanket: Rinsenji monjo #637.

201 When she finally left Echigo: Rinsenji monjo #637.

201 travelled the familiar road . . . thirteen days: Rinsenji monjo #2025.

202 a windy, rainy day: *Fujiokaya nikki*, vol. 3, 59–60.

202 less than a mile apart: Okazaki, *Tōyama Kinshirō*, 143.

202 near the Sukiyabashi gate: Ishii, *Edo no machi bugyō*, 19.

203 'This person – a woman': Saitō, *Shichiyashi no kenkyū*, 181.

203 believed that he had a responsibility: Fujita, *Tōyama Kinshirō no jidai*, 35–180.

203 His father: Okazaki, *Tōyama Kinshirō*, 26–50.

204 Tōyama was never sure: Okazaki, *Tōyama Kinshirō*, 76–86.

204 stories about Tōyama's misspent youth: Okazaki, *Tōyama Kinshirō*, 8–10; Fujita, *Tōyama Kinshirō no jidai*, 12–23.

204 haemorrhoids: Okazaki, *Tōyama Kinshirō*, 11–12.

205 died on the job: Beerens, 'Interview with a Bakumatsu Official,' 174; Minami, *Edo no machi bugyō*, 15.

205 broad, red-faced: Okazaki, *Tōyama Kinshirō*, 96.

205 He and his wife, Okei: Okazaki, ed., *Tōyama Kinshirō-ke nikki*, 11–13.
205 'subsidy assistants': Teeuwen and Nakai, eds., *Lust, Commerce, and Corruption*, 53–55.
205 personal retainers who helped: Minami, *Edo no machi bugyō*, 21.
206 obliged to live: On the details of the magistrate's living arrangements, Okazaki, *Tōyama Kinshirō-ke nikki*, 8–9. Hirosuke's letters were addressed to him at the office; see Rinsenji monjo #1972.
206 front gate was ominous: Sasama, *Zusetsu Edo machi bugyōsho jiten*, 39–41.
206 off duty: We know because he was on duty the following month; see Okazaki, *Tōyama Kinshirō*, 139.
206 still hard at work: Minami, *Edo no machi bugyō*, 15.
206 the great gate opened: Ishii, *Edo no machi bugyō*, 19; Sasama, *Zusetsu Edo machi bugyōsho jiten*, 40–41.
206 right gate: Minami, *Edo no machi bugyō*, 35–37; Sasama, *Zusetsu Edo machi bugyō jiten*, 40–41; Ishii, *Edo no machi bugyō*, 19–20.
207 left gate: Sasama, *Zusetsu Edo machi bugyō jiten*, 40–41.
207 the accused in criminal cases: On the process from apprehension to sentencing, see Botsman, *Punishment and Power*, 35–38.
207 giant key: Minami, *Edo no machi bugyō*, 36.
207 did not have time to review: Beerens, 'Interview with a Bakumatsu Official' (2), 177.
208 Tens of thousands of civil and criminal matters: Minami, *Edo no machi bugyō*, 40–41.
208 magistrate was always required: Beerens, 'Interview with a Bakumatsu Official' (2), 180.
208 'For the duration': Beerens, 'Interview with a Bakumatsu Official' (2), 180.
208 the dreaded compound at Kodenmachō: On the jailhouse and torture, see Botsman, *Punishment and Power*, 35–38, 62–66.
209 high-profile sentencing: *Tōyama Kinshirō*, 139–41; *Fujiokaya nikki*, vol. 3, 38. On Okada's job (as an *oku bōzu*), see Beerens, 'Interview with a Bakumatsu Official,' 389, 394.
209 execution: On beheadings, see Botsman, *Punishment and Power*, 25–26, 53; Beerens, 'Interview with a Bakumatsu Official' (2), 195.
209 Yamada Asaemon: Botsman, *Punishment and Power*, 20.
210 gallbladder: Ujiie, 'Hitokiri no ie, onna no ie.'
210 hundreds of people . . . twenty or more: 'Oshioki no setsu shusseki namae oboe-chō' (1844). Thanks to Daniel Botsman for sending me this document and the transcription.

210 commuted the sentence: *Fujiokaya nikki*, vol. 3, 89.

211 Their positions were hereditary . . . best possible form of protection: Minami, *Edo no machi bugyō*, 202–7.

212 discouraging civil litigation: See the examples in Saitō, *Shichiyashi no kenkyū*, 179, 188.

212 'This is a nice settlement': Saitō, *Shichiyashi no kenkyū*, 179.

212 bribes: Minami, *Edo no machi bugyō*, 192–95.

212 unlikely fashion icons: Minami, *Edo no machi bugyō*, 120.

212 collected information: See Miyachi, *Bakumatsu ishinki no bunka to jōhō*, on the political importance of rumours.

212 talking horse: Minami, *Edo no machi bugyō*, 43.

212 female calligraphy instructor: Miyachi, *Bakumatsu ishinki no bunka to jōhō*, 54–56.

212 giant carp: *Fujiokaya nikki*, vol. 5, 241–43.

213 groups of patrolmen made regular rounds: Minami, *Edo no machi bugyō*, 119.

213 suspicious drownings: *Fujiokaya nikki*, vol. 3, 92, 157, 162–63, 170.

213 'fingertips': Minami, *Edo no machi bugyō*, 120; Botsman, *Punishment and Power*, 87, 94.

214 formally appointed: See the example in Abe, *Meakashi Kinjūrō no shōgai*.

214 steady salaries: Tsukada, 'Meakashi.'

214 terrified of the fingertips . . . Confucian scholar: Minami, *Edo no machi bugyō*, 35–37.

215 pulled on his sleeves: Fujita, *Tōyama Kinshirō no jidai*, 22.

215 'very important position': Rinsenji monjo #637.

215 had tried to visit: Rinsenji monjo #2090.

215 accepting Tsuneno's gifts: Rinsenji monjo #637.

216 sent dolls: Rinsenji monjo #2084.

216 strangely vivid dream: Rinsenji monjo #2090.

216 'Your brother disinherited us': Rinsenji monjo #2084.

216 Unbeknownst to her: Rinsenji monjo #943.

216 magistrate's household was busy: Okazaki, *Tōyama Kinshirō-ke nikki*, 72.

216 miserable four days there: Rinsenji monjo #2042.

217 Tsuneno found Gisen: Rinsenji monjo #2084.

217 A priest had taken an inventory . . . to intervene: Rinsenji monjo #943.

217 'Grapes,' he said: Rinsenji monjo #2084.

217 summoned to Edo Castle: According to Hirosuke, Rinsenji monjo

#2088; according to Tsuneno, Rinsenji monjo #2084. In the Tōyama household diary, *Tōyama Kinshirō-ke nikki*, 73.

217 hearings were rare: Tsuneno said every ten or eleven years. Rinsenji monjo #2084. On the *kuji jōchō* Sasama, *Zusetsu Edo machi bugyōsho jiten*, 99–102; Fujita, *Tōyama Kinshirō no jidai*, 29–30.

218 news of Gisen's death: Rinsenji monjo #2079.

218 went to Kyōshōji at dawn: Rinsenji monjo #2090.

218 'When it came time to wash the body': Rinsenji monjo #2084.

218 Later, Gisen was dressed: On funeral rituals, and specifically those of Tsuneno's sect, see Hur, *Death and the Social Order*, 150, 161–62.

218 Then they carried Gisen's coffin to a temple by the Kozukappara execution ground: Rinsenji monjo #943.

218 He wrote and apologised: He says he is sending 'bones' (*hone*). Rinsenji monjo #1972.

219 'I poured the water over him myself': Rinsenji monjo #2084.

219 she admitted that his posthumous name: Rinsenji monjo #2090.

219 aftermath of Gisen's death: See the long discussion in Rinsenji monjo #2084 and Rinsenji monjo #943.

219 inventory: Rinsenji monjo #2086, Rinsenji monjo #943.

219 accounting: Rinsenji monjo #943.

219 kept a few items to place in his coffin: Rinsenji monjo # 2084.

220 burning at the stake: For a case of burning at the stake ordered by Tōyama see *Fujiokaya nikki*, vol. 3, 185.

220 He began to take months off: Okazaki, *Tōyama Kinshirō*, 150–52.

220 They discussed adopting a child: Rinsenji monjo #1972.

221 Giyū died: Rinsenji monjo #1231.

Chapter Nine: **Endings and Afterlives**

223 Commodore Matthew Calbraith Perry received a telegram: For the full account of his deliberation, Morison, *'Old Bruin,'* 261–75.

224 'learn to let our neighbours' affairs alone': Morison, *'Old Bruin,'* 273.

224 'a gift of Providence': Morison, *'Old Bruin,'* 268.

224 Perry asked for assurances: Morison, *'Old Bruin,'* 273–75.

224 the *Princeton*: Pineu, ed., *The Japan Expedition 1852–54*, 3, 29.

224 his old favourite: Walworth, *Black Ships off Japan*, 21–22.

225 gifts: Walworth, *Black Ships off Japan*, 23.

225 letter: 'Letter of the President of United States to the Emperor of Japan' reprinted in Pineu, ed., *The Personal Journal*, 220–21.

225 a large parchment: Pineau, ed., *The Personal Journal*, 98.

225 three feet deeper: Walworth, *Black Ships off Japan*, 28.

226 in service with yet another new master: This might have been Tsuneno, Hirosuke, or both of them; the letter isn't clear. Rinsenji monjo #2842.

226 only a block away: See the 'Surugadai' map in *Edo kiriezu*.

226 Tsuneno fell ill: Rinsenji monjo #2842. This document does not include the year, but I assume it is 1853, following the date of Tsuneno's death in Rinsenji monjo #670.

226 'cold sicknesses': *shōkan*; thanks to Waka Hirokawa for explaining the diagnosis and its modern equivalents.

226 'I'm not changing now': Rinsenji monjo #2842.

227 'I'm looking after her all by myself': Rinsenji monjo #2842.

227 'He must be so big now': Rinsenji monjo #1725.

227 polite message back: Rinsenji monjo #2027. 'Small gold coins' here are *shu*.

227 in Mauritius: Pineu, ed., *The Personal Journal*, 29–36.

228 'wretched, half-clad people,' 'poverty and filth': Pineu, ed., *The Personal Journal*, 54.

228 'the Chinamen must have thought': Speiden, *William Speiden Journals*, vol. 1.

228 the very beginning of Edo summer: Kishii, *Edo no higoyomi: jō*, 186–214.

228 the exact date: Rinsenji monjo #670.

229 'It is not extravagant': Pineau, ed., *The Personal Journal*, 57–58.

230 small slip of paper: Rinsenji monjo #670.

231 tributary state: on this complicated relationship, see Smits, *Visions of Ryukyu*.

231 'Japanese dependencies': Pineau, ed., *The Personal Journal*, 69.

231 'quite weak': Pineau, ed., *The Personal Journal*, 67.

231 'deceitful and unscrupulous': Pineau, ed., *The Personal Journal*, 69.

231 more taken with the Bonin Islands: Pineau, ed., *The Personal Journal*, 71–75.

231 liked the people: Heine, *With Perry to Japan*, 57–58.

231 When the divers went under: Sewall, *The Logbook of the Captain's Clerk*, 128.

231 Tsuneno's spirit was fully pacified: Hur, *Death and the Social Order*, 170–71, 177.

232 thick fog: Heine, *With Perry*, 63–64.

232 Immediately Perry's fleet was surrounded . . . 'queer sort of people': Speiden, *William Speiden Journals*, vol. 1.

232 News of the ships' arrival: Satō, *Bakumatsu ishin to minshū sekai*, 14.

232 City gossip turned: *Fujiokaya nikki*, vol. 5, 318–25.

232 Soon more boats: Speiden, *William Speiden Journals*, vol. 1.

232 a hundred Japanese ships: Speiden, *William Speiden Journals*, vol. 1.

232 steam whistle, an ear splitter: Heine, *With Perry*, 68.

232 Some of the men in the junks: Speiden, *William Speiden Journals*, vol. 1.

232 Others beat a path: Heine, *With Perry to Japan*, 68.

232 he went to shore on a barge: Pineau, ed., *The Personal Journal*, 98.

233 looked as if their last day had come: Speiden, *William Speiden Journals*, vol. 1.

233 Perry, accompanied: Pineau, ed., *The Personal Journal*, 98.

233 African-American bodyguards: African-Americans had served in the US Navy since its establishment. As of 1839, there was a ban on the employment of enslaved sailors, so these were freemen. Ramold, *Slaves, Sailors, Citizens*, 6–24.

233 to the strains of 'Yankee Doodle': Heine, *With Perry to Japan*, 75.

233 'It was deserted and lonely': Satō, *Bakumatsu ishinki no minshū sekai*, 14.

233 The rank-and-file samurai in the city prepared: Satō, *Bakumatsu ishinki no minshū sekai*, 14.

233 Meanwhile, high-ranking officials: These and other details about the complicated sequence of events leading to this decision from Jansen, *The Making of Modern Japan*, 256–332.

233 Commoners in Edo said: Satō, *Bakumatsu ishinki no minshū sekai*, 16.

234 For those who couldn't see: Dower, 'Black Ships and Samurai: Commodore Perry and the Opening of Japan.'

234 The commoner headmen in Edo had all been warned: *Fujiokaya nikki*, vol. 5, 610–11.

234 the menu: *Fujiokaya nikki*, vol. 5, 612–13.

234 The Perry expedition's artist: Heine, *With Perry*, 125.

234 'It cannot be said that Japan': Sewall, *Logbook of the Captain's Clerk*, 125.

235 one major disappointment: Heine, *With Perry to Japan*, 128–29.

235 Perry had wanted to anchor . . . turned them back: Pineau, ed., *The Personal Journal*, 198–200.

237 an earthquake: *Shinpen Chiyoda kushi: tsūshi-hen*, 727–31.

237 lords dressed in firefighting garb: Kitahara, *Jishin no shakaishi*, 329–31.

238 the people of Edo imagined that the black ships and the shaking of the earth were related catastrophes: Smits, 'Shaking Up Japan.'

239 'Stop this useless talk!': Smits, 'Shaking Up Japan,' 1065.

239 Ansei Treaties: Auslin, *Negotiating with Imperialism*, 1–2, 44.

239 he was adopted by the Lord of Kameyama: Ogawa, ed., *Kansei-fu ikō hatamoto-ke hyakka jiten*, vol. 5, 2574.

240 Tomosaburō suffered his worst crisis: Totman, *The Collapse of the Tokugawa Bakufu*, 14–15, 68–72; Jansen, *The Making of Modern Japan*, 314–15.

240 some of the British man's compatriots thought: E. H. House, quoted in Black, *Young Japan, Yokohama and Yedo*, vol. 1, 132–34.

240 roughly one or two hundred: Partner, *The Merchant's Tale*, Table Two.

241 the cost of living rose 50 percent: Jansen, *The Making of Modern Japan*, 314.

241 trade began to head directly to Yokohama: Makihara, *Bunmeikoku o mezashite*, 30–31.

241 Edo lost half its population: Smith, 'The Edo-Tokyo Transition,' in Jansen and Rozman, eds., *Japan in Transition from Tokugawa to Meiji*, 347, 350.

241 The last Tokugawa shogun: Totman, *The Collapse of the Tokugawa Bakufu*, 436–43.

241 'serious', 'frugal' and 'never wasteful': Katsu, *Musui's Story*, 2.

242 'Courteous, the Princes of Asia': Whitman, 'A Broadway Pageant' (1860).

242 'If you are bent on threatening weak people': Steele, 'Katsu Kaishū and the Historiography of the Meiji Restoration,' 307.

242 didn't burn: It didn't burn when the castle was surrendered. But subsequently, and to Kaishū's dismay, some of the shogun's troops rebelled, fought the imperial occupiers and lost a battle that burned down several neighbourhoods in northern Edo. Steele, 'Against the Restoration.'

243 Matsuo Taseko: Walthall, *The Weak Body of a Useless Woman*, 259–60.

243 never even seen Mt Fuji: Keene, *Emperor of Japan*, 5.

243 architects of the new regime argued: Kobayashi, *Meiji ishin to Kyōto*, 55–56.

244 Hoterukan: Coaldrake, *Architecture and Authority in Japan*, 216; also see, for example, Utagawa Hiroshige III, 'Tsukiji hoterukan omotegake no zu' (1869).

244 A grassy area nearby: *Chūō kushi: chūkan*, 125.

244 only in the twentieth century: Bestor, *Tsukiji*, 112.

244 *In Darkest Tokyo*: Matsubara, *Saiankoku no Tōkyō*.

244 cholera: Gramlich-Oka, 'The Body Economic.'

244 Sumiyoshi-chō: *Chūō kushi chūkan*, 193–94.

244 Ginza: Grunow, 'Ginza Bricktown and the Myth of Meiji Moderniza-

tion'; Grunow, 'Paving Power: Western Urban Planning and Imperial Space from the Streets of Meiji Tokyo to Colonial Seoul.'

245 permit to brew sake: Rinsenji monjo #1597.

245 donated fourteen yen for the construction of a public elementary school: Rinsenji monjo #1471.

245 six departures: Ōbuchi, ed., *Kisha jikokuhyō*.

246 hundreds of years in one generation: from the subtitle of Sugimoto, *Daughter of the Samurai*.

Epilogue

251 Hokusai's *Great Wave* is an icon: Guth, *Hokusai's Great Wave*.

BIBLIOGRAPHY

Abe Yoshio. *Meakashi Kinjūrō no shōgai: Edo jidai shomin seikatsu no jitsuzō.* Tōkyō: Chūō Kōronsha, 1981.

Aburai Hiroko. *Edo hōkōnin no kokoroechō: gofukushō Shirokiya no nichijō.* Tōkyō: Shinchōsha, 2007.

'Aiwatase mōsu issatsu no koto,' Kansei 10.7, Hasegawa-ke monjo, Niigata Prefectural Archives, Niigata City, Niigata Prefecture. Accessed through Niigata kenritsu bunshokan intānetto komonjo kōza. https://www .pref-lib.niigata.niigata.jp/?page_id=671.

American Citizen and General Advertiser, The (New York, NY).

Anderson, Clare. 'Convict Passages in the Indian Ocean, c. 1790–1860.' In Emma Christopher, Cassandra Pybus and Marcus Rediker, eds., *Many Middle Passages: Forced Migration and the Making of the Modern World,* 129–49. Berkeley: University of California Press, 2007.

Asakura Yūko. 'Kinsei ni okeru onna tegata no hatsugyō to Takada-han.' *Jōetsu Kyōiku Daigaku Kiyō* 23:1 (2003): 191–202.

Asano Shūgō and Yoshida Nobuyuki, eds. *Ōedo Nihonbashi emaki ezu: 'Kidai shōran' no sekai.* Tōkyō: Kōdansha, 2003.

Asaoka Kōji. *Furugi.* Tōkyō: Hōsei daigaku shuppankyoku, 2005.

Bacon, Alice Mabel. *Japanese Girls and Women.* Boston: Houghton Mifflin, 1891.

Beerens, Anna. 'Interview with a Bakumatsu Official: A Translation from Kyūji Shinmonroku.' *Monumenta Nipponica* 55:3 (2000): 369–98.

———. 'Interview with a Bakumatsu Official: A Translation from Kyūji Shinmonroku (2).' *Monumenta Nipponica* 57:2 (2002): 173–206.

———. 'Interview with Two Ladies of the Ōoku: A Translation from Kyūji Shinmonroku.' *Monumenta Nipponica* 63:2 (2008): 265–324.

Berry, Mary Elizabeth. *Hideyoshi*. Cambridge, MA: Harvard University Press, 1982.

Bestor, Theodore. *Tsukiji: The Fish Market at the Center of the World*. Berkeley: University of California Press, 2004.

Black, John Reddie. *Young Japan: Yokohama and Yedo. A narrative of the settlement and the city from the signing of the treaties in 1858, to the close of the year 1879. With a glance at the progress of Japan during a period of twenty-one years*. 2 vols. London: Trubner & Co., 1880.

Bodart-Bailey, Beatrice, ed. *Kaempfer's Japan: Tokugawa Culture Observed*. Honolulu: University of Hawai'i Press, 1999.

Bolitho, Harold. 'The Tempō Crisis.' In *The Cambridge History of Japan*, vol. 5: *The Nineteenth Century*, ed. Marius Jansen, 116–67. New York: Cambridge University Press, 1989.

Botsman, Daniel. *Punishment and Power in the Making of Modern Japan*. Princeton, NJ: Princeton University Press, 2004.

Chiyoda-ku, ed. *Chiyoda kushi*. 3 vols. Tōkyō: Chiyoda kuyakusho, 1960.
———, ed. *Shinpen Chiyoda kushi: tsūshi-hen*. Tōkyō: Chiyoda-ku, 1998.

Chūō-ku, ed. *Chūō kushi*. 3 vols. Tōkyō: Tōkyō-to Chūō Kuyakusho, 1958.

Clark, Timothy. 'What Is Ukiyo-e Painting?' Lecture, Art Institute of Chicago, November 15, 2018.

Coaldrake, William. *Architecture and Authority in Japan*. London: Routledge, 1996.

Corbett, Rebecca. *Cultivating Femininity: Women and Tea Culture in Edo and Meiji Japan*. Honolulu: University of Hawai'i Press, 2018.

Cornell, Laurel. 'Why Are There No Spinsters in Japan?' *Journal of Family History* 9:4 (1984): 326–89.

Dalby, Liza. *Kimono: Fashioning Culture*. New Haven, CT: Yale University Press, 1993.

Dobbins, James. *Letters of the Nun Eshinni: Images of Pure Land Buddhism in Medieval Japan*. Honolulu: University of Hawai'i Press, 2004.

Dower, John. 'Black Ships and Samurai: Commodore Perry and the Opening of Japan.' https://visualizingcultures.mit.edu/black_ships_and_samurai/bss_essay01.html.

Drixler, Fabian. *Mabiki: Infanticide and Population Growth in Eastern Japan, 1660–1950*. Berkeley: University of California Press, 2013.

Durham, Valerie R. 'The Scandalous Love of Osome and Hisamitsu: Introduction.' In James R. Brandon and Samuel L. Leiter, eds., *Kabuki Plays on Stage: Darkness and Desire, 1804–64*, 64–67. Honolulu: University of Hawai'i Press, 2002.

Edo kiriezu [map] (1849–1862). Accessed through National Diet Library Digital Collection, http://dl.ndl.go.jp/info:ndljp/pid/1286255.

'Edo no han'i.' Tokyo Metropolitan Archives, Tokyo, http://www.soumu .metro.tokyo.jp/01soumu/archives/0712edo_hanni.htm.

Edo shubiki zu [map] (1818). Tokyo Metropolitan Archives, Tokyo.

Ehlers, Maren. *Give and Take: Poverty and the Status Order in Early Modern Japan.* Cambridge, MA: Harvard Asia Center, 2018.

Emerson, Edwin, and Maurice Magnus. *The Nineteenth Century and After: A History Year by Year.* Vol. 1. New York: Dodd, Mead, and Co., 1902.

Emori Ichirō, ed. *Edo jidai josei seikatsu ezu daijiten.* 10 vols. Tōkyō: Ōzorasha, 1993–1994.

Ferguson, Niall. *Empire: How Britain Made the Modern World.* London: Penguin, 2004.

Frumer, Yulia. *Making Time: Astronomical Time Measurement in Tokugawa Japan.* Chicago: University of Chicago Press, 2018.

———. 'Translating Time: Habits of Western Style Timekeeping in Late Tokugawa Japan.' *Technology and Culture* 55:4 (2014): 785–820.

Fuess, Harald. *Divorce in Japan: Family, Gender, and the State.* Stanford, CA: Stanford University Press, 2004.

Fujioto Tokunin, ed. *Tsukiji Betsuin-shi.* Tōkyō: Honganji Tsukiji Betsuin, 1937.

Fujita, Kayoko. 'Japan Indianized: The Material Culture of Imported Textiles in Japan, 1550–1850.' In Giorgio Riello and Prasannan Parthasarathi, eds., *The Spinning World: A Global History of Cotton,* 181–204. New York: Oxford University Press, 2009.

Fujita Satoru. *Kinsei no sandai kaikaku.* Tōkyō: Yamakawa Shuppansha, 2002.

———. *Tenpō no kaikaku.* Tōkyō: Yoshikawa Kōbunkan, 1989.

———. *Tōyama Kinshirō no jidai.* Tōkyō: Azekura Shobō, 1992.

Fujiya Kichizō. *Bansei on-Edo ezu* [map] (1854). C.V. Starr East Asian Library, University of California, Berkeley. Accessed through 'Japanese Historical Maps: East Asian Library – University of California, Berkeley,' http://www.davidrumsey.com/japan/.

Fukai Masaumi. *Zukai Edojō o yomu.* Tōkyō: Hara Shobō, 1997.

Fukasawa Akio. *Hatamoto fujin ga mita Edo no tasogare: Iseki Takako no esupuri nikki.* Tōkyō: Bunshun shinsho, 2007.

Fukui Tamotsu. 'Edo bakufu nikki.' In *Kokushi daijiten* (accessed through JapanKnowledge).

Garrioch, David. 'The Everyday Lives of Parisian Women and the October Days of 1789.' *Social History* 24:3 (1999): 231–49.

Gaubatz, Thomas. 'Urban Fictions of Early Modern Japan: Identity, Media, Genre.' Ph.D. dissertation, Columbia University, 2016.

Golownin, R. N. *Narrative of My Captivity in Japan During the Years 1811, 1812, and 1813*. 2 vols. London: Printed for Henry Colburn, 1818.

Gordon, Andrew. *Fabricating Consumers: The Sewing Machine in Modern Japan*. Berkeley: University of California Press, 2011.

Goree, Robert. 'Fantasies of the Real: Meisho zue in Early Modern Japan.' Ph.D. dissertation, Yale University, 2010.

Gotō Kazuo. *Komonjo de yomu Essa josei no Edo jidai*. Niigata: n.p., 2016.

Gramlich-Oka, Bettina. 'The Body Economic: Japan's Cholera Epidemic of 1858 in Popular Discourse.' *East Asian Science, Technology, and Medicine*, no. 30 (2009): 32–73.

Grunow, Tristan. 'Ginza Bricktown and the Myth of Meiji Modernization,' https://meijiat150dtr.arts.ubc.ca/essays/grunow/.

———. 'Paving Power: Western Urban Planning and Imperial Space from the Streets of Meiji Tokyo to Colonial Seoul.' *Journal of Urban History* 42:3 (2016): 506–56.

Guth, Christine M. E. *Hokusai's Great Wave: Biography of a Global Icon*. Honolulu: University of Hawai'i Press, 2015.

———. 'Theorizing the Hari Kuyō: The Ritual Disposal of Needles in Early Modern Japan.' *Design Culture* 6:2 (2014): 169–86.

Hall, John Whitney. *Tanuma Okitsugu, 1719–1788: Forerunner of Modern Japan*. Cambridge, MA: Harvard University Press, 1955.

Harada Nobuo. *Edo no shoku seikatsu*. Tōkyō: Iwanami Shoten, 2009.

Hasegawa-ke monjo, Niigata Prefectural Archives, Niigata City, Niigata Prefecture.

Hayami Akira. 'Another *Fossa Magna*: Proportion Marrying and Age at Marriage in Late Nineteenth-Century Japan.' *Journal of Family History* 12: 1–3 (1987): 57–72.

Hayashi Reiko. 'Kasama jōkamachi ni okeru joseizō.' In Kinsei joseishi kenkyūkai, ed., *Edo jidai no joseitachi*, 221–86. Tōkyō: Yoshikawa Kōbunkan, 1990.

Heine, William. *With Perry to Japan*. Edited and translated by Frederic Trautmann. Honolulu: University of Hawai'i Press, 1990.

Hirai, Kiyoshi, ed. *Zusetsu Edo 2: daimyō to hatamoto no kurashi*. Tōkyō: Gakken, 2000.

Horikiri Tatsuichi. *The Stories Clothes Tell: Voices of Working-Class Japan*. Edited and translated by Rieko Wagoner. Lanham, MD: Rowman & Littlefield, 2016.

Howell, David. 'Foreign Encounters and Informal Diplomacy in Early Modern Japan.' *Journal of Japanese Studies* 40:2 (2014): 295–327.

———. *Geographies of Identity in Nineteenth-Century Japan.* Berkeley: University of California Press, 2005.

Hubbard, Eleanor. *City Women: Money, Sex, and the Social Order in Early Modern London.* New York: Oxford University Press, 2012.

Hur, Nam-Lin. *Death and the Social Order in Tokugawa Japan: Buddhism, Anti-Christianity, and the Danka System.* Cambridge, MA: Harvard Asia Center, 2007.

Igler, David. *The Great Ocean: Pacific Worlds from Captain Cook to the Gold Rush.* New York: Oxford University Press, 2013.

Ihara Seiseien. *Kinsei nihon engekishi.* Tōkyō: Waseda Daigaku Shuppanbu, 1927.

Inō Tadataka. *Dai-Nihon enkai yochi zenzu* [map] (1821). 108 vols. Accessed through National Diet Library Digital Collection, http://dl.ndl.go.jp/info:ndljp/pid/1286631?tocOpened=1.

Ishii Ryōsuke. *Edo no machi bugyō.* Tōkyō: Akashi Shoten, 1989.

Isoda Michifumi. *Bushi no kakeibō: Kaga-han osan'yōmono no Meiji ishin.* Tokyo: Shinchōsha, 2003.

Iwabuchi Reiji. 'Edo kinban bushi ga mita "Edo" to kunimoto.' *Rekishi hyōron*, no. 790 (2016): 60–73.

Janetta, Ann. 'Famine Mortality in Japan.' *Population Studies* 46:3 (1992): 427–43.

Jansen, Marius. *China in the Tokugawa World.* Cambridge, MA: Harvard University Press, 2000.

———. *The Making of Modern Japan.* Cambridge, MA: Belknap Press of Harvard University Press, 2000.

JapanKnowledge. https://japanknowledge.com.

Jōetsu shishi hensan iinkai, ed. *Jōetsu shishi.* 20 vols. Jōetsu-shi: Jōetsu-shi, 1999–2004.

Jones, Sumie, with Kenji Watanabe, eds. *An Edo Anthology: Literature from Japan's Mega-City, 1750–1850.* Honolulu: University of Hawai'i Press, 2013.

Kanamori Atsuko. *Sekisho nuke: Edo no onnatachi no bōken.* Tōkyō: Sōbunsha, 2001.

Kasaya Kazuhiko. *Shukun 'oshikome' no kōzō: kinsei daimyō to kashindan.* Tōkyō: Heibonsha, 1988.

Katakura Hisako. 'Bakumatsu ishinki no toshi kazoku to joshi rōdō.' In Sōgō joseishi kenkyūkai, ed., *Nihon joseishi ronshū,* vol. 6: *Josei no kurashi to rōdō,* 85–110. Tokyo: Yoshikawa Kōbunkan, 1998.

———. *Edo jūtaku jijō.* Tōkyō: Tōkyō-to, 1990.

————. *Ōedo happyaku-yachō to machi nanushi.* Tōkyō: Yoshikawa Kōbunkan, 2009.

————. *Tenmei no Edo uchikowashi.* Tōkyō: Shin Nihon Shuppansha, 2001.

Katō Takashi. 'Governing Edo.' In James McClain, John M. Merriman, and Ugawa Kaoru, eds., *Edo and Paris: Urban Life and the State in the Early Modern Era*, 41-67. Ithaca, NY: Cornell University Press, 1994.

Katsu Kōkichi. *Musui's Story: The Autobiography of a Tokugawa Samurai.* Translated by Teruko Craig. Tucson: University of Arizona Press, 1995.

Keene, Donald. *Emperor of Japan: Meiji and His World.* New York: Columbia University Press, 2002.

————. *The Japanese Discovery of Europe, 1720–1830.* Stanford, CA: Stanford University Press, 1969.

Kikuchi Hitomi. *Edo oshare zue: ishō to yuigami no sanbyakunen shi.* Tōkyō: Kōdansha, 2007.

Kikuchi Isao. *Kinsei no kikin.* Tōkyō: Yoshikawa Kōbunkan, 1997.

Kikuchi Kazuhiro. 'Benibana emaki o yomu.' *Mogamigawa bunka kenkyū* 5 (2007): 97–114.

Kikuchi Kazuo. *Nihon no rekishi saigai: Edo kōki no jiin kakochō ni yoru jisshō.* Tōkyō: Kokin Shoin, 1980.

Kinsei shiryō kenkyūkai, ed. *Edo machibure shūsei.* 22 vols. Tōkyō: Hanawa shobō, 1994–2012.

Kishii Yoshie. *Edo no higoyomi.* 2 vols. Tōkyō: Jitsugyō no Nihonsha, 1977.

Kitahara Itoko. *Jishin no shakaishi: Ansei daijishin to minshū.* Tōkyō: Yoshikawa Kōbunkan, 2013.

Kitahara Susumu. *Hyakuman toshi Edo no seikatsu.* Tōkyō: Kadokawa gakugei shuppan, 1991.

Kobayashi Takehiro. *Meiji ishin to Kyōto: kuge shakai no kaitai.* Kyōto: Rinsen Shoten, 1998.

Kodama Kōta. *Fukugen Ōedo jōhō chizu.* Tōkyō: Asahi Shinbunsha, 1994.

Koizumi Yoshinaga. 'Learning to Read and Write: A Study of Tenaraibon.' In Matthias Hayek and Annick Horiuchi, eds., *Listen, Copy, Read: Popular Learning in Early Modern Japan*, 89–138. Leiden: Brill, 2004.

Kokushi daijiten. Accessed through JapanKnowledge.

Kornicki, Peter. 'Women, Education, and Literacy.' In P. F. Kornicki, Mara Patessio and G. G. Rowley, eds., *The Female as Subject: Reading and Writing in Early Modern Japan*, 7–38. Ann Arbor: University of Michigan Center for Japanese Studies, 2010.

Krusenstern, Adam Johann von. *Voyage Round the World in the Years 1803, 1804, 1805 and 1806.* Translated by Richard Belgrave Hopper. London: C. Roworth, 1813.

Kubiki sonshi hensan iinkai, ed. *Kubiki sonshi: tsūshi-hen.* Kubiki-mura, Niigata-ken: Kubiki-mura, 1988.

Kurosu, Satomi. 'Divorce in Early Modern Rural Japan: Household and Individual Life Course in Northeastern Villages, 1716–1870.' *Journal of Family History* 36:2 (2011): 118–41.

———. 'Remarriage in a Stem Family System in Early Modern Japan.' *Continuity and Change* 22:3 (2007): 429–58.

Lindsey, William. *Fertility and Pleasure: Ritual and Sexual Values in Tokugawa Japan.* Honolulu: University of Hawai'i Press, 2007.

Long, David F. *Sailor-Diplomat: A Biography of Commodore James Biddle, 1783–1848.* Boston: Northeastern University Press, 1983.

Makihara Norio. *Bunmeikoku o mezashite.* Tōkyō: Shōgakukan, 2008.

Marcon, Federico. *The Knowledge of Nature and the Nature of Knowledge in Early Modern Japan.* Chicago: University of Chicago Press, 2015.

Markus, Andrew. 'The Carnival of Edo: "Misemono" Spectacles from Contemporary Accounts.' *Harvard Journal of Asiatic Studies* 45:2 (1985): 499–541.

Martin, Alexander. *Enlightened Metropolis: Constructing Imperial Moscow, 1762–1855.* New York: Oxford University Press, 2013.

Maruyama Nobuhiko. *Edo no kimono to iseikatsu.* Tōkyō: Shōgakukan, 2007.

Masuda Yoshimi. 'Yoshino Michi no shōgai: sono tegami o tsūjite.' In Kinsei joseishi kenkyūkai, ed., *Edo jidai no joseitachi*, 115–46. Tōkyō: Yoshikawa Kōbunkan, 1990.

Matsubara Iwagorō. *Saiankoku no Tōkyō.* Tōkyō: Minyūsha, 1894.

Matsudai-machi, ed. *Matsudai chōshi.* 2 vols. Matsudai-machi: Matsudai-machi, 1989.

Matsuo Bashō. *The Narrow Road to Oku.* Translated by Donald Keene. Tokyo: Kodansha International, 1996.

Matsuoka Hideo. *Torii Yōzō: Tenpō no kaikaku no dan'atsusha.* Tōkyō: Chūō kōronsha, 1991.

Maza, Sarah. *Servants and Masters in Eighteenth-Century France: The Uses of Loyalty.* Princeton, NJ: Princeton University Press, 1983.

McClain, James. 'Edobashi: Space, Power, and Popular Culture in Early Edo.' In James McClain, John M. Merriman, and Ugawa Kaoru, eds., *Edo and Paris: Urban Life and the State in the Early Modern Era*, 105–31. Ithaca, NY: Cornell University Press, 1994.

Mega Atsuko. *Buke ni totsuida josei no tegami: binbō hatamoto no Edo-gurashi.* Tōkyō: Yoshikawa kōbunkan, 2011.

Melville, Herman. *Moby-Dick; Or the Great White Whale* (1851). New York: Penguin, 2013.

Messenger, The (New Haven, CT).

Minami Kazuo. *Edo no machi bugyō*. Tōkyō: Yoshikawa Kōbunkan, 2005.

Miyachi Masato. *Bakumatsu ishin henkaku-shi: jō*. 2 vols. Tōkyō: Iwanami shoten, 2012.

———. *Bakumatsu ishinki no bunka to jōhō*. Tōkyō: Meicho Kankōkai, 1994.

Miyamoto Yukiko. 'Kakushi baijo to hatamoto keiei: *Fujiokaya nikki* o chūshin to shite.' *Komazawa shigaku* 55 (2000): 319–41.

Miyazaki Katsumi. *Daimyō yashiki to Edo iseki*. Tōkyō: Yamakawa Shuppansha, 2008.

Moring, Beatrice. 'Migration, Servanthood, and Assimilation in a New Environment.' In Antoinette Fauve-Chamoux, ed., *Domestic Service and the Formation of European Identity: Understanding the Globalization of Domestic Work, 16th–21st Centuries*, 43–70. Bern: Peter Lang, 2004.

Morison, Samuel Eliot. *'Old Bruin': Commodore Matthew Calbraith Perry, 1794–1858*. Boston: Little, Brown, 1967.

Moriyama, Takeshi. *Crossing Boundaries in Tokugawa Society: Suzuki Bokushi, a Rural Elite Commoner*. Leiden: Brill, 2013.

Morris-Suzuki, Tessa. *The Technological Transformation of Japan: From the Seventeenth to the Twenty-First Century*. Cambridge: Cambridge University Press, 1994.

Nagai Masatarō. *Ōishida chōshi*. Tōkyō: Chūō Shoin, 1973.

Nagano Hiroko. 'Nihon kinsei nōson ni okeru maskyurinitī no kōchiku to jendā.' In Nagano Hiroko, Sugano Noriko, and Sakurai Yuki, eds., *Jendā de yomitoku Edo jidai*, 173–212. Tōkyō: Sanseidō, 2001.

Nagatani Takaharu. *Kabuki no keshō*. Tōkyō: Yūzankaku, 2015.

Najita, Tetsuo. 'Ōshio Heihachirō.' In Albert Craig and Donald Shively, eds., *Personality in Japanese History*, 155–79. Berkeley: University of California Press, 1970.

Nakagawa Hōzandō and Hanasaka Kazuo, eds. *Edo kaimono hitori annai*. Tōkyō: Watanabe Shoten, 1972.

Nihon rekishi chimei taikei. Accessed through JapanKnowledge.

Niigata kenritsu bunshokan, ed. 'Shozō monjo annai.' Niigata Prefectural Archives, Niigata City, Niigata Prefecture.

Niigata-ken, ed. *Niigata kenshi shiryō-hen*. 24 vols. Niigata: Niigata-ken, 1980–1986.

———. *Niigata kenshi tsūshi-hen*. 5 vols. Niigata: Niigata-shi, 1995–1997.

Nishiyama, Matsunosuke. *Edo Culture: Daily Life and Diversions in Urban Japan*. Honolulu: University of Hawai'i Press, 1997.

Nishizaka Yasushi. *Mitsui Echigoya hōkōnin no kenkyū*. Tōkyō: Tōkyō Daigaku Shuppankai, 2006.

————. 'Yamori.' In *Nihon toshishi nyūmon*, vol. 3, edited by Takahashi Yasuo and Yoshida Nobuyuki, 224–25. Tōkyō: Tōkyō Daigaku Shuppankai, 1989.

Nojima Jusaburō. *Kabuki jinmei jiten*. Tōkyō: Nichigai Asoshiētsu, 2002.

Ōbuchi Wataru, ed. *Kisha jikokuhyō*. Shinshindō, 1894. Accessed through National Diet Library Digital Collection, http://dl.ndl.go.jp/info:ndljp /pid/805117.

Ōgata chōshi hensan iinkai, ed. *Ōgata chōshi, shiryō-hen*. Ōgata-chō: Ōgata-chō, 1988.

Ōgawa Kyōichi. *Edojō no toire, shōgun no omaru*. Tōkyō: Kōdansha, 2007.

————, ed. *Kansei-fu ikō hatamoto-ke hyakka jiten*. Vol. 5. Tōkyō: Tōyō shorin, 1998.

————. *Tokugawa bakufu no shōshin seido: Kansei jūnenmatsu hatamoto shōshinhyō*. Tōkyō: Iwata Shoin, 2006.

Ōguchi Yūjirō. *Edojō ōoku o mezasu mura no musume: Namamugi-mura Sekiguchi Chie no shōgai*. Tōkyō: Yamakawa Shuppansha, 2016.

————. 'The Reality Behind *Musui Dokugen*: The World of the *Hatamoto* and *Gokenin*.' Translated by Gaynor Sekimori. *Journal of Japanese Studies* 16:2 (1990): 289–308.

Ōishida kyōiku iinkai, ed. *Ōishida chōritsu rekishi minzoku shiryōkan shiryōshū*. Vol. 7: *Shūmon ninbetsuchō*. Ōishida-machi: Ōishida-machi kyōiku iinkai, 2001.

Okazaki Hironori. *Tōyama Kinshirō*. Tōkyō: Kōdansha, 2008.

————. *Tōyama Kinshirō-ke nikki*. Tōkyō: Iwata Shoin, 2007.

Ōshima-mura kyōiku iinkai, ed. *Ōshima sonshi*. Ōshima-mura: Ōshima-mura kyōiku iinkai, 1991.

'Oshioki no setsu shusseki namae oboechō' (1844). Vol. 4 of *Oshioki no mono obechō*. Beinecke Rare Book and Manuscript Library, Yale University.

Partner, Simon. *The Merchant's Tale: Yokohama and the Transformation of Japan*. New York: Columbia University Press, 2017.

Pflugfelder, Gregory. *Cartographies of Desire: Male-Male Sexuality in Japanese Discourse, 1600–1950*. Berkeley: University of California Press, 1999.

Pineu, Roger, ed. *The Japan Expedition 1852–54: The Personal Journal of Commodore Matthew C. Perry*. Washington, DC: Smithsonian Institution Press, 1968.

Platt, Stephen. *Imperial Twilight: The Opium War and the End of China's Last Golden Age*. New York: Knopf, 2018.

Rath, Eric. *Food and Fantasy in Early Modern Japan*. Berkeley: University of California Press, 2010.

Rediker, Marcus. *The Slave Ship: A Human History*. New York: Viking, 2007.

Rinsenji monjo (E9806). Niigata Prefectural Archives, Niigata City, Niigata Prefecture.

Roberts, Luke. *Performing the Great Peace: Political Space and Open Secrets in Tokugawa Japan*. Honolulu: University of Hawai'i Press, 2012.

Rubinger, Richard. *Popular Literacy in Early Modern Japan*. Honolulu: University of Hawai'i Press, 2007.

Saitō Gesshin. *Edo meisho zue* (1834). Accessed through JapanKnowledge.

Saitō Hiroshi. *Shichiyashi no kenkyū*. Tōkyō: Shin Hyōron, 1989.

Saitō Osamu. *Shōkā no sekai, uradana no sekai: Edo to Ōsakā no hikaku toshishi*. Tōkyō: Riburo Pōto, 1989.

Sakuma Tatsuo, ed. *Inō Tadataka sokuryō nikki*. 7 vols. Tōkyō: Ōzorasha, 1998.

Sakurai Yuki. 'Perpetual Dependency: The Life Course of Male Workers in a Merchant House.' In Sabine Frühstück and Anne Walthall, eds., *Recreating Japanese Men*, 115–34. Berkeley: University of California Press, 2011.

Sasama Yoshihiko. *Ō-Edo fukugen zukan: shōmin-hen*. Tōkyō: Yūshikan, 2003.

———. *Zusetsu Edo machi bugyōsho jiten*. Tōkyō: Kashiwa Shobō, 1991.

Sato, Hiroaki. *Legends of the Samurai*. Woodstock, NY: The Overlook Press, 1995.

Satō Shigerō. *Bakumatsu ishin to minshū sekai*. Tōkyō: Iwanami shoten, 1994.

Schwartz, Hillel. *Century's End*. New York: Doubleday, 1990.

Screech, Timon. *The Lens Within the Heart: The Western Scientific Gaze and Popular Imagery in Later Edo Japan*. Honolulu: University of Hawai'i Press, 2002.

Seki Jun'ichi. 'Shihon chakushoku "Ōishida kashi ezu" ni tsuite.' *Mogami-gawa bunka kenkyū* (2006): 39–53.

Sewall, John S. *The Logbook of the Captain's Clerk: Adventures in the China Seas*. Bangor, ME: s.n., 1905.

Shaw, Matthew. *Time and the French Revolution: The Republican Calendar, 1789–Year XIV*. New York: Boydell and Brewer, 2011.

Shiba Keiko. *Kinsei onna no tabi nikki*. Tōkyō: Yoshikawa Kōbunkan, 1997.

Shiga Shinobu. 'Sanseiroku kōhen' (1856). In Vol. 52 of *Edo jidai josei bunkō*. Tōkyō: Ōzorasha, 2000.

Shimazaki, Satoko. *Edo Kabuki in Transition: From the Worlds of the Samurai to the Vengeful Female Ghost*. New York: Columbia University Press, 2016.

Shimizu, Akira. 'Eating Edo, Sensing Japan: Food Branding and Market

Culture in Late Tokugawa Japan, 1780–1868.' Ph.D. dissertation, University of Illinois, Urbana-Champaign, 2011.

'Shinban Ō-Edo mochimaru chōja kagami' (1846). Kaga monjo 220. Edo-Tokyo Digital Museum, Tokyo Metropolitan Library, http://www.library.metro.tokyo.jp/Portals/0/edo/tokyo_library/upimage/big/013.jpg.

Shirane, Haruo. *Early Modern Japanese Literature: An Anthology, 1600–1900.* New York: Columbia University Press, 2002.

Shmagin, Viktor. 'Diplomacy and Force, Borders and Borderlands: Japan-Russia Relations in the Transformation of Japanese Political Culture in the Edo and Meiji Periods.' Ph.D. dissertation, University of California, Santa Barbara, 2016.

Smith, Henry D. 'The Edo-Tokyo Transition: In Search of Common Ground.' In Marius B. Jansen and Gilbert Rozman, eds., *Japan in Transition from Tokugawa to Meiji*, 347–74. Princeton, NJ: Princeton University Press, 1996.

Smith, Thomas C. *The Agrarian Origins of Modern Japan.* Stanford, CA: Stanford University Press, 1959.

Smits, Gregory. *Visions of Ryukyu: Identity and Ideology in Early-Modern Thought and Politics.* Honolulu: University of Hawai'i Press, 1999.

Speiden, William, Jr. *William Speiden Journals.* Vol. 1: *1852–1854.* Manuscript, Library of Congress, https://www.loc.gov/item/mss830450 001.

Spence, Jonathan. *The Search for Modern China.* New York: W. W. Norton & Co., 2013.

Stanley, Amy. 'Adultery, Punishment, and Reconciliation in Tokugawa Japan.' *Journal of Japanese Studies* 33:2 (2007): 309–35.

———. *Selling Women: Prostitution, Markets and the Household in Early Modern Japan.* Berkeley: University of California Press, 2012.

Starling, Jessica. 'Domestic Religion in Late Edo-Period Sermons for Temple Wives.' *The Eastern Buddhist* 43:1–2 (2012): 271–97.

Steele, M. William. 'Against the Restoration: Katsu Kaishū's Attempt to Reinstate the Tokugawa Family.' *Monumenta Nipponica* 36:3 (1981): 299–316.

———. *Alternative Narratives in Modern Japanese History.* New York: Routledge, 2003.

———. 'Contesting the Record: Katsu Kaishū and the Historiography of the Meiji Restoration.' In James C. Baxter and Joshua A. Fogel, eds., *Writing Histories in Japan: Texts and Their Transformations from Ancient Times to the Meiji Era*, 299–316. Kyōto: International Research Center for Japanese Studies, 2007.

Sugano Noriko. *Edo jidai no kōkōmono: kōgiroku no sekai.* Tōkyō: Yoshikawa Kōbunkan, 1999.

Sugimori Reiko. 'Furugi shōnin.' In Yoshida Nobuyuki, ed., *Akinai no ba to shakai,* 139–68. Tōkyō: Yoshikawa Kōbunkan, 2000.

Sugimoto, Etsu Inagaki. *Daughter of the Samurai: How a Daughter of Feudal Japan, Living Hundreds of Years in One Generation, Became a Modern American.* New York: Doubleday, Page & Co., 1925.

Suzuki Bokushi. *Snow Country Tales: Life in the Other Japan.* Translated by Jeffrey Hunter with Rose Lesser. New York: Weatherhill, 1986.

Suzuki, Keiko. 'The Making of Tōjin: Construction of the Other in Early Modern Japan.' *Asian Folklore Studies* 66:1–2 (2007): 83–105.

Suzuki Tōzō and Koike Shotarō, eds. *Fujiokaya nikki.* 8 vols. Vol. 1: *Kinsei shomin seikatsu shiryō.* Tōkyō: San'ichi Shobō, 1987.

Taguchi Akiko. *Edo jidai no kabuki yakusha.* Tōkyō: Yūzankaku, 1998.

Takahashi Satoshi. *Mura no tenaraijuku: kazoku to kodomo no hakken.* Tōkyō: Asahi Shinbunsha, 1995.

Takahashi Yasuo and Yoshida Nobuyuki, eds. *Nihon toshishi nyūmon.* 3 vols. Tōkyō: Tōkyō Daigaku Shuppankai, 1989.

Takai Hiroshi. *Tenpōki, shōnen shōjo no kyōyō keisei katei no kenkyū.* Tōkyō: Kawade Shobō Shinsha, 1991.

Takeuchi Makoto. *Edo shakaishi no kenkyū.* Tōkyō: Kōbundō, 2010.

Tamanoi, Mariko. 'Songs as Weapons: The Culture and History of Komori (Nursemaids) in Modern Japan.' *Journal of Asian Studies* 50:4 (1991): 793–817.

Teeuwen, Mark, and Kate Wildman Nakai, eds. *Lust, Commerce, and Corruption: An Account of What I Have Seen and Heard, by an Edo Samurai.* New York: Columbia University Press, 2014.

Tōkyō Daigaku Shiryō Hensanjo, ed. *Saitō Gesshin nikki.* In Vol. 24 of *Dai Nihon kokiroku.* Tōkyō: Iwanami Shoten, 1997–2016.

———, ed. *Shichū torishimari ruishū.* 29 vols. Vol. 6: *Dai Nihon kinsei shiryō.* Tōkyō: Tōkyō Daigaku Shuppankai, 1959–2010.

Tōkyō komonjo-kan, ed. *Edo: 1838–1841.* Tōkyō: Tōkyō komonjokan, 2014.

Tokyo Metropolitan Archives. 'Edo jidai no zumen o yomu (2): toire no iroiro.' Facebook post 8/24/2016. Accessed 12/14/2016, www.facebook .com/tokyo.archives.

———. 'Edo-jō no fuyu shitaku: hibachi.' Facebook post 11/6/2016. Accessed 12/14/2016, www.facebook.com/tokyo.archives.

Tōkyō-to Itabashi-ku, ed. *Itabashi kushi.* Tōkyō: Itabashi kuyakusho, 1954.

Totman, Conrad. *The Collapse of the Tokugawa Bakufu.* Honolulu: University of Hawai'i Press, 1980.

———. *Politics in the Tokugawa Bakufu. 1600–1843*. Cambridge, MA: Harvard University Press, 1967.

'Tsuji banzuke for Ume Saku ya Wakakiba Soga at the Kawarazaki Theater,' Tenpō 11.1, Publisher Ogawa Hansuke. Museum of Fine Arts, Boston. http://www.mfa.org/collections/object/kabuki-playbill-tsuji-banzuke -for-mume-saku-ya-wakakiba-soga-at-the-kawarazaki-theater-225317.

Tsukada Takashi. 'Meakashi.' In *Nihon toshishi nyūmon*, vol. 3, edited by Takahashi Yasuo and Yoshida Nobuyuki, 206–7. Tōkyō: Tōkyō Daigaku Shuppankai, 1989.

Tsukamoto Akira. 'Kariya ukenin.' In *Nihon toshishi nyūmon*, vol. 3, edited by Takahashi Yasuo and Yoshida Nobuyuki, 222–23. Tōkyō: Tōkyō Daigaku Shuppankai, 1989.

Tsukamoto Manabu. *Chiisa na rekishi to ooki na rekishi*. Tōkyō: Yoshikawa Kōbunkan, 1993.

Ujiie Mikito. *Hatamoto gokenin: odoroki no bakushin shakai no shinjitsu*. Tōkyō: Yōsensha, 2011.

———. 'Hitokiri no ie, onna no ie.' In Sakurai Yuki, Sugano Noriko, and Nagano Hiroko, eds., *Jendā de yomitoku Edo jidai*, 79–113. Tōkyō: Sanseidō, 2001.

Utagawa Hiroshige III. *Tsukiji hoterukan omotegake no zu* (1869). Museum of Fine Arts, Boston. https://www.mfa.org/collections/object/the-front -entrance-of-the-tsukiji-hotel-in-tokyo-tôkyô-tsukiji-hoterukan-omote gake-no-zu-129821.

Utagawa Kunisada. *Onoe Kikugorō no Omatsuri Sashichi, Onoe Eizaburō no Geisha Koito* [Onoe Kikugorō as Omatsuri Sashichi and Onoe Eizaburō as the geisha Koito], 1840. British Museum. http://www.britishmuseum .org/research/collection_online/collection_object_details.aspx?object Id=781668&partId=1&.

———. *Tsuragaoka kongen Soga*, woodblock print, triptych (1840). Victoria and Albert Museum, London. http://collections.vam.ac.uk/item /O33025/woodblock-print-utagawa-kunisada-i/.

Utagawa Kunisada I. *Actors Sawamura Tosshō I as Takeda Katsuyori, Iwai Shijaku I as Emon no Mae, and Iwai Tojaku I as Streetwalker Okimi, and Ichikawa Ebizō V as Boatman Sangorō* (Tenpō 11.11). Museum of Fine Arts, Boston.

———. *Memorial Portrait of Actor Iwai Tokaju I, with Iwai Kumesaburō III* (Kōka 4.4). Museum of Fine Arts, Boston.

Utagawa Kuniyoshi. *Actors Ichikawa Ebizō V as Yokozō, Iwai Tojaku I as Kansuke's Mother Miyuki, and Sawamura Tosshō I as Jihizō* (Tenpō 11.11). Museum of Fine Arts, Boston.

Utagawa Yoshikazu. *Kanda Matsuri dashizukushi* (1859). Museum of Fine Arts, Boston. https://www.mfa.org/collections/object/the-kanda-festival-parade-kanda-matsuri-dashizukushi-513212.

Vaporis, Constantine Nomikos. *Breaking Barriers: Travel and the State in Early Modern Japan*. Cambridge, MA: Council on East Asian Studies, Harvard University, 1994.

———. *Tour of Duty: Samurai, Military Service in Edo, and the Culture of Early Modern Japan*. Honolulu: University of Hawai'i Press, 2003.

Walthall, Anne. 'The Edo Riots.' In James McClain, John M. Merriman, and Ugawa Kaoru, eds., *Edo and Paris: Urban Life and the State in the Early Modern Era*, 407–28. Ithaca, NY: Cornell University Press, 1994.

———. 'Fille de paysan, épouse de samourai: Les lettres de Michi Yoshino.' *Annals Histoire Sciences Sociales* 54:1 (1999): 55–86.

———. 'Hiding the Shoguns: Secrecy and the Nature of Political Authority in Tokugawa Japan.' In Bernhard Schneid and Mark Teeuwen, eds., *The Culture of Secrecy in Japanese Religion*, 331–56. London: Routledge, 2006.

———. 'The Lifecycle of Farm Women.' In Gail Lee Bernstein, ed., *Recreating Japanese Women, 1600–1945*, 42–70. Berkeley: University of California Press, 1991.

———. *The Weak Body of a Useless Woman: Matsuo Taseko and the Meiji Restoration*. Chicago: University of Chicago Press, 1998.

Walworth, Arthur. *Black Ships off Japan: The Story of Commodore Perry's Expedition*. New York: Alfred A. Knopf, 1946.

Whitman, Walt. 'A Broadway Pageant' (1860). In Walt Whitman, *Poems of Walt Whitman (Leaves of Grass)*. New York: T. Y. Crowell, 1902.

Wigen, Kären. *The Making of a Japanese Periphery, 1750–1920*. Berkeley: University of California Press, 1995.

———. *A Malleable Map: Geographies of Restoration in Central Japan, 1600–1912*. Berkeley: University of California Press, 2010.

Williams, Duncan Ryūken. *The Other Side of Zen: A Social History of Sōtō Zen Buddhism in Tokugawa Japan*. Princeton, NJ: Princeton University Press, 2005.

Wills, Steven. 'Fires and Fights: Urban Conflagration, Governance, and Society in Edo-Tokyo, 1657–1890.' Ph.D. dissertation, Columbia University, 2010.

Wilson, Noell. *Defensive Positions: The Politics of Maritime Security in Tokugawa Japan*. Cambridge, MA: Harvard University Asia Center, 2015.

Yabuta Yutaka. *Bushi no machi Ōsaka: 'tenka no daidokoro' no bushitachi*. Tōkyō: Chūō kōron shinsha, 2010.

———. *Joseishi to shite no kinsei*. Tōkyō: Azekura shobō, 1996.

———. 'Nishitani Saku and Her Mother: "Writing" in the Lives of Edo Period Women.' In P. F. Kornicki, Mara Patessio, and G. G. Rowley, eds., *The Female as Subject: Reading and Writing in Early Modern Japan*, 141–50. Ann Arbor: University of Michigan Center for Japanese Studies, 2010.

———. '*Onna daigaku* no naka no "Chūgoku."' In Cho Kyondaru and Tsuda Tsutomu, eds., *Hikakushiteki ni mita kinsei Nihon: 'Higashi Ajia-ka' o megutte*, 140–62. Tōkyō: Tōkyō Daigaku Shuppankai, 2011.

Yamakawa Kikue. *Women of the Mito Domain: Recollections of Samurai Family Life*. Translated by Kate Wildman Nakai. Tokyo: University of Tokyo Press, 1992.

Yokoyama Yuriko. 'Jūkyū-seiki Edo, Tōkyō no kamiyui to onna kamiyui.' *Bessatsu toshishi kenkyū* (2009): 85–103.

Yonemoto, Marcia. 'Adoption and the Maintenance of the Early Modern Elite: Japan in the East Asian Context.' In Mary Elizabeth Berry and Marcia Yonemoto, eds., *What Is a Family? Answers from Early Modern Japan*, 47–67. Berkeley: University of California Press, 2019.

———. *The Problem of Women in Early Modern Japan*. Berkeley: University of California Press, 2016.

Yoshida Nobuyuki. *Dentō toshi: Edo*. Tōkyō: Tōkyō Daigaku Shuppankai, 2012.

———. 'Hitoyado.' In *Nihon toshishi nyūmon*, vol. 3, edited by Takahashi Yasuo and Yoshida Nobuyuki, 216-17. Tōkyō: Tōkyō Daigaku Shuppankai, 1989.

———. *Kinsei kyodai toshi no shakai kōzō*. Tōkyō: Tōkyō Daigaku Shuppankai, 1991.

———. *Mibunteki shūen to shakai, bunka kōzō*. Kyōto-shi: Buraku Mondai Kenkyūjo, 2003.

———. *21-seiki no Edo*. Tōkyō: Yamakawa Shuppansha, 2004.

———. *Toshi Edo ni ikiru*. Tōkyō: Iwanami Shoten, 2015.

Yoshida Setsuko, ed. *Edo kabuki hōrei shūsei*. Tōkyō: Ōfūsha, 1989.

Yoshida Yuriko. *Kinsei no ie to josei*. Tōkyō: Yamakawa Shuppansha, 2016.

Yoshihara Ken'ichirō. *Naitō Shinjuku*. Tōkyō: Tōkyō-to Komonjokan, 1985.

INDEX

Page numbers in *italics* refer to maps.